LIVING THE QUIETER ALGARVE DREAM

ALYSON SHELDRAKE

Tadornini Publishing

Free Photo Book

To view a series of free photographs which accompany this book, please visit my website:

www.alysonsheldrake.com/books/

Featured Painting

Alyson Sheldrake, (2016) *Alentejo Trees*.
Original Acrylic Painting on Board.
Private Collection.

Contents

Foreword

This is the continuation of the story of our life here in Portugal. It can stand alone as a book for you to enjoy, and it is also the sequel to *Living the Dream – in the Algarve, Portugal*.

In 2006, my husband Dave and I purchased a house in the picturesque fishing village of Ferragudo, in the Algarve. We had fallen in love with this charming place after spending many happy times on holiday here. Dave was nearing retirement from the police, after serving for over thirty years. I had a busy and rewarding, but exhausting job, working as a Director of Education.

We knew we wanted to do something different, something brave and positive with the next stage of our lives. No more rat-race, no more rainy, miserable, grey Britain. A new life in the sun beckoned.

Once Dave retired, our Ferragudo house kept enticing us over. In 2011, I handed in my notice from work. We packed up everything we owned and moved out here to live. I had long held a dream that one day I could become a professional artist, and Dave had always loved photography. Our plan was simple, move out to the Algarve, set up our own businesses and see what happened.

We battled with the dreaded Portuguese bureaucracy, mangled the Portuguese language beyond recognition, and deftly navigated around the expat world that exists here. We fell in love with a gentler way of life, made friends with our Portuguese neighbours and revelled in immersing ourselves in a different culture. We adopted a fantastic Spanish Water Dog that captured our hearts. Dave's sense of humour meant that we named her Kat the dog, and our home was complete.

Our creativity thrived. Living in such a beautiful place was inspirational, and both my art and Dave's photography grew in popularity. We organised our own pop-up exhibitions; I started painting commissions and selling everything I painted, and Dave launched himself as a professional photographer. He even ventured into the crazy world of wedding photography.

We were indeed living the dream. Our dream. And it was hugely exciting and rewarding. We had absolutely no regrets.

In 2018, we decided we wanted to slow down and move to a more peaceful location. Ferragudo had become more touristy and busier, particularly in the summer months, and the house we had bought still had a mortgage attached to it. We knew that selling would mean we could down-size and be more financially self-sufficient. We also both loved the beaches of the west coast, so we put our property on the market.

New adventures, and hopefully a slightly quieter way of life, awaited us.

1

Moving In

It was Friday the 13th of September and we had just completed the sale of our old house and purchase of what was to become our new home. The car was packed full, Kat was perched on top of one of her favourite cushioned beds on the back seat, and we were on our way.

The entire process at the notary office in Portimão had only taken an hour-and-a-half. We were expecting it to take much longer than that, based on our previous experiences of Portuguese bureaucracy. It was late morning, and we were travelling down the A22 motorway to its very end, which we always called junction 0. We turned onto the road to Aljezur, on the beautiful unspoilt west coast of the Algarve. Dave was driving and singing happily as we sped along. We kept smiling at each other and saying,

"We did it, we did it, we've bought our new house!"

It was a lovely warm sunny day. The roads were quiet, and as we turned onto the N120 single-carriageway road at the end of the motorway, we both sighed deeply and relaxed.

The entire process of selling and then buying had been an exhausting one and had taken several months. This was during an extremely busy period for Dave. Everyone seemed to want their wedding or event photographed that summer, which left me, as an artist, to put my work on hold and arrange everything. We have always worked as a team, and this was no exception, but it had been a difficult and fraught time. As we drove along, I exclaimed to Dave,

"I am never, ever, going through that again. You'll have to stay in this new house forever. I'm not selling and buying in Portugal again. Ever."

"Suits me," he replied, "I think we are going to love it here."

The N120 is not a busy road, even in the summer. You drive past open fields, small woodland areas, past a series of wind turbines and then out into more countryside. You pass by enticing signs that lead to the wonderful beaches of the south-west coastline of the Costa Vicentina.

As we entered Aljezur town, we were itching to get to our new house. We drove through the narrow main street with its shops and cafés, then took a sharp right turn over the old metal bridge which straddles the river. Then straight on past the fields that are all neatly divided up and owned by the locals who grow their own crops. We drove to the roundabout with its view ahead of the new church.

Most people turn left here, or go straight on, but we turned right, past the Junta de Freguesia and Câmara office buildings, and out onto the road that eventually leads to Monchique. A little way along this road you turn into the area known as Igreja Nova. Our new home was nestled in a small hamlet of houses, waiting for us to arrive.

As we parked outside and looked up at the house, I couldn't wait to put the key in the door and look around. I was delighted that the preceding owner's old wrecked car, with its flat tyres, was no longer parked to the side of the house. This would be our driveway. The garden was a mess, but we already knew that, and we had exciting plans for both inside and outside. But first, it needed a good coat of paint everywhere before we could do anything else. The house was about fifteen years old and was structurally sound. Sadly, the previous owner had neglected to maintain it, and it was the saddest-looking house in the street.

We opened up and scampered inside, looking around excitedly.

Without the large and imposing dark furniture that had been inside when we had viewed it with the estate agent, it seemed much lighter and brighter—and bigger—inside. It was as I remembered it, and the floors, shiny with their polished tiles, echoed to our footsteps as we marched around. We checked each room and exclaimed with glee at little things that we had forgotten, or not noticed, when we had seen it a few weeks before.

We emptied the car of a few basics, then left everything inside the house, locked up and walked Kat up the street. We were so happy to have finally made it, and as we walked around, several people said *"bom dia"* to us and introduced themselves. It seemed to be a pleasant, friendly, and quiet little neighbourhood, and we already knew that our immediate neighbours were Portuguese. It turned out that, except for one German lady, all the neighbours in the whole hamlet were Portuguese or Brazilian.

We drove back into town and parked beside the river in the market car park. It was lunchtime, people were milling around, and everywhere had a relaxed, unhurried air. No-one rushes in Aljezur. It has its own gentle pace, which is one of the reasons we were delighted to have found a suitable property to buy here. Having spent the previous seven-and-a-half years living in Ferragudo, we were ready for a slightly gentler and quieter way of life. We were also looking forward to enjoying the local beaches, which are some of the finest anywhere along the Algarve.

We walked over to the Café da Ponte, which overlooks the river and nestles alongside the metal bridge that links the old and new towns together. Ducks and geese swim below, waiting for a friendly tourist with some food to throw, and the trees along the small park area beside the café are full of birds singing.

There were lots of interesting things here for Kat to sniff. We slowed down, we were not in a hurry, and let her nosey along at her own snuffling pace. Our little rescued Spanish Water Dog garners attention wherever we go. She is black (although a little greyer now, as she is about eleven years old) and has a cute curly coat that makes her look like a little black sheep. People love to stop and fuss over her and say hello.

We spotted a free table at the café, and settled down with the menu, as the owner came over to greet us. We had been there before, but this time we could proudly tell him we were now officially 'locals'. He was delighted, and we started chatting, and then he said something we felt was the perfect phrase for us on our first day of our new life in Aljezur. He pointed to the cloud-free blue sky above us and said (in English),

"This place here is our little piece of sky."

The word for both heaven and sky in Portuguese is the same word, *céu*. Although he interpreted it incorrectly into English, we were thrilled with that translation, and thought it perfectly fitting for our new home. The skies do indeed seem a little larger and brighter here. You can stand in nature and see the dome of the sky stretching far above you. The thought of being able to own a piece of that, and it being representative of heaven too, seemed utterly appropriate.

We stretched out, ordered a *bica* coffee each, scratched Kat idly on the head, and settled in to enjoy the feeling of having finally moved to live in our own little paradise.

Our idyll, however, was rudely interrupted when we glanced at Dave's watch and saw the time.

"How can it possibly be almost 4 p.m. already? We arrived here at half-past one!"

We gathered up our things, paid the bill, and scurried back to the car. We had cleaners to meet at the house at 4 p.m.

✿❦✿❧✿

The first thing we had booked in the diary, once we knew the completion date for the purchase of our new house, was a company that specialised in industrial and residential property deep cleaning. Let's just say our new home had been sadly neglected. When we first viewed it and Dave casually leaned his hand upon the tiled wall in the kitchen, his hand stuck to the wall.

I was more than happy to stay there on our first night, and we had newly purchased inflatable mattresses in the boot of the car ready to unload. However, I had insisted the house had to be thoroughly cleaned before I would even contemplate moving in. We found the company via recommendation; I rang them and warned them about the state of the property. I negotiated a price that seemed fair for a top-to-bottom deep clean of a three-bedroom house that had two kitchens.

They arrived at 4 p.m. exactly. A cheerful husband and wife team marched in and got straight to work. They estimated they would need four hours. They seemed undaunted by the fact we had warned them that the only means of hot water available to them was by boiling a kettle (which we had packed for them). We could not arrange for the fitting of a new boiler until the following morning.

We took Kat out for a walk and left them to it. We popped back two hours later, and they seemed quite frazzled and busy. We said we were going down the road for some food and told them to call us if they needed anything. We shut the front door, feeling rather guilty.

One of our favourite restaurants in the area was now only a short walk away from our new house. Open since the mid-1980s, Pizzaria A Bica sells the best pizzas on the planet. We eagerly scoured the menu, enjoying all the original and unusual pizza options, before deciding eventually to plump for the aptly named 'Aljezur'. Local sweet potato, chorizo, pineapple, and garlic butter on a giant freshly made pizza base. A cold beer each, followed by their famous and utterly delicious chocolate mousse pudding, and we were happy. Kat sat contentedly beside us, listening intently to the sound of the frogs croaking away in the pond in the corner of the garden. She looked up expectantly each time Samuel the waiter approached us with a plate of food.

At 8 p.m. we paid the bill, and wandered home, expecting to see the cleaning company finishing up. We gingerly opened the front door and saw they were madly dashing around with mops and buckets scattered everywhere. Upstairs was finished, but they were still working away on the ground floor. They were looking much more frazzled by this time and hurriedly told us they thought they had at least another hour's work ahead of them. We retreated upstairs and started unpacking the contents of the car and inflating the mattresses.

Finally, at 9.20 p.m., they were finished. They had done a fabulous job but looked totally exhausted. We paid them extra, thanked them profusely, and helped them pack up their car, with their parting words ringing in our ears as they left,

"We know you told us it was very dirty, but it was much, much worse even than we had expected."

Oh dear. We thanked them again and watched as they drove away. We closed the front door and walked slowly round our new home, taking it all in. It was spacious, bright, and thanks to the cleaning company, now sparkling clean too.

We finished making the beds, made ourselves a hot drink, took Kat around the block before bedtime, then settled down on our extremely comfortable mattress beds for the night. I was fast asleep in under five minutes.

Sadly for Dave, I woke again about 2 a.m. with a start. The freezer! The previous occupants had left behind an old chest freezer in the garage. They obviously no longer wanted it, but couldn't work out how to remove it from the house before they left. This hadn't particularly bothered me when we had wandered around checking everything when we moved in, but in the middle of the night, in the dark, it haunted me.

The girlfriend of the preceding owner was, to put it politely, less than happy about the prospect of having to sell up and move to a new house. She was into voodoo and enjoyed slamming doors and windows. We had nicknamed her Voodoo Val on account of the collection of bones and dice that had been neatly displayed beside her bed. We had several giggles about her over the previous weeks, including a joke that when we moved into the house, she would still be hiding in there, refusing to leave. Suddenly I lay there thinking about her, and the freezer, and thought to myself, did we check there? What if she was inside, chopped up into small pieces?

Now you may think that to be faintly ridiculous and fanciful, until you find out that Dave (and I) were previously police officers in the UK. Dave had once discovered the head of a missing person hidden in a freezer whilst on duty. At 2 a.m. in the dark, in a new house, anything is possible. Poor Dave, I woke him up, and sent him off downstairs to the garage to check inside the freezer! Needless to say, it was empty, but I resolved to have it removed as soon as possible.

۞ ౾ ۞ ௸ ۞

The next morning we woke bright and early, and I took Kat out for her first walk in our new location. Our house is just up the road from the river path that leads into town, and it was a beautiful morning to explore this unspoilt and pretty area. Kat and I both returned delighted with our new walk, and I was thrilled to think I could stroll along the river with her every day.

9 a.m. and the doorbell rang, and we happily invited in the plumber we had booked to install a new hot-water boiler for us. It was a good job we had organised this quickly, as he took one look at the old boiler and pipework, whistled loudly, and set to work. Two hours later, we had a new shiny boiler, hot water, and a set of old pipes and the rusty boiler thrown into the back of his van. We then tentatively asked him if he could check out the other kitchen for us, which had a menacing pipe sticking out of the wall into the room.

The house has a second 'outside' kitchen, which is enclosed and leads off from the main kitchen. We later found out that the previous owner's ex-wife was a cook, and she used this area exclusively to create her locally famous sweet potato cakes and loaves. No wonder the walls were greasy.

There had been an oven in the corner of the second kitchen which had an interesting homemade pipe running from the room to the gas bottle cupboard outside. It was still live and needed soldering properly to ensure it didn't leak any gas. More work for our plumber. Whilst he was busy with that problem, we discovered the downstairs toilet wasn't draining away very well. In fact, not at all, if the amount of water swirling around the bowl was any indication. Our plumber to the rescue again as he helpfully said to us,

"I've got a set of rods in my van. I'll sort that out for you."

He ended up staying for the morning, and we would have offered him lunch if we had had any food in the house. We paid him, added extra for all the additional work he had completed, and he drove off waving happily to us. Job done.

The rest of our weekend was spent relaxing and walking and eating out. We hadn't packed any chairs, so we spent a lot of time out and about, only coming home to feed Kat or sleep on our extremely comfortable air beds. It was a good job they were so substantial. If we had known how long we were actually going to wait for our new beds to arrive, we might not have been quite so thrilled with the prospect of spending almost three months sleeping on mattresses on the floor.

✿ℬ✿ℭℛ✿

Monday morning finally arrived, the day the removal company was delivering everything for us. We cheered as we saw their van approaching, and then it was organised chaos as the team moved all our furniture and boxes in for us. Luckily, we didn't have any immediate plans for the garage, so anything we were not sure about was stacked in there. I had marked every box and item of furniture with its destination room, and the removal team seemed happy with this plan. I labelled each room and left them to it. The benefits of being an extremely organised person. Dave has a different name for this!

One of the bedrooms, on the ground floor, was the perfect size for our office space. When we first viewed the house, we decided the second outside kitchen could be my art studio, and the garage was big enough for Dave's home gym equipment. The car would live on the drive at the side of the house, and we had a small garden area that was just big enough for an outside covered seating area. The plans were already being drawn up in my head alongside a small area for planting. It was the perfect size for us to maintain easily. A lovely large open-plan lounge, a big kitchen, and two bathrooms and we were in house heaven.

By tea-time, we had started unpacking, and the kitchen was almost done. We went out for dinner, tired but happy.

The following few days were a flurry of unpacking and sorting.

Everything seemed to fit easily into place, and the house flowed nicely. We unpacked the decorating gear and I painted the office room, so we could assemble the office furniture and organise our computers. Working from home meant that we needed to be back online quickly, as we set up our 4G router and angled it towards the nearest mast. I was determined this would be a temporary measure until I could find a better solution to our internet requirements. If only I had known what pain and suffering that innocent-sounding idea would lead to, I might have been less keen to go down that route, but that's for another chapter.

2

Making our House a Home

We had already lined up our decorating team before we moved, as we knew that we had a lot of repair work to be completed on the outside walls of our new house. They needed re-rendering in places and desperately needed a decent coat of paint. Although the house was only about fifteen years old, I don't think it had been decorated since the builders had added their customary lick of paint upon completion. After years of sun and rain, the surface had crumbled away, and it needed to be repaired, before the winter weather set in.

I set to work as soon as we knew the house was going to be ours. August was a busy month for us, but it is notoriously difficult to find anyone in the construction world still working during the middle of summer. A photographer will usually find themselves fully booked during August out here, for obvious reasons, but the building trade pack up their tools and rest during the hottest month of the year. I can't say I blame them. With temperatures soaring into the high thirties, you don't want to be outside wielding a paint brush unless you have to.

I had two painters and decorators recommended to me. We contacted the first, a man called Glyn, and he kindly agreed to meet us at the house in August to give us a quote. We had advised the estate agent we wanted to visit the house to get a quote, but that we only needed to go outside. The back garden was at this stage open to the road, so we didn't need to bother anyone or have anything unlocked. Courtesy demanded we let the current owners know of our intended visit, and I didn't foresee any problems. We had already paid our ten percent deposit, and the promissory contract was signed.

We met Glyn at the house and instantly liked him. He was quiet and thoughtful, professional, and keen to impress us. He also had a good sense of humour, which is almost pre-requisite for getting on with us. Luckily, we had warned him about Voodoo Val.

We arrived, rang the bell, and waited. Two windows were open upstairs, but there was no reply. We shrugged and turned to look around, giving Glyn time to assess the state of the walls and give us his verdict. Out came his magic measuring machine, and he walked round making notes.

Out of his earshot, I said to Dave,

"I like him. I hope his quote comes back within our planned budget."

Ever the cynic regarding quotes and workmen, Dave merely replied,

"We'll see."

We went round to the back garden, where Glyn was busy checking the walls. Suddenly a window opened upstairs, a head thrust itself out and started shouting and hollering at us. All in Portuguese. Well, I didn't catch most of it, but I got the gist of it. Voodoo Val was not happy. At all. As fast as she had appeared, she shot back inside and closed the window with a loud bang. The entire house shook. Two minutes later, the front door slammed shut, and she marched off down the street, muttering and waving her arms around.

We glanced up at the house above us in the road. Their side wall backs onto our new house and there, looking over the top of the wall, was our new neighbour. We said hello to her, a little uncomfortably. What a great start to meeting the local residents.

She smiled back at us, said *"bom dia"* and shrugged her shoulders as if to say, don't worry, she does that all the time.

We had a quick chat with her and explained what we were doing there. She was very friendly and wished us well.

We glanced over at Glyn, who had retreated to the corner of the garden, and was grinning broadly. We promised him if he got the job, Voodoo Val was not part of the package. He looked relieved.

With the measuring-up completed, we shook hands, and he agreed to send us a quote within the week.

We drove away, still looking around, and half expecting Voodoo Val to jump out in front of our car and start shouting at us again.

We had always planned on getting three quotes. The second painter and decorator we contacted told us he didn't need to visit the property, and could we send him some photographs so he could get an idea of the size of the house? We explained over the phone to him that the walls were in a pretty bad state in places, and would need some rendering work completed too. He said that wouldn't be a problem. We were relieved that we didn't have to upset Voodoo Val again, but unimpressed that he wasn't interested in viewing the potential job. We decided to wait and see what his quote looked like.

Glyn was as good as his word, and one week later, he emailed us with his quote. It was just over five thousand euros, which was more than we ideally wanted to pay. We were, however, impressed with the paperwork which was on two sides of A4 paper. It covered in detail exactly what work would be undertaken, including the make and type of paint he would use.

We sighed at the price. Even buying a house that looked ready to move into was still going to be eating into our little pot of savings.

Quote number two came back a few days later. It was slightly less money, at around four thousand euros. Yes, that is what it said on the quote. Paint house outside. Around four thousand euros. And that was pretty much it. I am amazed he gets any work at all, if that is the response he gives to potential customers. Needless to say, he received a polite, but firm, "no thank you," as a reply.

The third quote was going to come from a local builder in Ferragudo. We had to wait until early September for the company to be back at work, and I met the boss outside the house in Aljezur one Friday afternoon. Our phone call to the estate agent this time paid off, and all was quiet when we arrived. One less thing to worry about. The Portuguese boss chatted happily to me as he looked around. He told me he loved Aljezur and would be willing to travel over with his team each day to complete the job.

"Well, that depends on your quote, of course," I told him, laughing.

"I will do you a good price," came his reply.

Well, if his quote was a good price, I would hate to see what the full amount would have been. We met him in his office a week later, and he produced his paperwork from the printer with a flourish. I am not particularly good at hiding what I am thinking; I have one of those faces you can read easily. I'm from inner-city Birmingham, and you learn quickly around there how to defend yourself with a look. Oh dear. I glanced at the quote and nearly gasped aloud.

Twelve thousand euros. To paint the house. And then, to top it all, he said to me encouragingly,

"If you pay an extra five thousand euros, I will use a special paint that means you will not need to decorate again for fifteen years."

A special paint? A total cost of seventeen thousand euros?! I only wanted the house painted; I didn't want him to build an extension on the house.

As politely as I could, I told him thank you, but no, shook his hand and wished him well.

As we walked back outside into the blazing sunshine, I said to Dave,

"Glyn it is then."

✿֍✿൏✿

It turned out to be an excellent decision, and not just from a financial perspective. Glyn arrived on the first day at exactly 8 a.m. along with his crewmate. We managed to mis-hear his name when he was introduced to us and thought he said he was called Shorty. He was quite short too. By the time we had realised our mistake, it was too late, and Shorty was his name for the whole two-and-a-half weeks that the boys were at our house painting. He didn't seem to mind too much.

We always intended to ask Glyn to paint our internal hall, stairs and landing for us as well. The height and turn of the stairs would have made it a difficult job for us to do without specialist ladders and equipment. He quoted us a fair price, and we set them both to work inside and outside.

I had quickly decorated our office room, and maybe I am getting older, but I don't remember decorating being such hard work last time I painted a room in our old house. I watched enviously as Glyn and Shorty jumped up and down off ladders, with a full roller of paint in hand. They made it look easy, and they certainly did a professional job. Every edge was sealed and finished, straight lines were painted with ease, and they cleared up behind themselves every day.

Asking them to paint the lounge as well was a straightforward decision. It was a large room, and not one we were looking forward to painting. In fact, if I am honest, the more we saw Glyn and Shorty work, the less inclined we were to paint anything else ourselves. We looked at our budget and wondered if we could ask them to do even more inside. We had already bought the paint for all the rooms, as they had a sale on in our local DIY store before we moved. I am sure the removal company were delighted to see all the enormous heavy tins of white paint stacked up ready when they loaded the vans on moving day.

Glyn's original quote included extra for the specialist paint needed for the outside walls, which in places were in a pretty bad way. He estimated that even after the walls had been re-rendered and repaired, we would need to use a Sandtex-type textured paint. We happily agreed to this. After a week of preparation, jet-washing, filling, and repairing, they were ready to start painting. Glyn quietly came into the house that afternoon and said,

"Can you come and have a look at one of the walls outside? We've put the first coat on and want to know what you think."

Our tired-looking dilapidated house now had one sparkling-white wall. It already looked transformed, and that was only the first of three coats of paint.

"It looks great," I replied, "much better than before."

"Well, that's good," said Glyn smiling, "because I've just used the external paint we normally use on a house, not the Sandtex we talked about. I don't think we need to use that after all."

I was delighted. The Sandtex would have been fine, but it was so much nicer to see a smooth finish to the wall. It was much more in keeping with the modern design of our house.

"The good news is this paint is cheaper than the other stuff would have been. Why don't I have a look round inside, perhaps we could decorate some rooms for you for the same price as the original quote?" said Glyn obligingly.

I was delighted with this suggestion and impressed with his honesty. I doubt I would have looked back through his quote and noticed the discrepancy at all. He ended up painting the rest of the rooms in the house for us at no extra charge.

The last decision we needed to make was the choice of colour for the decorative trim areas on the outside of the house. I knew I wanted a grey colour, and the artist inside me knew exactly which colour grey that was. Poor Glyn. He handed me the chart with thousands of colours on show and asked me to pick one.

"Well, it has to be a medium-grey colour, based on a Payne's Grey. With a blue undertone, I don't want it to have any yellow in there."

"Ok, well you have a look through the chart and tell us which one you like." Glyn replied.

I'm not sure he has many clients that describe their colour choice to him like that. I think most people simply say they want a nice blue colour and leave him to it.

I found the right page in the book and immediately spotted the perfect shade of grey. For fun, I took the samples out to Glyn and Shorty, and said,

"Which one of the greys on this page would you choose?"

They both picked exactly the same grey as I had. Dave wandered past, so I asked him the same question.

"That one," he said, pointing straight at the same colour.

"Well, that's settled then. That's the one for us, please."

The tin of paint was duly ordered and when it arrived, it was perfect and added the finishing touch the house deserved. We were done. Inside and outside looked amazing, almost unrecognisable from the dingy, tired building we had moved into only a few short weeks before.

We said goodbye to Glyn and Shorty and began the fun task of completing our shopping for furniture and making our new house truly a home.

✿❀✿❁✿

The recently opened Ikea store near Faro was about to become our favourite shop, and not for the first time. We have always loved their simple styling and reasonable prices, so we planned our furniture and furnishings around their catalogue. I was excited that we could start afresh in our new home, as we had left a lot of our old furniture behind for the new owners. This was our chance to select new items to enjoy rather than the hotchpotch of furniture we had ended up with previously. Our lounge was a blank canvas, and luckily Dave and I usually like the same things. We both chose the same large L-shaped sofa and selected the same muted-green colour choice on offer. That formed the basis for the room design that followed.

I got my tape measure out and carefully planned all the furniture and accessories we would need before I arrived at the Ikea store. I had everything printed out ready and I cornered the first friendly assistant I could find as soon as I arrived. Forty-five minutes later all the major furniture items were ordered for delivery the following week. I just needed to pick up some random items and a series of ceiling lights, and I was off for lunch. Meatballs, of course, in the Ikea restaurant, where I mused upon the fact that it seemed to be standard practice in Portuguese homes to take all the ceiling-light fittings with you when you sell up.

A week later and all our furniture arrived. We had paid extra for fitting, so we left the two delivery men to begin the unenviable task of building everything. The enormous sofa was the biggest job, but we had also bought three large bookcases, a TV unit and coffee table, a dining table and four chairs. And another large table for my art studio. They were still there working at 9 p.m. and gratefully accepted our offer of a beer and a sandwich each.

Once they had finished and drove away, we walked round each room grinning happily. It was perfect, and the furniture had helped to transform the house into our dream home. We could not have been happier and as we sat on our comfy new sofa and stretched out, we had the feeling we had arrived in exactly the place we were meant to be. We had finally embraced the minimalist layout we had longed for in our old home but never quite achieved.

Moving to a new house had given us the perfect opportunity to jettison so many things that were old or didn't really serve a purpose for us, and to only select the items we wanted to have around us. Now all we had to do was wait for our new beds to arrive and we could get rid of the airbeds we were sleeping on. We needed to order a new cooker and hob, and then we would be finished inside.

⊙ 🔊 ⊙ ⊂🔊 ⊙

The oven we had inherited was so old and dirty we didn't dare use it. The hob was ancient, but serviceable, but we decided to splash out and buy new appliances. Bizarrely, the kitchen already had a dishwasher that had never been used; it still had the original manual inside the machine, even though it was plumbed in.

Dave was passing one of the main homeware shops in Portimão one afternoon and popped in for a look. He came home delighted that they had a sale on, and he had spotted the perfect oven and hob. As he is the master in the kitchen, and I have absolutely no interest in cooking, it was simply left for me to go back to the store the next day and buy them. I walked in, found an assistant, and ten minutes later I was paying for the new appliances and arranging for the store to deliver and fit them.

The assistant looked amazed and said,

"You are one fast shopper. Normally, people come in here and wander around and take ages to make a decision."

It has always been my way. I like to go into a shop with a list, get everything on the list, and get out again as quickly as possible. I picked up my receipt, which was four sides of printed A4 paper, stapled in the top left corner. Every till receipt in Portugal seems to require a staple before it can be handed over to you. I went home content with my day's work.

Two days later the delivery arrived, and I was not so happy. Two giant bearded surly men knocked on the door, grunted unintelligibly at me, and staggered in carrying the new oven. This was closely followed by the hob, which they crashed down on top of the oven box. I pointed to the corner of the kitchen, rather unnecessarily, as it was obvious where the new appliances needed to go. They grunted again, and I left them to it.

Half-an-hour later I wished I had not bothered to pay extra for fitting. They were both useless, moaning about having to fit the oven into the space allotted. We knew the old oven would come out of the gap easily, as Dave and I had already pulled it out once to check the electrics behind it. The new oven was the same size as the old one. They fitted the oven then realised they needed to get to the space at the back to fit the gas pipe for the hob, so out it came again, accompanied by more grunting and moaning. Sometimes it is handy to understand the nuances of the Portuguese language, sometimes it isn't. I disappeared again.

Finally, they decided they had finished and called me back into the kitchen. I took one look at the oven which they had switched on to show me it was working, then I saw the hob. They gleefully switched on all four rings and snapped a photograph for their records. If the camera had a zoom feature, they certainly didn't employ it. If they had, it would have shown that the hob was raised up almost a whole centimetre from the work surface at the back, and about half a centimetre at the front.

I pointed out the obvious fault to them, and they brushed my indignant manner aside, saying,

"Oh, you just need to seal that with some filler. It will be fine."

"So, you don't have any filler then?" I asked.

"Oh no, we don't do that. We only fit things."

Yes, but not very well, I thought, but decided that, on balance, it was probably for the best they hadn't used any permanent filler on the hob.

Sometimes it is simply easier to cut your losses. I ushered the grumbling, useless fitters out the front door, whilst steadfastly refusing to give them a tip. I started again by hiring an actual plumber and gas fitter who knew what he was doing.

Lesson learnt. Don't bother paying extra for the fitting of appliances from that particular homeware store.

We did eventually get it all sorted out, and then we had the fun job of trying to understand the controls for the oven. It came with a fifty-two page manual, and it even has a Sabbath setting. Our last oven had two settings: on and off. It either veered towards burning and cremation, or it didn't cook things at all. This new-fangled, top-of-the-range number was going to take some getting used to. It does, however, have one fabulous feature — it cleans itself.

3

Fitting and Fixing

The next jobs on the list didn't go as well for us as the decorating and furnishing had. We had two old toilets that needed replacing, and in the downstairs cloakroom we needed a new sink and cabinet. The small corner shower required a shower cabinet adding before we could use it. The shower over the bath in the upstairs bathroom was missing a screen. We knew that our old plumber in Ferragudo wouldn't travel all the way to Aljezur to work. I checked online and asked around, and Paulo [not his actual name] came recommended. I rang him and he agreed to come out to discuss the job with us.

We had bought all the items we needed in a local DIY shop, and they were all delivered and stored in the garage waiting to be fitted. Paulo arrived, and he seemed like a nice cheery Portuguese chap. He said he could do the work, no problem, and could start the following week. Perfect.

The warning sign should have been that he could begin the job so quickly, but we didn't think about that until much later. Any decent workmen out here are booked up weeks ahead. Still, Paulo turned up the following Monday morning, toolkit in hand, and set to work. The toilets seemed to slot into place, although there was a lot of muttering about them being a 'different shape' and 'feeds going at an unusual angle'. We left him to it.

Then came the sink and under-cabinet for the downstairs bathroom. Paulo shook his head, saying that the 'feeder pipe was in the wrong place' and that he would have to fit the cabinet round the pipe. This meant we would only be able to use the two main cupboards, and not the lower drawer, once the unit was in place.

We were not duly concerned and said ok. Once he had fitted it, I checked to see how it looked. The cupboard had a great big pipe going right up the centre of the shelves, rendering a good third of the space unusable. And I couldn't even open the lower drawer. Still, the sink and tap section were fine, and they worked, so we figured it would have to do. It looked ok from the outside at least.

On to the shower cabinet downstairs. We had measured carefully and knew that the one we had bought would fit the space perfectly. Much cursing from Paulo ensued, as he tried to position it. After two hours, he sealed it all in, and told us not to open or close the doors until the next day. This was to allow time for the sealant to dry.

Finally he went upstairs to fit the glass shower screen along the bath. A simple job, we thought. We heard a lot of banging, and I held my breath, expecting to hear a loud crash at any moment. All went quiet, then Paulo bounded down the stairs.

"All finished," he said gleefully.

I popped upstairs, and the screen seemed to be in the correct place. I paid him what we had agreed, added another ten euros 'for a beer' and off he went.

The next morning I went for a shower upstairs, admiring the new shiny screen door over the side of the bath. After I had finished, I noticed in dismay that the bathroom floor was wet. I mopped it up and went downstairs, saying to Dave,

"I don't think much of that new shower screen. It leaked water all over the floor."

"It shouldn't have," Dave replied, "it is supposed to keep all the water inside, that is the whole purpose of having one."

He went upstairs to have a look but couldn't see anything wrong.

Then he went back downstairs to check the shower cabinet and found that the sliding doors didn't meet properly.

"Well, that's a lot of use, isn't it? The doors don't even shut." Dave was not happy.

I reached for the phone and called Paulo.

"Oh, I am sorry. I am busy today; I will come tomorrow to fix it for you."

The next day came and went. No Paulo. I rang him again.

"Oh, I am sorry, I was not well. I went to the hospital in Faro. But I will be better next week."

A likely story, I thought, but there wasn't much I could do about it.

The next day I took Kat out for her afternoon stroll, and who should I see in the road near us, chatting to a friend, and looking perfectly fit and well? Yes, that would be Paulo. He did, I admit, look a little sheepish. I greeted him and told him I looked forward to seeing him on Monday.

You can guess who didn't turn up the following week. I messaged him, but then gave up. I figured if he had done that bad a botch job the first time around, he was unlikely to fix it on a return trip.

Our newly appointed builders came to the rescue. The last work planned included having a covered area built in the back garden. Knowing how hot the summer can be, we wanted to have a secluded space where we could sit and eat, or simply recline and laze around.

Manuel the builder came highly recommended. We met him and he agreed to travel all the way from Albufeira each day to do the work for us. This meant adding an hour's travelling each way on top of his working day. He quoted us a fair price to build a large covered area, and a smaller separate little wood store to stash our winter fuel. We just had to wait for him to start.

Finally, in early November, he arrived with his team. We chatted to him about all the work he had recently completed, including building a new house from scratch.

"Oh, can you sort out our bathrooms for us then?" I asked, explaining the problems.

"Of course, let me have a look."

He went into the downstairs bathroom first and came out five minutes later shaking his head.

"Let me get my toolkit, I'll fix the shower for you," he said, "but I can't do much about the sink cupboard, I am afraid. I don't know what your plumber was thinking when he fitted it, but he was just lazy. It should have been cut properly, and the pipe moved back."

Half-an-hour later, the shower doors fitted perfectly. Manuel went upstairs to the other bathroom and came back down an hour later, looking slightly more flustered and tired.

"I can't believe what he did," he said, "he only put the shower screen on upside-down. I've had to take it all apart and start again. It's all fixed now though, you won't get any more water on the floor."

I was delighted. No more laying a towel down beside the bath before I could have a shower. Manuel was a star.

He also did a sterling job on our outside covered area, persuading us to expand our plans and have a three metre by four metre space enclosed. He recommended an insulated roofing panel which turned out to be a real bonus when the hot summer sun is beating down, as the temperature stays slighter cooler underneath. We now have a spacious outdoor eating area that even has room to fit in a large corner sofa. It is the perfect spot for a little afternoon reading and snoozing!

An offcut from the roofing material also formed the start of our log store. For the first time we have an open fire in our home, and I am thrilled with it. Not only does it create a warm cosy glow in the lounge, it also heats both upstairs bedrooms thanks to a pipe system in the chimney. We needed a storage area outside big enough to hold one tonne of wood, so Manuel marked it out and set to work. When our first delivery of wood arrived a few weeks later, the space he had created fitted the exact amount of wood we had to store. He had measured and planned it to perfection.

The last task was to transform the old vegetable plot into a small garden area. We visited a local garden centre and chatted to them about what we wanted to create and what things we liked. A week later a lorry arrived carrying five giant oleander bushes, and a small hedge of eugenia plants. They included planting in the overall price we paid, so the delivery men set to work, and by the end of the day, we had a mature garden ready to enjoy. It was worth paying the extra for. We added a riot of flowering African daisy plants and the outside area was complete. We could relax in our little retreat, sip a cold drink, and hide away from the world.

✿❧✿❦✿

When we left our old house in Ferragudo, we decided our waterbed was too old to move again, and we dismantled it. We had a nightmare of a job trying to empty it. I thought it would be a simple task as it had been in the past. We moved it over from the UK with no misfortune; however, since then, we had replaced the inner liner and the new one refused to budge. We even borrowed a friend's water pump to help us expel the eighty gallons of water inside. Eventually we emptied it enough to heave it over the first-floor balcony onto the ground below, where it landed in the perfect shape of a wrapped-up dead body.

After all that effort, we unceremoniously dragged it down to the bins and left it for disposal. Hindsight is a wonderful thing, and looking back I wish we had saved the wooden frame and structure from that bed, and simply bought ourselves a new inner liner. It was about twenty years old though, and we thought it was time to replace it all.

I started searching online, but I was disappointed to find that the business we had purchased our first waterbed from in the UK refused to deliver to Portugal. Their policy was simple, they insisted on delivering and fitting all their beds themselves and wouldn't entertain shipping it over without installation. We had to find another company.

"How hard can it be to find a waterbed company to help us?" I said to Dave, determined to replace our bed. "I thought waterbeds were more popular in Europe, surely we must be able to find someone local?"

I trawled the internet and Facebook with little success.

Eventually I found a distributor in the Algarve that said they sold waterbeds. I rang them up, thinking, at last I've found someone.

I was sorely disappointed with the person I spoke to.

"Hello, I believe you sell waterbeds?" I said.

"Erm, well yes," came the reply, from a woman who sounded less than positive.

"Well, do you have a catalogue or a website I can look at, please?"

"No, we haven't got anything like that. But I can get you a waterbed," she said, a little more brightly.

"That's great, but how do I know what I will get? Do you have a showroom?" I asked, not exactly holding my breath in anticipation of her reply.

"No, but we've got a waterbed here in our house. You can visit us and see it, if you like," she offered, "but we live miles from anywhere in the north of the Algarve."

"And how much are they?"

"Well, that depends. Come and have a look and we can talk about the price," she replied.

I politely declined and ended the phone call. I shook my head in amazement.

"How do these people hope to sell anything?" I asked Dave.

We were back to square one. I returned to the internet and found a company in the UK I had missed the first time around. On checking out their website, I could see they had a great range to choose from. I emailed them, and they replied that they could courier a bed down to the shipping company that we use in Andover, Hampshire. From there it could have onward delivery to Portugal, and then out to Aljezur. They were confident they could pack it securely.

I spent a while selecting a bed, then Dave decided he would like a waterbed too, instead of the old bed he had been using from Ikea. So we were in the market for two new king-size waterbeds. Our bedrooms had plenty of room to fit them in, and I love having an enormous space to stretch out on. Blame that on my long legs, and the fact that Kat takes up a fair portion of one side of my bed.

We hand-picked the beds we liked from their website. I was desperate to get them ordered and delivered as soon as possible. We were still sleeping on the airbeds we had set up the first night we moved into our new home. They were reasonably comfortable; it was late autumn, and we were still experiencing mild weather, but I knew once the nights drew in, it would get colder. Sleeping on a cold airbed was not my idea of fun. Not when I was dreaming about the luxurious warmth of a heated waterbed, softly cushioning me.

It's one of the real benefits of a waterbed. The water heats thermostatically, so you can turn the temperature up in the winter. You also get to wake up in a warm bed when it is cold outside in the morning. I have always loved them because they support your body and back in particular so well. No waking up with a dead arm or tossing around to find a comfy spot in bed. Kat seems to enjoy sleeping on a waterbed too!

Having selected our favourite beds from their extensive range, I rang the company to arrange payment and delivery.

"Aloo, Adam 'ere. Can I 'elp you?"

It was quite a bizarre conversation. Adam had a strong northern accent, one which I got to know rather well in the ensuing weeks. We called him Adam Ear, and went round saying 'Aloo' to each other for ages afterwards. I think that was a direct reaction to all the trauma that followed with trying to get the beds sorted out.

The first problem was that the bed I had selected online was not available for several weeks. It was out of stock until late November. At that rate, with Christmas in the mix, I could still be sleeping on an airbed in January. I had to choose another design. I had my heart set on the one I had chosen first, which had a lovely frame around it. The only other one they had in stock in the extra-long length I wanted was much plainer. It was just a box with a separate headboard. It would have to be that or wait until January.

Dave chose a leather-covered sleigh bed. That was in stock, so we placed our order, handed over my credit card details, and waited for the company to let us know they had sent the beds by courier to Andover.

We had several friendly phone calls from Adam Ear, including one where he explained he had personally built both our beds in the warehouse. He wanted to make sure all the pieces and fixings were there. He even sent us a video of himself building them. We hoped he had remembered to scoop up all the screws again and put them back in the bag.

Finally, our beds were ready to go, and the shipping company advised us of the date when they would arrive in Portugal. They arranged a day for delivery to Aljezur, and I cleared a space in each bedroom in readiness. By this time, it was the first week of November, it was getting cold at night and the airbeds were no longer amusing. The sooner we built the waterbeds, the better.

The packages arrived, and they were clearly labelled Bed One or Bed Two. I was surprised by the large number of planks of wood, foam pieces and assorted sections contained in the boxes. We arranged everything into two piles, assigning the correct mattress liner to each bed.

It took us the whole of one day to build the first bed, which was mine. We rang Adam Ear on three separate occasions to get his advice and help and watched the video he had made for us several times. What seemed to be a simple job turned out to be a bit of an epic struggle. Everything had to align perfectly for the liner to fit properly. Added to that was the fact I had organised my room to have the bed fitted on the back wall with a small open display cabinet on either side. The measurements were tight, but doable, if the bed was in the exact centre of the room.

Unlike our last waterbed, this frame seemed to have a mind of its own, and stubbornly refused to align itself. We took it apart and re-built it three times until Dave was happy with it. Eighty gallons is a lot of water to sit inside a frame on the first floor of your house. You must be sure the frame fits correctly to hold the inner liner that holds all the water.

Only then could we switch on the power and start heating the bed. One more night on the airbed, then I could enjoy my new waterbed.

The next day our friends Jan and Chris arrived. Chris and Dave made quick work of building the second bed together, along with much laughter and mirth. One of them let go of the hose pipe that was shooting water into the empty liner and sent water snaking across the floor. They refused to own up to who should have been gripping it! Jan and I stayed downstairs drinking tea and left them to it.

A week later, Adam Ear even rang us to see how things had progressed. I told him we were enjoying the luxury of our new palatial warm havens. I had packed away the airbeds at last, and as I answered the phone call, I glanced over at Kat, who was snoozing away on my bed, snuggled up with her head on a pillow. All was well.

4

Aljezur – Then and Now

Travel almost sixty kilometres by road along the coast from the most south-westerly point in Europe, the Farol do Cabo de São Vicente (The Cape St Vincent Lighthouse) and you will reach Aljezur. It is only sixteen kilometres from Odeceixe, which is the furthest location north before the Algarve ends. After this you enter the Beja district, and the region known as the southern Alentejo. Aljezur sits in the landscape of the Parque Natural de Costa Vincente, which is a protected area of the Portuguese west coast stretching all the way from Sagres to Odeceixe.

The name Aljezur derives from the Arabic word Aljuzur (الجزر), which translates as islands. It is a pretty market town often missed on the tourist trail with a population of less than six thousand people. For us, it has everything we need without feeling too big. It is large enough to have a primary and secondary school, health centre, Câmara and Junta de Freguesia (town hall and parish council), Serviço de Finanças (finances) and a post office. It has a pharmacy, a big supermarket and several other smaller food outlets and markets, and some tourist shops along the high street. It also has the main fire station for the region, two petrol stations and a spacious conference/multi-purpose hall on the edge of town. The Aljezur river divides everything in half, with the original town on the seaward side, and the new Igreja Nova development stretching across to the fields on the other side.

The old town nestles into a series of gently rolling hills, topped by the imposing remains of an old Moorish castle. All the houses are painted white and most of them have the wonderful red sandstone-coloured roof tiles typical of this region. I have no idea whether the Câmara insist on the choice of paint colour, or if people just instinctively re-paint their property each time to match. Door and window surrounds can be a range of different colours, but, from a distance, the entire town is colour-coordinated.

Aljezur is a land that has remote origins, as denoted by the various archaeological remains scattered around the region. Humans have inhabited this area since pre-history, as far back as 7000 BCE. Nomadic tribes would have hunted and fished here and searched the land for tubers or roots that made up their basic diet. The humble sweet potato grown here might well have been sustaining people for far longer than we think. According to the records, it was during the Neolithic and Chalcolithic periods (3000-2500 BCE) and Bronze Age (1200-800 BCE) that more permanent settlement happened in the area.

Aljezur was invaded and conquered in the 10th century by the Moors, who quickly began to expand the town, until around AD 1250, when they were defeated by the Christians. Aljezur would have been a key town in the region, as it had a port capable of hosting large boats. The Aljezur river surrounded the village and turned it into an island, hence the Arabic name. Agriculture was the main economy here, and the cargo was shipped out through the port, which was near a creek close to the edge of the old town.

The Moors built the imposing Aljezur castle on the highest hilltop to protect both the inhabitants of the town and also the port. In its commanding position, it must have been a majestic sight when it was first built. During the Christian conquests it was the last castle to be conquered in the Algarve. I would love to transport myself back in time to that moment and walk around this structure in all its finery. It would have been polygon-shaped, with one circular and one square tower. Inside there would have been a cistern, storage area and a barracks.

I was intrigued why the towers were two different shapes, especially with one of them being circular. I already knew that a round design would make a good lookout tower and afford them better protection against arrows and other projectiles. A quick bit of research revealed that a spherical configuration would also have been easier to defend if someone tried to advance up the stairs of the tower. The tower would have a spiral staircase built in with steps curving up to the right. As most people are right-handed, the soldiers defending would have the advantage. Attackers coming up the stairs could not swing their swords, whereas the soldiers descending to defend the castle could wield their swords with ease and use their shields to protect their bodies.

The walk to the castle is steep, but worth it. Or you can cheat and drive there. The view from the top is spectacular, stretching across Aljezur town all the way to Monchique. In the other direction you can see the river meandering through the fields to Amoreira beach and the Atlantic Ocean.

The castle proudly flies a Portuguese flag from the top turret. Some mornings, when I am out walking Kat along the river, you can see it enveloped in a sea mist, and it is a wonderful local landmark and slice of history. It is an impressive sight at night too, as the castle wall is illuminated by clear white lighting. There are also four green spotlights perched on the hillside below. At Christmas it becomes even more resplendent, decked out with extra twinkling lights and a *Boas Festas* sign.

The castle also made it onto the town's coat of arms, which depicts the tower, alongside the images of both a Christian and a Moorish king. It sits above a series of wavy lines that represent the sea. The coat of arms also has a mural crown incorporated in the image. It interested me to discover that all Portuguese municipal coats of arms have a coronet in their design. The outline of the crown is extremely specific, according to the size of the urbanisation it portrays. Villages have three visible peaks illustrated on the crown, towns have four, and cities have five peaks. I checked, and yes, Aljezur's crown has four distinct peaks.

The devastating earthquake of 1755 damaged much of the original old town and resulted in a new settlement being built on the other side of the river. Francisco Gomes de Avelar, the local bishop of the time, ordered the new building plan, to encourage people to remain living in the town. The resulting development was called Igreja Nova, which translates as New Church. The plans apparently met with considerable local resistance, and it wasn't until the end of the 19th century that the planned building programme was finally completed.

The 1755 earthquake also silted up the river, rendering it impassable to boats, and forcing trade to continue via the road to Lagos. In places, the river is little more than a trickling stream now. If you walk through the small gardens and across the footbridge near to the municipal market, you can spot a blue-tiled panel on the wall. This depicts the site of the old Medieval bridge over the river. The original three-arched bridge was sadly washed away in foul weather and flooding in 1947.

There is so much history to enjoy in this town, including four museums that can be visited on one combined daily pass or ticket. The old blue and white Town Hall which dates back to 1883 is now the location of the Aljezur Municipal Museum. It houses a display of archaeological remains found in the area from the Neolithic period. These include farm tools and ploughs, fishing boats and nets, and an old horse-drawn carriage. You can also see a selection of Islamic coins and pottery. They sometimes use the space for art exhibitions too.

Next stop is the Aljezur Museum de Arte Sacra (Museum of Sacred Art). This museum showcases various religious artefacts donated by the former Monsignor Canon Manuel Francisco Pardal, who was born in 1896. Next door is the Igreja da Misericórdia (Church of Mercy), which was the original parish church. Built in the 16th century, it was rebuilt in the 18th century after the 1755 earthquake. If you ask at the Museum of Sacred Art, they might let you into the church as they have a key.

The Casa Museu Pintor José Cercas (House of José Cercas), was the former residence of this locally born artist. Some of his work along with paintings by other Portuguese artists are on display in this tiny traditional house.

The fourth museum is the Museu Antoniano, in what was the 17th century chapel of Santo António of Aljezur. In 1995 it opened as a museum dedicated to Saint Anthony, displaying medals, coins, books, and paintings all related to this revered saint.

Saint Anthony was a Portuguese Catholic priest and Franciscan friar. He is one of the most well-known saints in history, but I did not know he was Portuguese. Born in 1195, he came from a wealthy family. After attending the local cathedral school in Lisbon, and aged only fifteen, he entered the Augustinian community and was ordained as a priest. At the age of nineteen, whilst in the nearby monastery in Coimbra, he met some Franciscan friars who were staying at a hermitage dedicated to Anthony the Great of Egypt. He joined the Franciscan order and adopted the name Anthony. He died in 1231, aged only thirty-five, and is best known as the patron saint of lost things. I often tease Dave he should pray to Saint Anthony more often as he is always losing his keys.

✧ℬ✧ℬ✧

A significant piece of local history I would love to have seen in all its splendour is an ancient ribat on the cliffs near to Arrifana beach. You can still see the ruins which have been partially excavated, giving a tantalising glimpse of what must have once been an impressive site. It was a fortress convent, occupied by warrior monks, who were dedicated to prayer, and watching over the coast. This is the only Muslim ribat identified in Portugal - there is a second, the Ribat de Guardamar, in Alicante, Spain. It was constructed around AD 1130, probably by Abū'l-Qāsim Ahmad ibn al-Husayn ibn Qasī during his reign in the 12th century. He was a Sufi, born in Silves, and was the governor of Silves for the Berber Muslims.

Ibn Qasī wrote his most famous work, *The Removal of the Sandals* during this period, but the locals assassinated him in 1151, after accusing him of betraying Islam. This was because of a non-aggression pact he signed with Dom Afonso Henriques, forging two independent states in the Algarve region. They agreed they would divide the area up with the north being Christian and the south Muslim.[1]

In recent years, many teams searched for the remains of the ribat, but it wasn't until 2001 that the site near Arrifana was discovered. A scientific team was assigned to the archaeological investigation. They remarked that the remains of the buildings, built in stone and mud, showed that the ribat would have covered a vast area. They calculated there would have been nine mosques, all with their respective mihrab oriented towards Mecca. They believed there might also have been a Koranic school or *madrassa* on the site.

They also discovered a vast necropolis, and counted sixty-one graves, seven of which they excavated. Low, earthy burial mounds with stone monuments marked each of the graves. All the graves, except three, orientated northeast to southwest. This would have ensured that the face of each body turned towards Mecca. The other three orientated north to south, and were separate to the other graves, which led the team to believe those three graves were of Christian origin.

To the west, where the peninsula narrows, they discovered another complex of buildings. These formed four mosques, surrounded by a group of houses. On the south side, they identified a mosque overlooking the sea and a further set of buildings at the tip of Ponta da Atalaia. This area would have been the most sacred place in the ribat and is where they located the remains of a prayer wall.[2]

The Prince of Saudi-Arabia declared these ruins to be the most important place for the Islamic religion across the entire Iberian Peninsula when he visited the site. In July 2013, the ribat was classified as a National Portuguese Monument. Sadly, the excavation work halted soon afterwards. We have visited the location several times since this time, marvelling at how something so significant and historical could be left unattended and abandoned.

In November 2018, the local Jornal do Algarve newspaper featured a story on the ribat. This resulted in the government,

Aljezur Council, Lisbon University, and the Aga Khan Trust for Culture signing a protocol to "investigate, preserve and publicise the archaeological site."

The Regional Directorate for Culture of the Algarve defined the site as follows,

"Classified as a national monument, the Ribat da Arrifana is considered one of the most important archaeological discoveries of the 21st century."

They planned to create a working group, that would define an action plan, that would create and manage an interpretative centre for the ribat.[3]

To date, nothing seems to have changed, and the site is still abandoned. Perhaps Dave is not the only person that needs to pray to Saint Anthony for some help.

Another historical site that seems to have fared better in recent years is the fortress of Arrifana. Built in the year 1635, during the reign of Filipe II, it was both a lookout point and coastal defence. The front part, behind the entrance, consisted of a guardhouse and lodgings. The battery, with two artillery pieces, faced the sea. It was destroyed by the 1755 earthquake and subsequent tsunami. According to a report of the then parish priest of Aljezur,

"The sea reached thirty fathoms (fifty-four metres) and returned three times, crashing against the walls of the fortress with such impetus... [it left] standing only the battery and the walled curtain of the entrance door."

Due to its strategic position, the fort was rebuilt in 1762 by orders of the fantastically titled Governor of the Kingdom of the Algarve, the Marquis of Louriçal. Sadly, its location also meant it was further damaged several times by storms and left in an awful state of repair. It was rebuilt during the Portuguese Civil War (1828-1834) then abandoned again.[4]

Finally, in 2007, Aljezur Council reconstructed the front wall and entrance area and added a new fence, walkways, and a car park. It is now a busy place at sunset, as many people travel there to watch the setting sun disappear into the sea.

Back in the old town, you can visit the Associação de Defesa do

Património Histórico e Arqueológico de Aljezur (Aljezur Archaeological and Heritage Defence Association) building. They have a long name plaque on the wall outside. Here you will find a wealth of tourist information and artefacts, including original pieces of a German fighter plane that crashed near Aljezur in 1943. Portugal was neutral during World War II; however, a little-known fact is that they saw aerial combat over the skies around Aljezur.

The Allied forces were aiming to control the Mediterranean region. On July 9th, 1943, the Allies began the launch of Operation Husky, which was the invasion of Sicily and the first amphibious assault on occupied Europe. The area was the focus of fierce fighting as 2,590 allied ships gathered around Malta. Transport aircraft and gliders from North African airbases began inserting troops into Sicily from the British 1st Airborne and the US 82nd Airborne Divisions. German airfields in Sicily, Italy and Crete were also being hit, to provide air superiority over the enemy.

But the Germans were fighting back, attacking the ships around Malta, and targeting convoys passing from the Atlantic into the Mediterranean, both from the air and from U-Boats.[5]

The German forces tried to control Cabo de São Vicente, bribing the lighthouse keeper so he would pass them information about the approach of enemy ships. Based on the information gathered, four Focke-Wulf Condor fighter planes from the Third Reich appeared on the horizon. The RAF, however, had three aircraft nearby. Two Bristol Type 156 Beaufighters from 248 Squadron whose UK home base was Predannack Airfield, near Mullion on Cornwall's Lizard Peninsula, and a Hudson from 233 Squadron, which came from Gibraltar, were ready and waiting.[6] Perhaps the lighthouse keeper had been passing on information to both sides.

An aerial battle ensued, until the German planes fled north, dropping bombs as they disappeared. At Atalaia, near Arrifana, one of the German Condor planes was left behind, which was then hit and set on fire by one of the Beaufighters. The plane crashed into a cliff just south of Atalaia Point, Vale da Telha, resulting in the death of seven German airmen. Local people transported the bodies to the parish church in Aljezur.

Later that day, the Assistant of the aeronautical attaché of the German embassy in Lisbon, Major Karl Spiess, arrived to watch over the bodies. He was joined by members of the Portuguese Legion and local residents. They buried the soldiers the next day in Aljezur. Major Spiess, along with numerous Portuguese and German individuals, then visited the cemetery to pay tribute to the fallen airmen.

This battle is of particular importance as it is the only conflict of the Second World War recorded on Portuguese soil. Adolf Hitler even decorated some of the inhabitants of Aljezur with the Cross of Merit of the German Eagle, in recognition of the help they gave.

Today, there are seven graves in the cemetery of Aljezur where you can read the names of the aviators engraved on military crosses. For years, money came from Germany to help with the upkeep of the graves, and German soldiers stationed at the airbase at Beja looked after the graves. Even today, some Germans living in the vicinity still travel to the cemetery, especially on the anniversary of the event, to pay their respects.[7]

If you head up into the Igreja Nova side of town, you cannot miss the Igreja Nossa Senhora da Alva (the parish church). The square surrounding the church is a lovely place to enjoy a coffee or lunch and watch the world pass by. Just be warned that the clock in the tower chimes loudly every fifteen minutes. One strike for quarter past the hour, two strikes at half past. Three strikes at quarter to, and a full four strikes, followed by a bong for every hour, on the hour.

It is great fun arriving at one of our favourite restaurants for lunch, the Taberna do Largo, a few minutes before midday. We grab an outside table and wait for the midday chimes. You get sixteen chimes and bongs in total, and it is hilarious to spot the tourist who did not know it was about to happen. I've even seen a cup of coffee go flying as a person shot off their seat as the first chimes sounded. I mentioned how loud they are, didn't I? We can hear them from our house, and I like to count them as they chime out the hours. It's handy if you need to know the time, the first chimes are at 7 a.m. and the last bongs signal 10 p.m. each night.

The new church is also worth a detour—if you can catch it when it is open—if only to explore the legend of the skulls. This is one of the oldest stories from the area and dates back to the time when King Dom Manuel I reigned from 1495 to 1521. At the same time, in Aljezur, there were two farmers, a father and son, called João and Pedro Galego, respectively. They were described as being dedicated to their work, just and virtuous, and they were famous for being able to cure sick people by simply breathing on them. It was said that their very breath had healing powers and could heal people who had been bitten by dogs or other animals. They could even help those who had heart problems, headaches, or toothache.

The legend continues that, even after their deaths, their skulls continued to perform miracles. The skulls were placed in a box in the parish church, and they are still there to this day.[8]

It's not all history in Aljezur, though. Many people visit the area and its local beaches for the surfing and water sports, or to go fishing. It is a great place for walking and hiking too. It is part of the 300-kilometre-long Via Algarviana which runs from Alcoutim in the west to Cabo de São Vicente in the south. It is also on the 400-kilometre walking route known as the Rota Vicentina.

We are delighted with our move to live in this peaceful and traditional rural market town. For day-to-day life, it has everything we need. The people are friendly, and there is a genuine sense of community here. Finding out about the local history of this place has been a fascinating exercise. Now every time I glance up at the castle, or hear the church bells chime, I am reminded of the centuries of stories and legends that underlie the fabric of this old town. It is a privilege to live here.

1. National Geographic (s.d.). Website article *As ruínas arqueológicas da Arrifana*. Accessed 14th July 2020 through https://nationalgeographic.sapo.pt/historia/grandes-reportagens/2072-o-ribat-da-arrifana
2. Fondation Max Van Berchem Genève (s.d.). Website article *The Arrifana Ribât (Algarve. The Study of the Necropolis | 2014*. Accessed 12th September 2020 through https://maxvanberchem.org/fr/activites-scientifiques/projets/archeologie/11-archeologie/60-the-arrifana-ribat
3. Jornal do Algarve (18.07.2019). Website article by N Couto *Ribat da Arrifana vai finalmente ser requalificado*. Accessed 14th July 2020 through https://jornaldoalgarve.pt/ribat-da-arrifana-vai-finalmente-ser-requalificado/

4. Wikipedia (collated from 11.12.2018) Website article *Fort of Arrifana*. Accessed 14th July 2020 through https://en.wikipedia.org/wiki/Fort_of_Arrifana
5. Amovate (20.12.2010). Website article by Matt D'Arcy *When World War II Came to Vale de Telha*. Accessed 5th September 2020 through http://amovate.com/index.php/2010/12/when-world-war-ii-came-to-vale-da-telha/
6. Aljezur Câmara (s.d.). Website article *História*. Accessed 14th July 2020 through https://cm-aljezur.pt/pt/menu/66/historia.aspx
7. Wikipedia (collated from 12.08.2013) Website article *Batalha de Aljezur*. Accessed 14th July 2020 through https://pt.wikipedia.org/wiki/Batalha_de_Aljezur
8. Aljezur Câmara (s.d.). Website article *História*. Accessed 14th July 2020 through https://cm-aljezur.pt/pt/menu/66/historia.aspx

5

The River Walk

O ne of my favourite parts of Aljezur has always been the river walk. Each time we visited the town, we would park in the small car park beside the old metal bridge near the market and take Kat for a walk along the river. We would wander a little way along the path, then double-back and continue our exploration of the village.

I could not contain my excitement when we had agreed to buy our new house in Igreja Nova once I realised that, virtually at the end of the road, we could walk round and join the other end of the same river path. Fifteen minutes ambling along the most beautiful trail and I am back at the same car park in town, travelling from the other direction.

Two small rivers, the Alfambres and the Cercal, join at Aljezur and travel west for almost ten kilometres to the mouth of the Atlantic Ocean at Praia da Amoreira.

By the 16th century, ships up to 150 tonnes could navigate the river all the way to the castle until the earthquake in 1755. The pier at Aljezur could dock ten ocean-going vessels at the same time. It is hard to picture this now; the river is so narrow in places, and for many months in the summer it is just a dry riverbed.

Today, it is a wonderful little natural habitat and home to numerous animals and birds. Some of the most exciting creatures to see are the otters that dance and play in the river under the pedestrian bridge. Spotting them is always a genuine thrill. They share the water with the Mediterranean or Spanish pond turtles, alongside the resident greylag goose husband and wife team. The mother goose is so tame that Paulo, the owner of the local café, can hand-feed her pieces of bread.

You can see many local birds along the river, including kingfishers, herons, marsh warblers, and grey wagtails. We have our own resident white storks that have a nest in the fields on top of an old water mill. The river is also home to mallards and Muscovy ducks. Watching the newly hatched chicks paddling along the river is such a delight. Sometimes there are as many as twelve ducklings in a family, all eagerly exploring and making adorable shrill whistles and quacks as they go. I am sure there is a local nursery or creche for the ducklings nearby. I have seen a female herding and shepherding up to thirty babies at a time in one of the more sheltered corners of the river.

Kat and I must walk quietly, as we startled a purple heron one morning that was busy drinking water from the river. It rose up out of the riverbank right beside me and swooped away, beating its enormous wings directly over my head. I was staggered at the size and power of the bird; it was a remarkable sight. We regularly see the white storks parading around the field or flying overhead, and sometimes we are lucky enough to observe them standing still on the path in front of us. Even Kat is in awe of these magnificent birds that stand so strong and tall. To watch them whirl and soar in the sky above is wonderful, and it is a real feat of nature that such a large bird can fly so elegantly.

Mediterranean tree frogs create a noisy, if not a little discordant, backdrop of sound to the river with their loud mating croaks. For me, the most enjoyable thing is to stand quietly and listen to the wind rustling through the trees and hear the myriad bird calls that fill the air every morning.

The path that runs alongside the river is only a little more than the width of a truck, with grasses growing down the middle of the track. On one side are the small plots of land that are managed by local people. These parcels of land continue on the other side of the river all the way to the main road into town. They utilise all the terrain, with grain crops edging the fields, and immaculately tended and well-marked out plots covering the remaining land. I love walking along and seeing all the different plants and vegetables being grown, all laid out in neat rows, and mostly tended by hand or small machinery. There is apparently a long waiting list of people who would like to rent one of the plots. The land here is extremely fertile and well protected, with natural waterways. The perfect location for budding gardeners, with no chemicals or pesticides allowed.

The path is lined with ornamental bushes and trees. My favourite are the poplar trees that sway in the breeze. Their flowers are drooping catkins that arrive before the tender green leaves appear. In late spring, the floor around the trees is covered in cotton wool, as they disperse their seeds. Tufts of fluffy cotton are everywhere, and from a distance it looks like snow has fallen. The trees create a peaceful backdrop to the river. The name Populus dates back to Roman times when the trees were often planted around public meeting places. They are certainly a welcoming sight each morning.

Less inviting is the invasive bamboo that grows with abandon along the side of the paths. No sooner is it chopped down, often quite brutally, than it returns, sending its powerful shoots to the sky. Local people use the canes for their plants, so it has some purpose, but it is definitely not welcomed by all. There was a particularly comprehensive culling last spring, when the entire riverbank was decimated by large machines cutting absolutely everything back to the ground. A week later, the bamboo was shooting up again. One section of the path had a tunnel of bamboo to walk through. The plants on either side of the path had grown so tall they were bending over and reaching to touch each other across the path. It was magical to walk through in the early morning light. Sadly, since the spring cull, the plants have never reached the same height again.

There are so many flowers that grow along the side of the path. I adore the sight of the wild red poppies that come to life in the late spring, against a backdrop of light-yellow corn stalks and fresh green grasses. Nature doesn't need a flower vase to create a beautiful display. If you are lucky, you can also spot the larger and more mysterious purple poppy flowers that appear. They usually only last for a day or two, but they are magnificent. You would think an ex-police officer might have recognised them as opium poppies, but no, I just referred to them as the pretty purple poppies. I now know their proper name. Perhaps that is why they only survive for a day or two, if they even make it as far as flowering.

The poppies are unlikely to last longer than a particular day in May, however. The Dia da Espiga is a Christian festival, although probably pre-Christian in origin. It translates as 'the day of the wheat stalk' and always lands on a Thursday in late May. Historically, no work happened on that day, and at noon people would go into the fields to collect a specific set of flowers and wheat stalks to make up a bouquet. They would keep this arrangement for an entire year, either pinned up behind the front door, or on the highest shelf in the house, until they replaced it with a new bouquet the following year.

My Portuguese friend, Maria Victoria, told me about this tradition and explained you must select the plants and flowers carefully as they are all symbolic. The bouquet comprises a set number of different plants and flowers. A white and a yellow flower stand for silver and gold respectively, (i.e. money or wealth) and the poppies represent joy and life. A wheat stalk symbolises bread, and an olive branch is there to represent not only food but also peace and light.

The next day, I saw Maria Victoria and several other ladies down in the fields collecting their bunches of flowers and leaves together. I had no idea the tradition was still followed here so faithfully, and it was a lovely sight.

❀ ❧ ❀ ❧ ❀

One creature which is a less welcome visitor on our morning walk are the *javali*, or wild boar. You can see the evidence that the local herd has been roaming along the path at night by the devastation the following morning. They love to dig and uproot plants to get to the root balls, which they devour. They can be aggressive with very sharp teeth and have a strong instinct to protect their young. Portuguese wild boar are generally smaller than others found in central Europe, although an adult male can still weigh about eighty kilograms. The adult size ranges from 120 to 170 cm in length, and about 50 to 70 cm in height. They like dense shrubland with a water supply, so the river walk is perfect for them. They venture out when it is dark, which is why I wait until first light before I walk Kat each day.

We were caught out one morning though as we walked quietly along the river. I could hear squealing ahead; we turned a corner and there, in front of us on the path, was a young *javali*. It was obviously upset and had been left behind by the herd, presumably it was so busy snuffling and chewing roots that it missed the time to leave. It looked healthy and its lungs were certainly working well. The baby didn't concern me; it was about the same size as Kat, and it was too distraught to pay us much attention. What worried me was the fact that at any moment mom or dad would appear and spot us as well as their missing youngster. Not a prospect that I relished. Suddenly it scampered off to the riverbed, and Kat and I sidled past and then hot-footed it away from the squeals. We took the long route home that morning and hoped the little one found its herd again.

We spotted a larger *javali* about a month later, but this one was busy down at the riverbed. We walked along and something interested Kat in a particular spot along the river path, and she kept returning for a better look. Initially, I couldn't see what she was so enthralled with, then suddenly I saw it. A rear end sticking up out of the far side of the riverbank, head and body submerged in the bushes. It was the back end of a *javali*. Luckily, it was so busy eating whatever it had found, it paid us no attention at all. Kat fancied a longer look, but I wasn't going to risk it and urged her on.

The hunting season in Portugal normally starts in August and continues until the end of March. It is extremely confusing to work out exactly when the shoots are going to occur. The *javali* are the main quarry, and the local hunters create groups called *montaria* and drive out the herd with beaters and dogs. *Montaria* hunting can only take place on Thursdays, Sundays, and public holidays. They are also targeted from something called a 'blind' which can be erected for ten nights each lunar month. Very specifically, these ten nights are detailed as follows: eight nights before the full moon, the night of the full moon, and the following night only.

Where we live, they seem to alternate between several locations, and I never know when they are going to be in our local area. The sudden burst of shotgun fire, complete with the sound of howling and baying dogs, can be a real shock early in the morning, and has set Kat off before now. She really doesn't like loud bangs, and on one occasion she was so spooked she shot off back home at full pelt, with me in pursuit.

Of much more interest to Kat are the mounds of earth that we frequently spot on our travels which signal the home of a *toupeira*, or mole. Specifically the native Iberian mole. These little fellows dig small mounds along the riverbank and especially in the grass outside the Câmara building. Kat loves to spend ages watching the soil fly upwards in the vain hope she will spot the elusive creature below. It is not uncommon for Kat to keep me waiting a good ten minutes while she watches to see if the earth will move.

At night-time, Kat delights in trying to spot the family of hedgehogs that live in the fields. Their loud snuffling and chomping tend to give them away, and they are easy to find. They seem oblivious to most things around them, although if they catch a scent of us, they stop stock still until they think the danger has passed. I am sure Kat would be more at risk of injury than the hedgehogs; their spines always look so impressive in the moonlight.

Some nights you can even spot the bats flying overhead. The local information boards describe them as being *Morcego-de-água*, or Daubenton's bat, which I had never heard of before. It is a Eurasian bat with short ears, that roosts near water, hence its nickname, the water bat. The information on them is fascinating:

"This species is easily recognised in flight by its low, level flight a few centimetres above the surface of lakes, slow-moving rivers and canals. It skims like a hovercraft above the water in search of caddisflies, mayflies, and midges, and may even scoop prey from the water surface using its big feet. Many other bats feed over lakes and rivers, but none has such a close association with water as the Daubenton's. The Daubenton's bat can even swim if it makes a mistake and ends up in the water."[1]

I love walking past the fields and smelling the wild thyme and rosemary that grow with abandon amongst the grasses. Less welcome, but just as pungent, is the scent of wild garlic you can also catch on the breeze. The garlic here has a gentle, sweeter flavour and we use it a lot in our cooking.

My favourite tree is the magnificent pine tree standing majestically in the field at the far end of the river walk. I was reliably informed it is an edible pine tree, which sent me scurrying off to research this in more detail. Pine nuts for pesto sauce I knew about, but I did not understand how useful this tree can be. The pine needles are perhaps the most versatile part:

"Externally, pine needles are added into salves for skin care 'because pine is astringent, it reduces pore size and fine wrinkles. And pine is a powerful antioxidant which means it may help to prevent premature aging and may even help to reverse skin damage.' Adding pine needles to homemade bath salts can help relieve headaches, soothe frazzled nerves, relieve muscle pain, and treat skin irritation. A pine needle hair rinse can be used to treat dandruff and eczema while adding shine to your hair. Internally, pine is high in vitamin C, which makes it perfect in a nutrient-rich pine tea or pine needle soda. Pine needles are also naturally antibacterial, antifungal and expectorant, so they make a great pine cough syrup when combined with honey."[2]

That is only the beginning though:

"The inner pine bark is edible, and it can be eaten raw, boiled, fried or roasted over a flame. Male pine cones found near the tips of the branches can be eaten, boiled, or baked. The male cones will produce pollen in the spring that can be collected and used as a thickener for broths, stews, and added to flour or even used as flour. The male pine cone is smaller than the female cones. Pine resin can be applied directly to cuts, abrasions and even to deep slashes to help kill bacteria, to prevent bacteria growth and to keep it from getting into the wound. It can be chewed like gum and Native Americans routinely chewed and consumed the resin for its anti-bacterial properties and for joint pain. The resin can be steeped in hot water to make a tea that is said to help with arthritis and stomach problems."[3] I'm not sure I am brave enough to try drinking that.

Along the river we also have the *freixos* or European ash trees with their pretty flowers reminiscent of a lilac tree. The *salgueiros* willow trees hang their fronds over the river and create a peaceful rustling sound as the wind picks its way through the delicate branches. The *amieiro* or alder buckthorn tree don't have thorns, but they do have black berries that the birds love to eat. It is a long-standing inhabitant of the region, as it was first registered in Portugal in the year 907.

It is thrilling to think the trees along the banks of this beautiful little river walk may have their origins so many centuries ago. Although the riverside with its bustling port are merely stories in the history books now, this is still a delightful and peaceful place to stroll. I am grateful that Kat and I can enjoy its beauty and nature every day.

---

1. Bat Conservation Ireland (s.d.). Website article *Daubenton's Bat*. Accessed 10th September 2020 through https://www.batconservationireland.org/irish-bats/species/daubentons-bat

2. Practical Self Reliance (11.12.2018). Website article by Ashley Adamant *How to eat a pine tree (and other conifers)*. Accessed 10th September 2020 through https://practicalselfreliance.com/edible-pine/

3. Preparing for SHTF (s.d.). Website article *The Incredible and Edible Pine Tree*. Accessed 10th September 2020 through http://prepforshtf.com/incredible-edible-pine-tree/

6

The Fibra Fiasco

Our last house had 4G, and even though we were within a stone's throw of a giant mast, it seemed as if we were at the mercy of the wind whether we had a decent internet signal. And by decent, I mean around 5 Mbps. It was woeful really and made much worse because our office area was technically underground. Add to that, the summer influx of tourists put even more strain on the signal, and we could often be found shouting at the little box in the hallway, begging it to go faster. We wanted to have better internet provision in our new house, especially with Dave needing it for his work. Uploading large image files to his online site for delivery to clients could be a painfully slow experience.

I bounced off to the local Vodafone shop and asked them what they could do for us. We have been with them for years and have always found the staff in the shop to be helpful and knowledgeable. I should warn you, this was the last time I was cheerful when talking about the internet for several months, as you are about to discover.

All went well to begin with. The salesperson tip-tapped on their computer for ages, then looked up and said to me,

"We can install fibre-optic internet for you; we call it Fibra. It will be much faster than 4G, and it is unlimited too."

I was delighted and signed all the paperwork in record time. They promised they would call me to let me know which day they would install it.

Well, that was easy, I thought, grinning to myself, and grabbed my phone out of my pocket to call Dave to tell him the good news straight away.

"You'll never guess what," I told him excitedly, "we can have Fibra. They're going to let me know when they are coming. We are going to have super-fast broadband."

"Really," he said, slightly sceptically, "are you sure? I'll believe it when I see it."

"Pfft!" I replied, "Oh ye of little faith. Wait and see."

If only I had known how long we would have to wait, I might have been slightly less perky on the phone.

A week passed, then two weeks, and we had still not heard anything. I was back in the Aqua shopping centre in Portimão, where the Vodafone shop is located, so I popped in, picked up the ubiquitous ticket, and waited. Unusually, the same assistant that had helped me before, was there. I don't think I have ever been served by the same person twice in that store. He remembered me and my glee at being told we could have Fibra. He tapped away on his computer, then said to me,

"I'm sorry, it says here they cannot fit it at your house."

"But why?" I replied. "You said we could have it and I filled in all the paperwork."

"I don't know why, but the technical team at headquarters in Lisbon have said it is not possible to install it. I am sorry."

"When were you going to tell me then? I have been waiting for your team to call for the last two weeks."

The assistant was apologetic but said there was nothing more he could do. I left the shop frustrated, and more than a little fed up.

I walked past another internet-provider's shop and stopped to look in the window. Let's call them ZIP to save me from being sued. I had heard horror stories about them and how difficult it is to get out of one of their contracts, but they were advertising Fibra, so I thought to myself, well, it's worth asking, and went inside.

An assistant came over, I explained what I wanted, and she checked on her computer.

"Yes, that's fine, we can install Fibra at your address, no problem at all. It will be super-fast, over 100 Mbps. Our best package."

"Are you sure?" I said to her. "Only I went to Vodafone, and they told me they could, and then they said they couldn't do it where we live."

"Oh no, I am sure, we use different cables to them. It will be fine," she replied confidently.

I have since discovered this is, at best, shall we say, a fabrication. They all use the same cable system, which is owned by a third-party company, but I digress. Suffice to say, I believed her at the time.

We arranged a date for connection; I completed another small rainforest of paperwork and left the store.

I got home and told Dave what had happened. He was, predictably, as cynical as before, and hardly filled me with confidence. Looking online at the horror stories other customers had posted about ZIP on Facebook probably did little to allay the disturbingly uneasy feeling I had about signing up with them. But I thought it was worth a shot at getting decent internet provision. We were still muddling along with our 4G set-up, which was as slow as it had been in our old house.

The big day came, and at 4 p.m. on the dot, two ZIP technicians arrived and began work. An hour later, we had a wrecked connection socket on the wall in the hall, and a flashing box beside the computer attached to an ominous yellow cable. They proudly informed me,

"You now have the internet."

They started to pack up to leave.

"Hang on a minute. I want to check it all before you go. Can you wait, please?" I said firmly.

I logged on to my computer, linked up to the new system, and went online. I don't know what made me do it, but I found a free internet speed tester and pressed all the buttons required to test the download and upload speeds the new connection was providing. I was less than impressed with the results: 30.23 Mbps download and 2.98 Mbps upload.

I checked back with our current 4G provision, which yielded 73.92 Mbps download and 25.3 Mbps upload. I made a screenshot of each result and showed it to the ZIP technicians.

"Oh don't worry about that," one lad replied, "it always starts slowly, then over the next twenty-four hours it will speed up for you once it has settled down."

Now I might not be a technical expert, but years of policing gave me a strong 'bullshit' detector, and I was not impressed—at all.

"I'm sorry, can you explain to me exactly how it will miraculously get faster once you have disappeared out of the door, and I have signed up to a two-year contract with you?"

If they had known me, they would have recognised the tell-tale sign of my folded arms and sarcastic response, and backed off at this point.

"Oh, it just does; it speeds up after a few hours. It will be fine, don't worry."

"Right, I see, so it just magically speeds up does it. Overnight. Great. Well, I'm sorry, but the only thing that is going to magically speed up here is you. Pick up your box, disconnect it, remove all those wires you have scattered all over the place, and take it away. I am not accepting that. I was promised over 100 Mbps. Let's see, 2.98 is not one hundred, is it now?" I was losing my patience.

"But if we remove it, we won't get paid for the job."

The lad looked desperately sad, and I felt sorry for him. He was only doing his job, but I knew if I accepted the box, I would be stuck with it, and ZIP, for the length of the contract. All those warning posts on Facebook flashed before my eyes, and I politely, but firmly, declined and told them to remove it all. They did as I asked and left without a backward glance or even saying goodbye. I sighed, shut the front door, and went back to sit in the office and stare at my computer screen.

"Oh well," I said to Dave, "I guess we will have to put up with Vodafone 4G."

❊ෆ❖ගෙ❊

We continued for several more weeks with our current system, which was pedestrian but just about did the job. Then, late one afternoon in the depths of winter, I saw two workmen out in the street, packing up their white van. I saw a flash of red T-shirt and a distinctive logo and thought, that's Vodafone, and scampered out of the front door to look. Sure enough, it was Vodafone, and I walked over and said hello. My husband calls me cheeky—I call it initiative—and I certainly wasn't going to let this opportunity pass me by.

"Excuse me, are you installing Vodafone here?"

"Yes," came the reply, "we are fitting Fibra into your neighbour's house."

"But they told me we could not have it fitted here in this road."

"Oh no, that is not true. You can have Fibra here. Who said you could not have it?"

This was music to my 4G ears.

"The Vodafone shop in Portimão said they could not do it. I tried to get it fitted. Does that mean we can have it after all?" (I held my breath at this point!)

"Yes, of course you can. We are the engineers from Lisbon. We do all the installations round here. Which house is yours? I will come and see you once we have finished here and sort everything out for you. And I speak English too."

I couldn't wait to go back inside and tell Dave the good news. We waited, and after a while the doorbell rang, and our Vodafone angel, as he became known, was outside. His name was Nélio, he was at least 6'3" tall, and had the longest beard I had ever seen. Not quite your standard angel attire. He was holding a clipboard and said,

"Let's get your paperwork sorted. I have a friend in the primary accounts office, I'll ring him up and we can fill in everything here, and then they will arrange for me to return and fit your Fibra for you."

I could have kissed him as I danced around in excitement. If I had known how long the process would take, and how many problems we would have, I might have been dancing a little slower.

I filled in the forms, kept a copy, wished Nélio a good evening, thanked him again, and sat down to eat dinner, excited that [I thought] we had fixed it at last. Now we only had to wait for a call to arrange the fitting. Simple.

Oh dear. Nothing out here appears to be that straight-forward, does it? We waited, and waited, and then finally we had a text message from Vodafone saying they would fit our Fibra the following Tuesday, between 4 and 6 p.m. Perfect. Except Tuesday came and went, no Vodafone. No Fibra.

Nélio had kindly given us his mobile phone number, and I hesitated to bother him, but decided a quick call wouldn't hurt. He was his usual cheerful self and was puzzled why he had not had our address included on his itinerary.

"Don't worry," he said, "I will fix this. You will have Fibra soon."

I lost count of the number of times we heard Nélio say this in the ensuing weeks. It became a mantra, and he seemed to take us on as his personal mission. He was determined to get everything sorted for us; however, it wasn't that simple. He was frustrated when he rang us one afternoon to explain that the reason we could not have Fibra installed was because our house was mapped wrongly at the head office in Lisbon.

"What do you mean, we are mapped incorrectly?" I asked Nélio.

"Well, your house is marked up as having your front door facing out onto the main road. That road does not have any connections available."

The side of our house runs parallel to the main road, but the actual entrance to our house is on a side street. The same street we first saw Nélio installing Fibra in our neighbour's house. Their front door, unsurprisingly, opens out onto the same street. The main junction box for the area is on the far side of the main road, about twenty metres away. We know this by the number of times we have seen the manhole cover sticking up and watched someone disappear down into the depths of the underworld. How the main road did not have any connections marked up was an amusing thought, as it was the major arterial route for the entire estate of houses.

"Would you like me to send a photograph of our front door to Lisbon?" I was getting desperate by this stage.

"No, no," said Nélio laughing, "don't worry, I'll fix this. You will have Fibra, I promise."

Two or three weeks passed by, then late one afternoon, the doorbell went and there was Nélio outside, along with his much shorter colleague. Both of them were grinning broadly.

"I have come to fit your Fibra!"

"But we have not heard anything. Are you sure?"

"Yes," Nélio replied, "I have sorted it all out. I will fit it today for you."

I didn't enquire too deeply how he had sorted it out for us. Knowing Nélio, he probably re-drew the map for us, or moved our house to a new geographic location. Either way, we were delighted and welcomed them in.

Two hours later, and after much cable-winding and hole-searching, we finally had Fibra. It transpired that Nélio's colleague did all the tunnel-work. I can't even imagine how Nélio would have fitted through the manhole in the road outside. We had special cables fitted so our computers were hard-wired into the system. Dave had speeds of over 100 Mbps upload and download, and my computer reached the equally dizzy heights of around 95 Mbps. We had a shiny new wi-fi box, and Portuguese TV channels all linked up to our television in the lounge.

We were away.

Spring came and went, and our super-fast internet was brilliant. We were even a little smug when friends told us about their painfully slow internet in the summer months, as they struggled with the influx of tourists draining their service. We should have known better than to gloat. Suddenly, one morning we awoke to find we had no internet at all. Puzzled, we did all the usual technical things: that is; we unplugged everything, then plugged it all back in and switched it on. Nothing. Just an annoying red flashing light on the connection box.

I went through our files and found the helpline number for Vodafone, and sat back in a comfy chair with a cup of tea and the phone in hands-free mode. My plan to settle in for a lengthy and boring wait was a sensible one. Forty-five minutes later, I was still there, thinking that if I had to listen to the same music looping round one more time while they put me on hold, I was going to scream. If only I had known how many times I would end up listening to the same track over and over in the coming weeks, I would probably have cried! It consisted of a man telling me he wished he had found me a long time ago. Needless to say, I told him exactly what I thought of that idea—several times.

The phone was eventually answered and the helpful assistant promised to send someone round as soon as possible. The next morning, the lovely Nélio appeared at our door. Two hours later, after an extensive search above and below ground, he concluded there was a problem with the main box. Another two hours passed, then he returned, tested everything, and declared that it was fixed. We were back to normal. For one week. Then the same thing happened again. The helpline ended up on speed-dial; I called them so often. Suffice to say that for several months we did not have to pay anything when our monthly bill arrived, as they added credit to our account each time we lost our service. It was so frustrating.

Then one day, a different team of engineers appeared. Nélio had moved back to Lisbon to work. We knew he had a young family, and he had been staying in a cheap B&B all week whilst he was working down here. I was sure he would be glad to be back nearer home, and far away from Aljezur and its connection problems! We missed him, though.

The new team came inside, and one man immediately said,

"I know what the problem is. You have a rat."

"Sorry," I replied, "did you say a rat?"

"Yes, that is what's wrong. You have a rat chewing your cable. Come outside, I will show you."

He led the way to an unused old telephone connection cover on the wall of our house and showed me inside. There was the usual dust and debris, nothing spectacular. No rat peeping out from inside.

"I will prove it to you," he said, undeterred.

We left him to it and tried to ignore the ensuing mess as he dismantled the inside connection box in our hallway, leaving a trail of dust, broken cable pipe and paintwork all over the floor. We have learnt when someone comes to repair something out here, they rarely clean up behind themselves. I think they just assume we will do it for them.

Finally, we heard an exclamation of delight and went over to see the engineer pulling out metres of cable from inside the wall of our house, at the end of which was a giant mess of chewed and damaged wire. It was almost one metre of wrecked cable.

"You have a rat!" he said, proudly holding up the ruined cable.

Well, we couldn't argue with the evidence.

"What can you do about it?" I asked warily.

"We will replace the cable. It will be fine."

I wasn't convinced that was the solution but left them to it. An hour later, we had a green light on our connection box and the internet was back.

I couldn't understand why a rat would want to chew a cable unless they were bored. I also figured that if they had chewed the first cable, presumably they would be back to nibble the next one. I wasn't wrong.

We ended up calling the helpline again, and again—every single time we lost our connection. Sometimes twice in one week. One day, we saw the engineers pull up outside our house, and I thought, hang on, we haven't called them today, have we? They were visiting our neighbours opposite, who had also lost their internet. This was one busy rat! We put down rat poison and tried to seal things off, but it was impossible. The road underneath the houses was a warren of tunnels and connections for all manner of services. We named the rat Basil, and anyone familiar with the television series *Fawlty Towers* would understand the joke. Except it wasn't very funny.

Then one day the engineers arrived and gleefully informed us that the rat was dead. They even held up a dead rat to prove it. I turned to Dave and said,

"Don't rats have big extended families? I thought they liked to breed; you know, have nice large families to keep them comfortable and look after them in their dotage?"

It did, however, seem to have done the trick. I no longer had to spend hours of my life on hold listening to the same singer telling me he wished he had met me sooner. No more waiting for engineers to arrive and decimate our hallway with debris.

We have—touch wood—and anything else you can think of to ward away evil spirits and hungry rats, only lost our connection once since Basil passed on to the great rat cage in the sky. That was a main box fault, apparently. It took three weeks to fix, during which time we despaired of ever seeing a green light appear on our connection box again. Finally it was fixed, we had been upgraded, we had new rat-proof cabling (I'm still not convinced) and all is whizzing along again in the world of super-fast Fibra.

Well, that is, until one of Basil's cousins moves into the neighbourhood.

7

Portugal's Rich History

The name Portugal comes from the Roman name for the town Portus Cale, and the area we now know as Portugal was originally settled by local tribes, particularly the Lusitanians. Early in the first millennium, the Celts from Eastern Europe appeared. The Roman invasion in the 3rd century lasted several centuries, and their influence can still be seen today throughout the country. Add to that rich history, the Moorish invasion in the 8th century where they proceeded to conquer the Iberian Peninsula and settle here for several hundred years. History, myth, legend, and stories abound, and many of the local names and places that we know today have their origins in the tapestry of history woven throughout the landscape.

Portugal is located on the west side of the Iberian Peninsula. Spain is its only bordering country. Depending on which article you research, o ilhéu do Monchique, a small uninhabited islet off the coast of Flores in the Azores, is the most westerly point of Europe. Others will say that Cabo da Roca, west of Sintra, is the westernmost point of continental Europe. Both could be seen as correct, based upon how you define your European map boundaries.

What is undisputed is that Cape St Vincent is the most south-westerly point in Europe.

Today, you can visit the Cape and see the St Vincent Lighthouse. Safeguarding one of the world's most hectic shipping lanes, it hurls an impressive white beam sixty kilometres into the dark expanse of the Atlantic Ocean. It is the second most powerful lighthouse in Europe after Phare du Créac'h in Brittany.[1] It is also the perfect spot to witness the spectacular sunsets that dip into the ocean here.

The Cape St Vincent also has an interesting story behind its name. As with so many towns here, it is named after a venerated saint who, it would be fair to say, had a rather tumultuous end to his life.

In the 4th century, a pile of human remains came ashore in the far corner of what was then called Lusitania. This was the ancient Iberian-Roman province located where modern Portugal (south of the Douro river) and part of western Spain now sits.

The gruesome remains belonged to Vincent of Saragossa, who was a Christian martyr slaughtered by the Roman emperor Diocletian. When the emperor began persecuting Christians in Spain, Vincent was brought before the Roman governor, Dacian, in Valencia. According to tradition, as a punishment for refusing to perform pagan sacrifice, Vincent was imprisoned. The Bishop Valerius of Saragossa, who was with Vincent at the time and also arrested, was merely banished. The report of Vincent's subsequent time in jail makes for some gruesome reading:

"Vincent was subjected to fierce tortures before ultimately dying from his wounds. According to details of his death [which seem to have been considerably elaborated upon at a later date] his flesh was pierced with iron hooks. He was bound upon a red-hot gridiron [sic] and roasted and then cast into a prison and laid on a floor strewn with broken pottery. But through it all his constancy remained unmoved (leading to his jailer's conversion) and he survived until his friends were allowed to see him and prepare a bed for him on which he died."[2]

When Dacian heard Vincent was dead, he decided that wasn't sufficient punishment. He cast his body into a field to be devoured

by the beasts and wild birds. The legend continues that a raven came
and drove away all the other animals and protected his body. Dacian
wasn't happy with this and commanded that Vincent should be
thrown into the sea with a millstone tied around his neck. If he
couldn't be devoured by animals on the ground, then his plan was
that he would be eaten by whales and fish instead.[3]

That explains how his body ended up in the sea, to be washed
ashore at the place that was later christened Cape St Vincent. The
legend also states that ravens continued to watch over his body as it
washed ashore. A shrine was erected over his grave, which was
guarded by flocks of ravens. In the time of Muslim rule in the
Iberian Peninsula, the Arab geographer Al-Idrisi made note of this
constant vigil by the birds, and he named the location كنيسة الغراب
Kanīsah al-Ghurāb (Church of the Raven).[4] Even today, ravens can
still be seen circling around the Cape St Vincent promontory.

In 1139, Afonso Henriques became the first king of Portugal, and
he recaptured Lisbon from the Moors. Christian remains were seen
as important relics to be celebrated at that time. As a symbol of the
liberation of the city, the king sent a team down to recover Vincent's
bones. They were placed on a ship and brought to Lisbon,
apparently accompanied all the way by ten ravens flying overhead.
Vincent was declared Lisbon's patron saint, and his remains were
interred in the newly formed Lisbon cathedral, which was built over
the site of an old mosque.

King Afonso Henriques also had the Igreja e Mosteiro São
Vicente de Fora built on a hill overlooking the city. They dedicated
the church and monastery to St Vincent's name. The city's coat of
arms even includes a ship with two ravens in its design. Today, St
Vincent is the patron saint of a wonderfully eclectic mix of objects
and professions, including bakers, roof-makers, sailors, schoolgirls,
vintners, tile-makers, and roofers.

✧ℰ✧☙✧

Being the most south-westerly point in mainland Europe, the Cape
has historically been considered sacred ground. The ancient Greeks

named it the Land of Serpents, and the Romans called it Promontorium Sacrum (Holy Promontory). This is the Latin origin of the name of the town of Sagres (from Sacrum). It was also known as the Edge of the World, and this idea persisted throughout the Middle Ages until Prince Henry the Navigator arrived on the scene in the 15th century.

Interestingly, Henry, or to give him his proper title, Infante Dom Henrique of Portugal, the Duke of Viseu, was neither a sailor nor a navigator. Henry was the fourth child of the Portuguese King John I and sponsored a series of journeys into African lands.

The coast of Africa was unchartered territory for Europeans. Their ships were too slow and heavy to make the long voyage. Under Henry's direction, they developed a new and much lighter ship, which they called the caravel. A ship with a distinctive triangular sail, it was able to sail much further and faster. This meant they could travel into the prevailing winds on the open seas and explore rivers and shallow waters.

Legends at the time spoke of huge sea monsters that could allegedly swallow entire ships whole. Henry ordered his sailors to explore beyond the Cape, avoiding the ocean demons. They discovered, and later colonised, the islands of Cape Verde, the Azores, and Madeira. They were responsible for mapping the area and documenting the trade winds that dominated the North Atlantic Ocean.

Prince Henry used the town of Lagos as his base, and from here he funded voyages that explored the Mediterranean and African coasts. One historical voyage, in 1434, commanded by the famous captain, Gil Eanes, sailed past the Cape of Bojador in the Western Sahara. Before this, most explorers had considered this point to be the end of the world, calling the ocean beyond that the Sea of Darkness.

Henry secured significant trade routes for Portugal, making the country one of the world's major economic powers of the time. The Algarve Trails website describes this position as follows:

"The astronomically lucrative spice trade between Europe and the Far East was dominated by Arab merchants and their über-rich

Venetian allies. 'Why not bypass the infidel middlemen, locate Prester John, expand Christianity and humiliate the Muslim enemy?', Henry thought. The way to achieve those ambitious goals, he realised, was to send heavily armed flotillas into the perilous Atlantic to chart 'New Worlds' and new oceanic routes to India. It was a giant leap of faith because nobody knew for sure whether the Earth was round or flat, or even if there was a feasible sea lane into the mysterious Far East. Such purpose demanded new technologies, great fortitude, and a lot of brainpower. But this far-sighted venture paid off in spades. In 1498, almost 40 years after Henry's death, Vasco da Gama finally landed in Calicut, India. The fates of East and West, India, China and Japan, Africa, and Europe, started to diverge that same year. Portugal became the forerunner in the Age of Discovery."[5]

These early voyages, sponsored by Henry, laid the knowledge base of the sea routes necessary for Vasco da Gama to sail successfully around the Cape of Good Hope for India in 1498.

Sadly, Henry was not only known for trading in spices and gold, he was also attributed with being the founder of the Atlantic-African slave trade. The Portuguese captured slaves through raids on the coastal villages of Gambia and Upper Guinea. Henry justified this on the grounds that he was converting these captives to Christianity.

The history surrounding these intrepid adventures, and the belief that Henry founded a nautical school at Sagres, was lost forever during one fateful day. The 1755 earthquake that devastated so much of Portugal hit Sagres as well as many other Algarvian towns. It was the strongest earthquake with the highest tsunami ever recorded in European history.

On the 1st November 1755, at 9.40 a.m. a huge earthquake struck in the Atlantic Ocean, about one hundred-and-twenty miles off Cape St Vincent on the Portuguese coast. Modern scientists believe it measured between 8.5 and 9 on the Richter Scale. Over a ten-minute period, three shocks are said to have occurred.

Unfortunately, that was not the end of this terrible natural disaster. About forty minutes after the initial shock, tsunami waves said to have been more than eighteen feet (six meters) in height reached the shores of Lisbon. Before they struck land, the water retreated, draining the estuary of the River Tejo and revealing a number of shipwrecks in the basin. Many individuals rushed to claim treasure that might have been aboard, unaware of the impending tsunami. Others had loaded themselves onto boats and rowed out away from the shore to avoid the earthquake and its after-effects. Many vessels were overturned and sunk by the tsunami.

The 1st of November is the holy feast day of All Saints. Lisbon's churches and cathedrals were packed full of people celebrating this important day in the church's calendar. Every candle was lit, and the chapels were decorated with flowers and flammable decorations. As the tremors rocked the churches, the candles tipped over and ignited the decorations. The resulting fires raged for five days after the initial shock waves had rocked the city.

Although this became known as the Lisbon Earthquake, the entire western Portuguese coast was devastated including much of the Algarve. The worst damage occurred in the city of Lisbon because it was the most populated area in Portugal at that time. Tremors were felt as far afield as the southern coast of Ireland and Great Britain, and tidal waves reached Brazil on the far side of the Atlantic Ocean.

In Lisbon, eighty-five percent of the buildings were destroyed, and it was estimated that between thirty and forty thousand inhabitants in Lisbon perished from a total population of around two-hundred thousand. It was one of the most devastating earthquakes in history. In purely financial terms it cost Portugal almost half of its Gross Domestic Product and put an end to any future hopes of Portuguese exploration. Many historic buildings, artefacts, books, and works of art were destroyed and lost forever.

By the end of the week an estimated seventy thousand people had died as a direct result of this natural disaster.

Sadly, with their days of exploration and discovery over, partly because of the devastating effects and cost of the earthquake, by the 1900s Portugal's influence and position in the world had shrunk. In 1932, António Salazar became prime minister, and for forty-two years, first Salazar and then Marcello Caetano, ruled Portugal under a dictatorship. In 1974, a left-wing military coup, more or less peacefully, took over control of the country. Far-reaching reforms were made, including granting independence to all of Portugal's African colonies.

Portugal joined the European Union in 1986, instigating another major overhaul of the country. It is now established as a European democracy, far removed from the dictatorship of the early 1970s. Workers, however, still earn only about a third of the pay of their counterparts in the United Kingdom. Here in the Algarve, most people rely on tourism in one form or another for their work.

The European Union, and other investors, have funded the start-up of new industries and the future does look a little brighter for the country. Portugal's infrastructure has also been improved in recent years, with a better railway system, new roads, and fast motorways. Telecommunications and internet coverage are impressive in almost ninety percent of the country. Lisbon and Porto have thriving tech scenes, boosted by the annual International Web Summit, which is hosted in Lisbon each year. Presumably Basil the rat is still waiting for his invitation to attend the summit.

There is a general feeling of optimism in Portugal that combines with its wonderful history and culture, to create a country full of future possibility and old-world charm. Old fishing villages have ancient properties sitting alongside modern buildings, and many derelict houses are being sympathetically restored.

The Algarve, from the Arabic Al-Gharb meaning The West, is seen by many as the jewel in the crown, particularly in terms of tourism. Portugal is the third safest country in the world, and the Algarve is often voted the world's best golfing location and Europe's best beach destination. Always near the top of any Quality of Life surveys, and with easy residency and citizenship requirements, the Portuguese passport is much sought-after as an option for visa-free travel across Europe and beyond.

With over three hundred days of sunshine a year, and over one hundred miles of beautiful coastline, the Algarve is a wonderful place to live. There are soft sandy beaches, blue skies, clifftop walks, great food, generous and friendly people, and a relaxed way of life. It is no wonder that so many of us think this is our own little slice of heaven. I'm not sure why Prince Henry was in such a hurry to depart these delightful shores to explore the world. Every time we leave here, we can't wait to return. And every time we visit Sagres and Cape St Vincent, we check overhead to see if there are any ravens circling above us.

---

1. Walk Algarve (s.d.). Website article 10 Curious Facts about Cape St Vincent. Accessed 30th August 2020 through https://www.walkalgarve.com/attractions-and-things-to-do-in-algarve/cape-st-vincent

2. Catholic Online (s.d.). Website article St. Vincent Saragossa. Accessed 30th August 2020 through https://www.catholic.org/saints/saint.php?saint_id=724

3. Columbia University - Treasures of Heaven Project (s.d.). Website article *Saints & Martyrs - Saint Vincent of Saragossa*. Accessed 31st August 2020 through https://projects.mcah.columbia.edu/treasuresofheaven//saints/Vincent.php

4. Medium.com (22.01.2020). Article by Father Troy Beecham *Today, the Church remembers St. Vincent of Saragossa, Deacon and Martyr*. Accessed 31st August 2020 through https://medium.com/@Troy_Beecham_Episcopal/today-the-church-remembers-st-vincent-of-saragossa-deacon-and-martyr-1ef1898cf049

5. Walk Algarve (s.d.). Website article 10 Curious Facts about Cape St Vincent. Accessed 30th August 2020 through https://www.walkalgarve.com/attractions-and-things-to-do-in-algarve/cape-st-vincent

8

Golf, Charities, and Cataplanas

I was keen to talk to our friend Dave D about his experiences of moving here to live, especially as he has settled down in our much-loved old town of Ferragudo with his wife and son. We have had some wonderful evenings out with him and his family, enjoying his robust sense of humour and teasing him about his golf swing.

Dave D was born in Sunderland, he graduated in maths from university in 1979, and ended up running and owning computer companies in and around North London. He moved here to live in the Algarve at the end of 2016. His wife had retired, and together with their son, she had relocated here six months earlier. Dave D commuted back and forward whilst working his notice until he could finally make the permanent move to be with his family.

He first explored the Algarve in the early to mid-1990s when he came out to stay near Almancil to play golf. He rediscovered the region in the early 2000s and formulated a plan to live here after retirement. I asked him what swayed his decision.

"The clincher was a half-term break at Center Parcs with some friends where I saw a daytime TV show about a couple who had relocated to the Algarve. Ironically, after we bought our first place here in 2014 and watched the show on repeat, we discovered we had chosen the same town (Ferragudo) as the couple in the show!"

His favourite thing about living here was easy for Dave D to answer:

"Waking up for six months of the year and realising you only need your swimming shorts and a T-shirt."

He admitted, though, that he missed seeing live rugby matches.

"I used to go to at least one rugby international at Twickenham each year. Watching it on TV here just isn't the same."

Initially, Dave D said he and his wife had grand plans to buy a large house in the countryside. They quickly realised they didn't want to spend three or four days a week maintaining it and driving backwards and forwards to restaurants, so they settled for living in a town. They found it straightforward to find a property to purchase but admitted that 'authentic towns' like Ferragudo have a price premium attached.

He has an interesting perspective on the value of genuine friendships, especially once you move abroad to live. It is easy to meet lots of new people, although not all of them are going to become friends.

"I was sixty just over a year after we moved out here and held two parties, one in the UK and the other in a local restaurant. I had more people at the Portuguese event than the UK (it cost less than half the price of course!). I realised that you make many acquaintances very quickly but soon the real friends list is whittled down."

Dave D's outlook is similar to our own view of friendship. Dave and I have always maintained we have many acquaintances, but few friends. It is a word of caution we often give to new people that have recently moved here to live. Take your time meeting people, don't be drawn into new groups and social events so quickly that you do not take time to take stock of everything and everyone.

Some people will want to be your friend, in our case, because they are also British, but sharing a nationality is not usually enough reason to befriend someone. Many so-called friendships are often only on a very superficial level in the sunshine, surrounded by a few beers or glasses of wine. Which is fine if all you are looking for is some company. Real friendships can take much longer to cultivate but are priceless when you find them.

Dave D plays golf but has decided not to base his social life around the golf course and the 19th hole.

"There are golf clubs all over the Algarve and many people live in that expat bubble, which is fair enough. I still play regularly but prefer to organise my social life with a more varied set of people—a mix of Europeans from all over. I volunteered for a local soup kitchen in Portimão, but since that was closed because of Covid-19, I now support a charity called Algarve Families in Need."

I had heard about both charities and was keen to find out more about them. The Portimão soup kitchen started in May 2010, run by the local International Christian Fellowship church. At their busiest, they feed up to sixty people per session. They provide meals on Mondays at 4 p.m. and Wednesdays at 6 p.m. They offer a larger meal on Sundays at 2 p.m. On Friday mornings they open their doors to distribute used clothing. At Christmas they feed around one hundred people for a special festive dinner. Solely funded by charitable donations and private sponsors, their work adds a valuable contribution to the local area and is sadly much needed.

The Algarve Network for Families in Need is a longstanding and well-developed charity in the Algarve, concentrating primarily on acquiring items for families that need help. People who no longer require an item donate it to the charity and they then forward it on to someone in need. They have an online network of supporters and put out requests for items that are required, like a second-hand bed or fridge. They also have collection points situated outside major supermarkets and shops across the Algarve. Once a week, volunteers man these points and collect dried goods and foodstuffs which are then bagged up and distributed to low-income and struggling families.

The Covid-19 virus has made matters even more severe here in the Algarve, where so many people rely on tourism for their work and livelihood.

Bernadette Abbott is an English sociologist who moved to live here eight years ago. Her background was in social justice and human rights, as well as social care management. Bernadette became a volunteer for Algarve Network for Families in Need charity and was interviewed in a local paper about her work.

"One of the main problems for Portuguese families is that the minimum pay has been low and there has been no correlation between pay and the minimum amount it is possible to live on. Too many people work without contracts and on minimum pay only during the tourist season. They are without work or income in the winter months. For workers without a contract or the self-employed without work through the winter, there is no eligibility for social security payments. The Algarve has become far too dependent on summer tourism and little else. Winter is a nightmare for those on minimum pay in seasonal work. Families run up debts on rents, utilities, and other essentials. They have to spend the whole of the summer repaying them."[1]

The work of charities like this becomes a vital lifeline for such families. This is the hidden side of the Algarve that tourists, and sadly many locals, often fail to see. Dave and I are looking at ways we can use our skills to promote this charity, and support Dave D, Bernadette, and the other volunteers who give tirelessly of their time and knowledge to help others.

❀❧❀❀☙❀

Having a friend called Dave who has the same name as your husband is a tad confusing. For the purposes of this chapter I have called him Dave D. In real life, we call him 'Red Dave' on account of his strong political views, which align nicely with our own. We do tease him that his altruistic and fervently socialist stance is slightly at odds with his love of golf, though.

The Algarve is a golfer's paradise, boasting some of Europe's finest championship courses, all set in magnificent surroundings, and many have breath-taking views of the coastline. It's not difficult to see why people like playing golf here.

The first golf ball was struck in Portugal in 1890 when British port producers formed the Oporto Niblicks Club, now known as Oporto Golf Club. In the 1920s, golf first made its way to the Algarve. Reports suggest the first golf course in the Algarve was built between Portimão and the beach of Praia da Rocha. I cannot find any more information about this course, other than they mysteriously constructed the greens from sand and oil.

Golfers then had to wait until 1966 and Sir Henry Cotton, who built the first traditional grass course in the Algarve at Penina, which is now called the Sir Henry Championship Course. The resort's website describes the lengths he had to go to build the course, which is on a 360-acre estate. He planted 360,000 trees and shrubs to create a woodland environment and added streams and lakes to the layout.[2]

Not only was Sir Henry responsible for the Penina course, but he also drew up the original layouts for the courses at Vale do Lobo, Pestana Alto near Alvor, and Benamor Golf in Tavira. The mild winter weather in the Algarve meant that golfers could extend their golf season and enjoy their game almost all-year round. As a result, a new branch of tourism was born for the region. By the end of the 1980s, Portugal had twenty-three courses, with thirteen of those here in the Algarve. By the start of the year 2000, Portugal had over fifty courses, with thirty-one located locally. Most of these are centred around purpose-built resorts. Dave D will never be short of somewhere to play a round of golf here.

I asked Dave D if he had encountered any problems here (apart from some tricky holes on his local golf course). He replied that inevitably there is a lot of paperwork when you move here and sometimes the process can be slow. His advice was sensible and succinct: just go with the flow.

I wondered if his Portuguese language was also flowing nicely now.

"I have been on two courses and really struggled. Like many Brits I don't excel at languages, but by spending more time with the local communities I am gradually picking it up. I speak baby Portuguese, but this will get better!"

I asked Dave D about his retirement, teasing him that he is not old enough to have stopped working.

"Thankfully, I don't have to work—a near impossibility for me given my language skills—but I could spend every day at the golf course or local gym if I wanted to. I try to mix it up, some local lunches, long dog walks, some leisure time, and some charity work. I did a remote contract in the UK initially, but soon concluded I was doing it because I was scared of being bored. When I stopped working, I realised I am rarely bored living here."

Dave D moved over here with his wife and teenage son. Their son was starting his GCSEs within a year of moving out here and they sent him to a fee-paying international school which Dave D described as of 'mixed quality'. The school had some good teachers, and some who were, in his words, 'only here for the wine and sun.' He recognises there are limited job opportunities here in Portugal for the young.

They have a cottage in Finland, which they visit every summer. They lived in the Netherlands from 1998 to 1999 and enjoyed it, but found it very different. They especially loved the beauty of Amsterdam.

Moving to the Algarve was a simple decision for them. The climate, the wine and the food make Portugal a special place.

"It has an amazing history of achievement, education, and culture, all of which are prized more than wealth."

I was interested to find out what living in different countries had taught him and, in particular, his experiences here in Portugal.

"I have learnt to adapt—you are the migrant. The Portuguese are generally a lovely bunch of people, if you respect their culture, their food, and their pace of life, you will settle quickly."

I asked him about shopping out here, and if there were items he missed from back home.

"You can get anything you like over here if you are prepared to pay for it. We mainly stick with local brands; they are cheaper and usually better quality. White and brown goods and cars are more expensive here."

Dave D gave away a few secrets for me with some of his special places and favourite foods:

"Rui's bar also known as The Yacht Club on the main beach here in Ferragudo is a lovely beach bar to sit and watch the world go by. I love *cataplana* which is a fish soup. There are nearly forty restaurants within walking distance of our house, but I would single out Aria and Sanleti, two locally run restaurants, as my favourites."

His perfect day out would include walking their dog along a deserted Alvor beach with his family, followed by coffee and toast at a local restaurant. He would have a friendly game of golf, a late lunch at a local chicken restaurant, and then a quiet glass of wine sat outside.

I asked him where he sees himself in five years' time (and resisted the urge to tease him about still being stuck on a green somewhere). His reply was reassuring and positive,

"More or less the same (hopefully). I realise how lucky I am to retire early. When I think that by the age of seventy-five most people have ailments of one sort or another, enjoying life as early as possible is crucial."

I had to ask him about the UK's decision to leave Europe, as this has been a sore topic for many people out here. I knew that Dave D would give me a forthright answer.

"This is a disaster waiting to happen; the ramifications are likely to be dire, particularly on those Brits living in the EU—many of whom still don't get it—and some even voted for it!"

His advice for anyone considering a similar move abroad is sensible.

"Find a local tax expert who can advise you in advance of what you need to do. Timing is crucial in tax matters, and it is so easy to get it wrong. Don't listen to anybody who says you can live for next to nothing over here. And join as many local expat online communities as you can."

Dave D seems to have hit a good balance out here. He enjoys his life and his family, and has a healthy and satisfying social calendar, surrounded by special friends, and wonderful food and wine. He has found a niche with his charity work and is sanguine about the bureaucratic paperwork processes we all come up against living here. It is lovely to chat to other people who have moved here to live, and discovered things to be as fantastic as we have, despite the problems we all face from time to time. I just hope he gets his golf swing sorted out soon.

---

1. Cited via the Portugal Resident (11.05.2020). Website article by Len Port *Algarve Network for Families in Need: insight into a charity whose efforts have become vital.* Accessed 16th September 2020 through https://www.portugalresident. com/algarve-network-for-families-in-need-insight-into-a-charity-whose-efforts-have-become-vital/
2. Penina Hotel and Golf Resort (s.d.). Website article *History of Golf in the Algarve.* Accessed 16th September 2020 through https://www.penina.com/penina-hotel/the-algarve/history-of-golf-in-the-algarve/

9

Aljezurenses

O ne thing about living here in Aljezur that has amazed me is how welcoming our neighbours have been. Right from day one, they have made us feel part of this wonderful little local community. Everyone has been very patient with us and our appalling Portuguese language skills. They are fantastically generous, bringing round bags of fruit and vegetables with amazing regularity. There is rarely a week that passes without someone knocking on our door with another gift from their *horta* or allotment. Many of our neighbours own a plot on the shared field below us, and whatever is in season ready to harvest they share with us. Everything is chemical-free and tended by hand. You cannot get much more local than the end of your road. I often find I am not alone as I rinse a cauliflower just handed to me from our neighbour's garden, as I watch all the slugs and snails crawl out to say hello.

I have never tasted such fresh fruit and vegetables as those we have been eating here. Even the colour of the produce seems brighter and more natural. The strawberries and blueberries, in particular, taste nothing like the bland supermarket-packaged ones, even their so-called organic range.

One of my absolute pleasures has been discovering the daily market in the old town beside the river, and especially one of its stallholders, Petra. She is Dutch, married to a local Portuguese man, and has become a dear friend and trusted food seller. There is nothing she doesn't know about the wonderful and varied products she sells at the market, and she has taught me so much about how to prepare and eat food. She has also introduced me to so many new flavours, fruits, and vegetables, some local and most surprising. I did not know that the leafy tops of the little baby broccoli tasted as good as the actual vegetable. Or that you can cook the leaves of the Portuguese cabbage plant, which the locals call *grelos de couve*. You fry it in a wok with some coconut oil, diced onion, garlic, fresh mushrooms, and bacon bits. It makes the most amazing and filling lunch in under ten minutes. The little yellow flowers on the top of the plant are edible too.

I have learnt that bananas from Madeira have a denser and sweeter flavour than ordinary bananas, and that the lettuces, carrots, and green beans from Petra's garden are possibly the best in the world. The blueberries come from Rogil, just up the road, and the sweet potatoes are from São Teotónio, about ten miles away. I have also discovered that broccoli, and some sweet potatoes, can be a bright purple colour. Purple mashed potatoes are an impressive addition to any plate of food.

Petra's stand is a veritable feast of colourful produce and it is a delight to shop there each week. Not to mention the fact that Petra, and her colleague Graça, are so helpful. Petra has run the stall for about seven years, and I meet her early each morning at Paulo's, the local café. We have discovered we have the same naughty sense of humour and a similar outlook on the world. Kat adores Petra, and the never-ending supply of biscuits hidden in her pocket, and the café is a lovely natural half-way point on our river walk to stop and have a coffee and chat.

Other neighbours have been so helpful when we have been stuck. We have a narrow-ish driveway for our car, which we always park facing inwards and then reverse out. I clipped the wall with my offside mirror one morning, whilst reversing. Initially, I rolled down the window, looked at the offending item and thought I had got away with my little escapade. I tapped the top of the mirror to say, 'well done' and it promptly fell off its perch and ended up dangling at an alarming angle, wires askew.

I got out to take a better look, just as one of our neighbours, Ricardo, drove past. He works in a local car repair garage, and when he had finished laughing at my predicament, he promised to pop round later to mend it for me. Ricardo came that evening after work with the kit that he uses to cement windscreens in place. He admitted he had done the same thing with his own wing mirror some months ago, and after using the fixative, it set like concrete. I soon had a bandaged mirror, which he assured me would be fine by the following day. The next morning he returned before he went to work and checked over his handiwork. We had to force him to accept some 'beer money' as a thank you, as he refused to take any payment at all for his efforts.

Another neighbour came round to give us a hand to change the ceiling light in our kitchen. I knew he worked for the local electrical company and assumed that he could help us. When he had finished fixing it, I said to him,

"You must be fed up fitting another light, having been working all day."

He replied,

"But I am not an electrician. I just work in the office."

We also have our own local neighbourhood watch too. I thought I would miss our neighbour António and his vigilance walking up and down our road when we left our old house. Readers of my first book might remember him, as he was the man that sprouted an entire new set of gleaming white teeth. He went from being toothless and easy to understand, to a pin-up for dental implants and completely unintelligible.

Our new neighbour, José, has a less impressive set of teeth, but a shock of white hair for a man approaching his eightieth birthday. You can find him all day either leaning on his umbrella or a long stick of bamboo cane, watching his beloved chickens scrabble around the land outside his house. He does not miss a trick, observing every person and vehicle entering or leaving our little estate. The only time you could get past him unnoticed would be during his nap hour when he settles himself into a comfy old armchair in his garden, nestled under the veranda, and has his constitutional forty winks. It's often nearer eighty winks, though.

He plays a mean game of dominoes with one of our neighbours every weekend at lunchtime. I love walking past their garden and hearing the clack of the dominoes hit the table alongside the guffaws of laughter and chatter. That, and the clink of the wineglass as they both drink their daily red wine apéritif. It's good for the heart, you know!

José is also an absolute stickler for the midday tradition of changing the *bom dia* morning greeting to the afternoon *boa tarde*. If it is even only a minute past noon when I pop outside to walk Kat for her lunchtime stroll up the road, and I get it wrong and say *"bom dia"* to José, he mutters *"não, não,"* and shakes his head at me, saying,

"Boa tarde, boa tarde, é meio dia." ("Good afternoon, good afternoon, it is [after] midday.")

Now and then I catch him out, usually when he has had an early nap and missed the church clock chiming twelve. I say *"boa tarde"* to him and he says *"não, bom dia."* Back and forth we go until he reaches into his jacket and pulls out his old and much-loved pocket watch. His face, if I am right and he is wrong, is priceless.

He is naughty sometimes too. At the end of our little estate of houses, the road turns into a dead-end track. José delights in seeing a caravan or campervan travel past him, knowing there is nowhere for them to go other than to execute a tricky three-point turn and backtrack. He waits until they are going back down the hill, then gives them a cheery wave and a hearty chuckle.

His long-suffering wife, Fernanda, is an amazing woman in her late seventies, who spends every day feeding and cleaning their chickens and rabbits, not to mention looking after José. I often see her digging over their vegetable plot, or returning from a quick trip down to the fields around the river, laden with grass cuttings for the animals to eat.

She had an ancient wheelbarrow that squeaked and swayed as it trundled along on an almost flat old wheel. Sometimes it was piled so high you couldn't see who was behind the mound of grass and weeds as it trundled up the hill. Dave and I frequently helped her as she pushed the ancient contraption back to their house. I appreciate that José's health meant he could not assist her as much as he might have liked to; however, I teased him one day he should try to help Fernanda more.

The next time I saw José, he informed me he had indeed decided to assist Fernanda. He pointed down the road, where I could see her approaching me, pushing her usual mountainous mass of greenery up the hill. Except this time, she was brandishing a brand-new shiny green wheelbarrow with a bright yellow wheel.

"You see," said José with pride, "I am helping her. I bought her a new wheelbarrow."

☼ॐ☼ֆ☼

Walking Kat means that I see many of our neighbours every single day. One local man, Fernando, has a daily walk around the river, and I often stop and talk to him. I would always call him *senhor* Fernando, which is a respectful form of greeting for someone older or more senior. One morning I saw him and, as usual, said,

"Bom dia, senhor Fernando."

"No," he replied in Portuguese, "it is not *senhor* Fernando anymore. Now we are friends and you must call me just Fernando."

There are so many wonderful, simple moments like this that remind me why we love living here.

If only all the names of the locals were as easy to remember as Fernando's though. There are some amazing men's names round here, including an Ederlazio and an Amilka. There is also an Abelha, which I thought was another strange male name. It translates as 'bee' and is the nickname of one of our neighbours. I have no idea what his actual name is, as everyone calls him Abelha.

It is much easier to remember local women's names as most of the women here are called Maria. I know so many Marias; I need a way to differentiate them all. So there is my dear friend Maria Victoria, then there is Maria, who is Maria Victoria's neighbour, (are you confused yet?) and Maria the street sweeper. Then there is Tia Maria, who is Maria the street sweeper's aunt, and Maria from the padaria, who works in the local bakery, called A Padaria. (They make the best cakes in town, but I digress from the Maria-fest). Finally, we have a Maria round the corner, and a Maria up the hill. It can all get very confusing.

My name causes even more problems. I am used to having to spell my name, as I am an Alyson with a 'y'. It is almost impossible to find anyone locally that can say my name correctly – not that I mind at all. The closest alternative that most of my neighbours manage is to call me Alice. Which is pronounced 'A – leese'. One of the many Marias knows that Alice is not quite right, and that there is an 'on' to be added somewhere. Whenever she sees me, she says "Olà, A – leese". Then there is a pause—imagine the time it would take for her to inhale deeply and count to four—then she says, "on" with a smile. I'm sure she wishes I was called Maria, the same as all the other women around here.

Dave gets off lightly, as he is always called David. It is just pronounced differently; it is more like 'Da – veed'. You can see him wince slightly every time he hears that, as the only time his parents ever called him David was when he was in trouble.

Every Saturday morning you will find most of the Marias are up at the farmer's market, which takes place on the edge of town. It is a curious mix of local, elderly people, selling their home-grown fruit and vegetables; together with the local travelling community touting all manner of home-made items. You can find jams and chutneys, knitted baby clothes, home-made cakes and bread, and weird and not-so-wonderful balms and remedies all lined up on adjoining tables. It is also the meeting place for the travelling community, who then transfer themselves up to the cafés at the square in Igreja Nova afterwards and sit chatting in the sunshine.

This Saturday lunchtime festival is often called the local

Woodstock event. It is not always described in the most glowing of terms, it must be said. I have no idea where most of these people live or park their vans, as you rarely see that many travellers around during the week. But every Saturday, the square is full of hippie-chicks and chickens. Sometimes there are well over a hundred people, including children, families, and wandering minstrels (literally). You can usually find a couple of tattooed and dreadlocked Buddhas sitting contemplating life whilst drinking coffee and eating dubious-looking sushi as well.

Aljezur seems to draw in more than its fair share of alternative lifestyle travellers. I have nothing against them and their ambition to live a different way of life, and many will explain they want to leave a gentle footprint and respect the planet. What I do object to is that, for some of them, their desire to be ecological doesn't extend to not leaving soiled toilet paper along the river path. I have sadly had the dubious pleasure, on too many occasions, of watching both men and women saunter out of their camper vans and crouch down to pee (or worse) in the bushes. Some of them don't even look embarrassed when they see me walking past them.

Award of the year, however, must go to the man I walked past one morning along the river. It was summer solstice, which I guess was his reason for sitting on the path, cross-legged, waiting for the sun to rise. Nothing wrong with that, you are probably thinking. Except for one slight problem. He was wearing only a pair of baggy and soiled pants. Nothing else. Kat trotted up for a better look, and I tried to sidle past him, which was hard to do. He then decided as it was such a delightful morning he wanted to chat to me. I am quite a gregarious sort, but I didn't fancy spending any length of time talking to 'pants man'. Luckily for me, Kat got the whiff of a different and more interesting scent ahead of us, and shot off, giving me the perfect excuse to leave him to it.

He should have taken a leaf out of the locals' books and worn something more appropriate. If it had been wintertime, he could have wrapped up nice and warm and covered up his dirty pants. Winter is the time to strut your stuff wearing the latest female fashion - flannelette pyjamas, worn under a big fluffy dressing-gown.

It is almost standard cold-weather attire here, especially the dressing gown. I regularly see one lady walking her dog whilst wearing a patterned fleecy little number and furry slippers, and the locals think nothing of popping to the local shops similarly attired. It must be a British thing, but I wouldn't be seen dead outside in the road wearing my night clothes, let alone go shopping in them! Here, nobody bats an eyelid.

Older women tend to wear a housecoat, often topped with a straw boater in the summer, or a more substantial hat in the winter. There is a local shop in town that sells these old-fashioned housecoats. I walked past one day, and they had an entire rack of them on display for sale. I had to stop myself from going in; the thought whizzing through my mind was that one of those might be handy for when I am painting. However, I didn't have my purse with me, and the feeling passed.

One place that is worth visiting is the traditional market that takes place on the second Monday of each month. The usual bric-à-brac, shoes and clothes, and small kitchen appliances are on display, alongside some very impressive (and sharp) garden tools. Boxes of chickens and rabbits are on sale and I always struggle to walk past them as they look so fed up and lonely. However, by the end of the morning, most of them are sold and are on the way to some (hopefully) larger accommodation. You can buy fresh fruit and vegetables, herbs, and plants here, which are strategically placed next to the stall selling pairs of extra-large pants and wellington boots. Who says that rural life is boring?

✿❧✿☙✿

One of my favourite things has been making friends with the locals, and one friendship has blossomed. Maria Victoria is now seventy and lives a little way away from me. I often go past her house walking Kat, and her daughter is one of our neighbours. Maria Victoria leads a simple life, tending to her many chickens, rabbits, and vegetables on her little plot of land. We started chatting one day and became good friends. I knew she had accepted me the afternoon she invited me in to sit inside her covered patio area beside the house and talk to her.

She is very patient with me and my poor grasp of Portuguese, and as she speaks no English at all, she has forced me to improve my language skills. It has been worth it to listen to her tell stories about her childhood and growing up in the town.

I had been busy creating a painting of the local windmill at Rogil and showed Maria Victoria the picture of my finished work one afternoon. She launched into a fabulous story about growing up nearby, and the windmill being the local source of wheat and bread. The owner's wife, Clara, was also famous for her poultices and potions. Maria Victoria explained that if anyone in your family was ever ill, if you had a cold, for example, you would be packed off to see her. Clara prepared a poultice of herbs and wild plants for you, which you would attach to the soles of your feet overnight. In the morning, miraculously, you would feel better. Legend has it that Clara even cured herself. A scorpion bit her on the arm and she created a special remedy which healed the bite. Well, even if it is not true, it is still a novel way of marketing your products.

Maria Victoria leads an uncomplicated life that involves rearing chickens and rabbits from the monthly market and collecting large bundles of grass and wild plants for them to eat. Female chickens are bred for their egg-laying capacity, but the males are for the pot. Rabbits arrive at the same sad ending. I grew up in a big city, where the only meat I ever saw was already dead hanging up in the butcher's shop window. Living in a rural area takes some getting used to. The first time I saw a bunch of baby rabbits lolloping around in their makeshift shelter, I fell in love with them. They were so cute with their floppy ears and inquisitive nature. I had no idea they were being fattened up for Maria Victoria and her family to eat. Call me a naïve city girl, but I thought they were going to stay there and grow old together.

Once I found out their true purpose, I was gutted. I went home and wrote out a petition notice, complete with photographs of the bunnies, and space for signatures underneath. Dave and I signed it, I added a paw print for Kat, then printed it off and laminated it. Next time I visited her and her fluffy companions, I pinned it to the outside fence of their little home. Maria Victoria and her daughter and family all thought it was hilarious. Almost eighteen months later, the sign is still there, a bit faded, but still attached to the fence. Sadly, the rabbits have long gone into her cast iron cooking pot that is over one hundred years old and hangs above an outside fire oven in the garden.

The next batch of rabbits fared no better. My face is always a study when I find out what she has planned for them, which makes her chuckle. I even walked past one afternoon, just as she had slit the throat of one of the rabbits. It was hanging upside down, blood still dripping, as she skinned it with a small sharp knife in one straight manoeuvre. I bet she bought the knife, as well as the rabbit, from the monthly market.

Baby chickens must be some of the cutest animals on sale there at the market. Maria Victoria often has chicks instead of rabbits in her 'abattoir corner' as I have nicknamed it. It is perfect for Kat, who loves visiting as she can observe the inhabitants from a higher vantage point. There are stone steps outside that give her an unobstructed view down into the covered area below. Lots of local people see us walking up to Maria Victoria's and shout "off to see the chickens again?" as we pass by.

Watching her latest batch of chickens grow up has been a delight. Kat and I often arrive in time to see them get their afternoon feed, and one day I said to Maria Victoria,

"Can I bring some lettuce for them to eat tomorrow?"

"Of course," she replied, "if you want to."

I had an idea. Petra always has leftover food at the market that I know she takes home to feed her own animals, so I figured she would have some old lettuces for me. Sure enough, the next day, Dave collected our order, and there was a big bag of green leaves waiting for me. I walked to Maria Victoria's house, and she smiled at me as we arrived. Kat settled down in her usual spot, and Maria Victoria assumed I was going to throw the food for the chickens onto the ground.

"Oh no," I said, "I'm going to feed them by hand."

She looked at me with an amused expression that roughly translated as 'mad English-woman' but left me to it.

There is a small-holed plastic fence that covers the side of their little enclosure. Inside there is an old ramp and stacked-up tables that allow the chickens to climb up to the fence to say hello to us. Kat can see them but can't touch them, although I have known her to sniff a chicken's rear end rather enthusiastically. She has never tried to hurt one, even though José's chickens are often loose in the road outside our house. She is just fascinated by them, so I thought if I could train them to come and eat the lettuce through the fence in front of Kat, she would have a ring-side seat to enjoy the show.

It took a couple of days, then one of cockerels, the little runt of the litter, spotted the lettuce and scrambled up to eat it. I named him Eric as he reminded me of Eric Idle (with apologies to the Monty Python genius), and he was quickly followed by Bonita (Beautiful), Curiosa (Nosey) and then Ovozinha. Maria Victoria tipped her head to one side and chuckled as I explained the last name to her,

"It's a made-up name from *ovos* (eggs) and *vizinha* (neighbour)."

If she didn't think I was daft feeding the chickens by hand, she did once she found out some of them now had names. I am sure none of her brood has ever been given a moniker before.

"But look," I continued unperturbed, "Eric knows his name. Watch."

I called out "Eric," and sure enough, he turned around and trotted right up to the fence to say hello to us.

I'm not sure what she replied in Portuguese at that moment. Some things are maybe better left untranslated.

It became an afternoon ritual to take lettuce leaves up for them to eat. After a few days, I arrived to find that Maria Victoria had added some fine mesh to the outside of the fence to stop birds, especially sparrows, from getting into abattoir corner. She came over and saw I was struggling to reach the chickens through the extra layer of fencing.

"What I need is a little window to feed them through," I exclaimed.

The next afternoon I returned to find she had cut a large slit in the mesh which was now held in place by two clothes pegs. The opening was the perfect size for me to roll back and secure with the pegs. Now who was being soft about feeding the chickens?!

As I write, Eric continues to entertain the three of us every afternoon, and I am busy petitioning for him to beat the pot and live out his days being hand-fed and pampered.

10

The Dog Whisperer

I have always loved animals, and particularly dogs, from an incredibly young age. We always had a dog at home when I was a child, and they were part of the family and much loved. Some of my earliest memories are of Jane, a lovely gentle dog that was a cross between a Dalmatian and a Spaniel. She was the most patient little girl, never minding when I played roughly with her as a toddler and joining me in my playpen. Once she passed, we had an old fat Labrador that came to stay as her elderly owner could not manage her. Sadly, she did not live much longer, and my mom decided that next time we would have a younger dog so we could enjoy more time with them.

No doubt fuelled by the Andrex toilet paper adverts that abounded on television at that time, mom invited a breeder to visit us. They had two young yellow Labrador puppies available and they looked exactly like the pups used in the adverts. It was an impossible task for my mom to choose one. She would have taken both of them immediately, had my dad allowed that... so it was left to me, the teenager, to select my favourite. One of the pups was sleeping peacefully in her basket, the other jumped and leapt around, gnawing anything and everything, and went outside with me into the garden where she promptly did a poo! You can guess which one I chose. Susie, as we named her, remained a monster all her life, chewing things, racing around, and enjoying life to the full.

My knowledge of how to work with a dog and train them gently was non-existent then. I gleefully taught Susie tricks that included being able to pull the tablecloth off from under a fully laden table of food and plates in one flourish. The resulting mess on the table was a bonus. My poor mom, I look back on my exploits now with a sheepish grin, but still chuckle at Susie's antics.

Once I was away at university, and subsequently working full time, it was not possible for me to have a dog, much to my bitter disappointment. I did not fully realise how much I missed having a dog beside me until we adopted our darling rescued Spanish Water Dog, Kat. The day we collected her was the most wonderful, transforming moment. We instantly fell in love with our little scrap of fur with her trusting yet sad eyes. We will never know the extent of her life before she was rescued, and perhaps it is for the best we do not know her history. We now have the most adorable, quiet, yet slightly mischievous monkey we could have ever hoped for.

I found Kat extremely easy to train; in fact, she needed very little training at all. As an older dog—she was about five when she was rescued—she was already house-trained. She walks well on a lead, and perfectly off a lead, and just wants to please us. My connection with her was instant. I can read her and know what she wants by glancing at her. If she needs something, for example, to go outside, she comes over to me and gently nudges my side to tell me. The bond between a dog and their owner can be magnificently strong, and her loyalty is immense. The few occasions when I have been in any danger (like the time feral cats attacked us and chewed chunks out of my leg) she was there defending and protecting me.

I have never thought of my view of animals, and dogs in particular, to be anything other than normal. I love to greet other dogs on our walks, and they always seem calm and pleased to see me. Maybe they simply know that I like them.

I realised I might have a natural gift with dogs the day I met one of our neighbours, who lives up the road from us. They have a garden that overlooks the main road, with quite a high wall with a hedge growing on top. There is a small hole in the hedge and their cute little dog, a typical crossbreed type that defies description, always pops her head through the gap for me to say hello to her. She has lovely soft caramel eyes and a very waggy tail, as I could see through the hedge. I spent many weeks fussing over her on our lunchtime walks but had no idea what her name was. Kat would happily sit beside me as I played with my new friend.

One lunchtime I walked past her house when I heard a gate opening and the little dog came bounding up the road. She sat in front of me and started wagging her tail. Naturally, I bent down to give her some attention, and the next thing I knew, my neighbour, her owner, came over and said to me,

"What are you doing with my dog?"

"I'm sorry," I replied, "what do you mean, I'm only fussing her."

"Yes, but you cannot do that," she said, looking more confused than angry.

"Why not?" I said, still scratching her dog's head and giggling at how happy she was to see me. Kat was saying hello to her as well, and all seemed fine. I could not understand why my neighbour was upset.

"Because she will not let you do that. She does not like anyone except our immediate family to touch her, and she doesn't like other dogs either."

"Oh, well, she seems fine with me," I replied, "in fact I fuss her most days through the hedge." (I wasn't sure whether to admit that or not!)

"What's her name?"

Her owner stood beside me, looking bemused, and replied,

"Cindy."

I carried on stroking her head, wondering what all the fuss was about.

"How do you do that?" her owner, whose name I discovered was Paula, asked me.

I was confused; all I had done was what I would do with any other dog I met that wanted some attention. Paula explained that

Cindy would bark and growl at anyone passing by, would let no one touch her, and was aggressive towards other dogs. I looked down at the little grinning dog squirming around to get her back rubbed as I played with her. She seemed happy to have Kat sat beside her. I found it hard to reconcile the dog and the description.

I left Paula scratching her head, and would not have believed her at all, had I not walked up the road one lunchtime shortly after this, with both Dave and Kat in tow. We reached Cindy's garden; she spotted Dave and started barking and growling menacingly, teeth bared. Dave stepped back, I walked forward towards her, and she instantly stopped barking, wagged her tail, and licked my nose in greeting!

She has done this every time since when she sees Dave. With me, whenever Paula opens their gate, Cindy comes hurtling towards me, tail wagging, looking for fuss. Paula spent months shaking her head at me when she saw this happening; now she has simply accepted her dog seems to love me and happily chats to me whilst I play with Cindy.

✿❧✿❦✿

We have another street dog I have also started to teach basic commands to, mainly because I got fed up with him misbehaving. I nicknamed him Wolfie because he can often be found out in the road on the night of a full moon howling away to himself. He has a most impressive cartoon howl; he holds his head back and really goes for it. He is a type of Springer, with long black wavy hair, although that description does make him sound rather handsome. In reality he is a scruff, with matted fur full of grass and seed heads. He has a tail that has some white hair scattered on the top that makes him look like he ran past a building that had just been freshly painted and managed to rub his tail along the wall. He also has four paws that seem to run in four different directions as he hurtles past you down the road, woofing at nothing in particular.

His name is apparently Valente. Or Valence, as his owners are Brazilian, which translates as Valiant. I prefer Wolfie. He is quite a sweetie with me, and no trouble at all, although neighbours will tell a different story of him terrorising their dogs and even biting one of them.

He has a small kennel outside his house which he sleeps in, unless it is raining, when he is put in the garage. He spends his days wandering up and down the road, or sleeping under a car, waiting for his owners to come home or someone to give him some love or food. One of the neighbours did make a complaint about him, much to his owner's consternation, and the GNR Police were called. Advice was sternly given, and for about two weeks Wolfie was chained up outside his house. The resulting howls of indignation and the pitiful expression on his face meant that idea was quickly squashed, and he was soon back to his old tricks in the road again.

He loves to come for a walk with Kat, which for a while caused me some problems. He is a bit of a rogue, and likes to race along, obviously not on a lead. Which is fine when we are walking beside the river where Kat is also off-lead and walks perfectly, sniffing and snuffling along. Wolfie likes to hurtle around, but he is oblivious to traffic on the main road. After a few disastrous walks where he ran in front of a bus and a few near misses with cars, I gave up and taught him the command of 'casa' or 'home' and sent him back to his kennel.

In the winter months, Kat and I walk along the road first and do a circuit which leads us back along the river walk on the way home. The looks of anger and shouts from car drivers when they saw Wolfie hurtling towards them was too much for me. It is impossible to explain in a single gesture to the driver whizzing past me that he is not mine, he's the neighbour's dog. Or to explain that I can't really control him, he's just come along for a walk with my dog.

In the summer months, I swap round and walk first along the river, as it is lighter much earlier and the chances of seeing a *javali* or wild boar are slim. In the winter, in the half-light, as I previously explained, we have seen several, and they are a scary sight. Wolfie seems to know when we change direction, and he can come with us again for a walk. Most mornings I wake before 6.30 a.m. and I can usually hear him outside our front gate waiting for us. By the time we leave at about 7 a.m. he is beside himself with excitement, howling and racing around.

I taught him to sit outside the gate until we are ready, which he now manages to do well, but I have yet to learn a command for keeping him quiet! I think the neighbours are used to him now, yelping and whirling around in a circle. The minute we open the gate he is off down the road towards the river at full pelt, with Kat trotting behind him with an amused expression on her face. He has never been anything other than well-behaved with Kat, who is definitely the boss around him, despite her smaller size. She seems happy to have some company on the walk, so I let Wolfie tag along.

We walk to a local café every morning, which Wolfie knows he is not allowed to visit, so he turns around and races off back home again along the river on his own. Dave calls him Scooby-Doo, as we decided if he could talk, that is what he would sound like. He really is a goofball of a dog, but we have grown fond of him now, and as long as he behaves himself, he can continue to keep Kat and me company on our walks.

✿ℬ✿ℚ✿

The land around the river can bring up some surprises too. Kat and I were walking along the road near our house one afternoon when I noticed a flash of yellow beside one of the storage areas for farm tools. By the time we reached the spot, I could see a young dog racing away into the fields. The dog was obviously frightened and alone, as there was no-one else around. It ran off, and I initially thought I wouldn't see it again, and went to walk on. I then noticed the dog had doubled-back and was now standing about one hundred metres away from me, watching carefully. I whistled gently, and it took a few tentative steps forward. Slowly it kept moving towards me, hesitating, and hiding from view, then reappearing each time I whistled or called it.

Finally, the dog was within about ten metres of me, still hiding in the long grass and crouching down. It was extremely nervous and wary, although Kat, standing patiently on her lead beside me, was obviously of interest. I could see the dog was young and shaking all over. Gently, I called again, and it came towards me, bounding out of the grass and landing in front of me.

I always carry a small bag of kibble food in my pocket for Kat, so I scattered some on the ground in front of me, and the dog gobbled it up. I could then have a better look at the dog, and saw that she was a girl, a young pup I would guess no more than a year old, and dreadfully skinny. Interestingly for me, Kat normally pounces on any food on the ground, but on this occasion, she carefully turned her back slightly and sat down, away from the young dog. It was as if Kat was giving her permission to eat her food.

The dog ate everything I put down and was eagerly looking for more. She bounced up to me, spun around several times, then sat and stared at me. She was a pretty dog, despite the bedraggled appearance and dreadfully skinny body. You could see all her ribs, but her face was sweet, and she had cute ears that stuck straight up in the air.

"Well, what am I going to do with you then?" I asked her and received a wag of the tail as a reply.

I looked over at some elderly neighbours who lived opposite, who were stood watching this episode with great interest, no doubt thinking, daft English lady, she's just gained another dog.

We had always said only one dog at a time, and Kat seems perfectly happy to be the only four paws in our house. Although she is fine around other dogs, she has never particularly shown much enthusiasm in playing with them, preferring to potter along at her own speed. It would be fair to say she happily tolerates Wolfie, but if he tries to come into the front garden, he is met with a low, quiet growl of disapproval. He knows who the boss is.

I started to walk home with Kat on her lead and the new young dog walking along happily beside us. Dave had popped out with his camera, so I figured I would see if she followed us home. I could feed her and give her some water, and then decide what to do. She walked alongside me all the way home, and Kat let her into the front garden without any problems. I am sure Kat recognises when another dog is in trouble; she has a tenderness about her that accepts me feeding strays without a murmur. I took Kat inside and then brought out food and water for the little one who devoured everything, knocking the water bowl over in her excitement. It was at that moment Dave came back, pulling the car onto the drive. He got out, took one look over the wall and said,

"Uh-oh!"

"It's ok," I said, "I don't want to keep her, but I couldn't leave her. She's starving, and such a sweet thing."

"Well, what are you going to do then? Kat won't like her in the house, and she is probably covered in ticks and fleas."

Luis, one of our neighbours, walked past with his dog, and I jokingly said to him,

"Would you like another dog?"

"No thanks," he replied, laughing. "One is enough, you'll have to ring the *canil*."

The *canil* is a local kennels for stray animals, and luckily for us we know Kerry, an English lady who manages a local charity-based rescue centre. The charity is called AEZA (Associação Ecologista e Zoófila de Aljezur). I called her, explained what had happened, and asked if she could help.

"Can you keep her overnight?" she replied.

"Not really," I said, "Kat won't like her in the house, and we can't leave her in the garden, she'll jump over the wall."

"Ok, I'll come and get her now."

I explained where we lived, and Kerry said she was nearby. While I waited, I continued to fuss my little rescue, and I talked to her explaining what was going to happen. I thought to myself, if I were keeping you, I would have called you Amber. She was such a pretty thing, and once her nervousness had disappeared, she had a sweet and gentle nature. She was as bouncy and energetic as you would expect a young dog to be. Although I did have a few moments of thinking about keeping her; I knew Kat would be unimpressed with a second dog in the house. I reasoned that someone else would delight in this youngster, and the kennels would do everything they could to find her a new home.

Not ten minutes later, Kerry arrived in a pickup truck with a secure cage in the back. Amber was loaded into the back without a murmur. Kerry explained she thought she was probably a failed hunting-dog that had been released as she was no good to the farmer.

She asked me how I had managed to get her to come to me, and I explained what had happened.

I jokingly said to her,

"I'm a bit of a dog-whisperer. Dogs seem to like and trust me."

"Well, don't make a habit of it!" she laughingly replied.

I was incredibly grateful that she had arrived so quickly, or even agreed to take the dog at all. Most rescue kennels out here are full and rely on donations and sponsorship to survive.

Kerry drove away, and I wistfully cleared up the food and water bowls and hoped they would indeed find a family and a new home for Amber. Even after half-an-hour, I had grown fond of the little scrap, but as I went back inside and made a fuss of Kat, I knew I had done the right thing.

Amazingly, only a few days later, the charity contacted me to say Amber had already been adopted by a German couple. They sent me a photograph of her lying on her new bed, upside-down, and smiling. It was a wonderful sight.

11

SEF Delight

I t started out as quite an innocent thought. I was going through all our files and checking off things I needed to update with our new address. Then my heart sank. Of course, we would have to update our Certificado de Residência Permanente or Permanent Residency Certificate.

Readers of my first book, *Living the Dream*, will recall the absolute horror attached to mentioning the name of the SEF office in Portimão. Or to give it the correct title, the Serviço de Estrangeiros e Fronteiras (the Foreigners and Borders Service).

Even getting an appointment there was a tall order, and the entire process of gaining our ten-year residency was a complete nightmare.

I tentatively approached Dave and said to him,

"You know what we have to update, don't you?"

"No, what?" came his disinterested reply.

"Our residency."

"What... at the SEF office? With Mrs Happy at desk number seven? No way!"

His horrified expression made me giggle. We had given her this nickname after our first forays into the SEF office.

"Yes, Mrs Happy again. I can't wait!" I replied evilly.

"No, no chance, I'm not going there again. We'll just keep our old address on the cards. No-one will know," Dave said, looking desperately at me.

"We can't, there's a fine if you don't update your address. You've only got thirty days from a change of address to inform them. It's a legal document, we have to renew it."

Our fate was set from that moment.

I hesitantly logged onto the SEF website, shuddering at the memory of how difficult it was the first time to even get an appointment. That was only just over a year ago; how ironic that a ten-year document was only going to last us such a short time. Oh well, I thought to myself, at least we get to update the useless pieces of folded cardboard they presented us with. I knew they wouldn't last five minutes when we received them. Our ten-year cards consisted of a triple-folded piece of card with a smudged fingerprint, that conveniently did not fit into a wallet space, and had curled corners straight away. We had copies certified at our local parish council office straight away, in order to salvage what we could of the originals.

My first surprise was that they had updated the SEF website. I logged in, and it instantly gave me the option of booking an appointment online. Five minutes later, I had secured a date and time for myself: Tuesday 8th January, 10 a.m. I logged on again as Dave and was amazed to find I could book him in for the same day, at 10.30 a.m. It was only early October, but I wasn't concerned; as long as I had the dates booked, the fact that our address was incorrect on our documents would not matter. The appointment was the important thing. I printed off the information and set it aside, shaking my head in amazement. The panic of Brexit, and the flurry of hurried applications, had impacted upon their system. It had been upgraded and now seemed to be working well. Perhaps all would flow smoothly for us this time, I thought. How naïve I was.

I downloaded the required forms, which were identical to the ones we tried to fill in last time. There was a tick-box option for updating or changing an address, so I filled in the basics and left it at that. There didn't seem to be much guidance about what information they would require; however, experience told me to just gather everything up and take it along. It is almost always a surprise to discover how much paperwork Portugal likes to generate. The SEF office likes copies of everything, often in triplicate, so I was prepared for that too. We had copies made of the deeds of our house purchase, so I took those along to our local Junta de Freguesia and asked them to complete an *Atestado de Residência* form for each of us.

The *Atestado* is a stamped and signed form that proves the validity of your address in the parish in which you live. I assumed it would be a pre-requisite for anything to do with the SEF office and residency applications. The only problem was that as I gathered up the household bills for our new address, I realised that every single bill had a slight variation to our address written on them. It seemed that we lived in about five different locations. I hoped I could sort it out at the Junta.

I walked in and immediately breathed a sigh of relief. No ticket machine, simply a carpeted entrance with art displayed on the wall beside some comfy chairs, and then a smiling face at the desk. Hang on a minute, isn't that our neighbour who lives opposite us? I thought to myself.

"Boa tarde, vizinha!" ("Good afternoon, neighbour!")

That jolly welcome came from what indeed turned out to be one of our neighbours.

Brilliant, I thought, she will know our address, she lives on the same street!

We chatted and laughed our way through the formalities, and Anabella, our neighbour, kindly offered to knock on our door and inform us when the forms were ready for collection. The joys of living somewhere local. I waltzed out of the Junta thinking this was turning out to be a doddle. SEF office, here we come.

Tuesday, January 8th dawned, and we set off for Portimão clutching a folder full of paperwork, as prepared as we could be.

Our first surprise, as we greeted the friendly security man at the entrance, was that we were each given a ticket for table number one instead of number seven as we were expecting.

We shrugged and sat down.

"Perhaps Mrs Happy has retired?" I said to Dave.

My hopes were soon dashed as she walked in and sat behind desk number seven.

"Oh well, at least she's not sat at desk number one today," I said, "perhaps they have shuffled things around."

The SEF was the usual mix of new people arriving, looking keen and expectant. They were sat amongst rows of glum-faced customers who looked like they had been there since the previous week and had almost lost the will to live. I wondered how long it took for the eager faces to drop and slump into the hunched-over, desperate expressions of the forgotten. I figured about two hours would do it.

Our numbers came up quickly, and we walked over to desk number one and sat down. Nobody was there, and we sat waiting for at least ten minutes.

"Perhaps they are all in the back room, drawing lots. They've seen us and they are trying to decide who gets the short straw," I said, remembering the fun we had last time we were there.

Eventually a nice friendly lady emerged, and we handed her all our paperwork and explained we needed to update our address.

"Oh, you are in luck," she said, "we've just changed our system. Yesterday was the first day we issued the new style residency cards. You will get a new card."

She told us they were phasing out the old tri-fold paper cards in favour of a new plastic credit-card style. The new card would have everything on it in one place for us to carry around more easily. They had started issuing them the day before, their first day back after the Christmas and New Year break. We were to be one of the first British people issued with the new cards.

She went through all our paperwork, then said to us,

"What are your *numeros do utente* please?"

Our health centre numbers. I had no idea. They were not on the list of things needed last time for residency, so I did not have them in the pile of paperwork. We were stuck.

"Hang on a minute," I said, suddenly remembering, "they are in the car, in our special folder. I can go and get them; can you give me five minutes?"

"Of course," she replied.

I scampered back to our car and returned with the required numbers.

Then came the fun part. Everything was now computerised, and they had a fancy new machine to take our photograph and a single fingerprint. She asked our height, then the machine raised itself up to the correct position to fill the screen with our image, eyes in exactly the right spot. It was very clever.

Fifteen minutes later, we were all done. Nice and simple. Then the lady said the infamous words,

"I will send everything off to Lisbon, and you should get your cards within two weeks."

"Really, two weeks?" I said, incredulously.

"Oh yes," she replied, confidently nodding her head.

We walked out of the SEF office, clutching our folder and two new pieces of paper, stamped and dated to prove we had applied for our new residency cards.

"Two weeks?" I said to Dave. "Two weeks? Really? We'll see."

I didn't hold out much hope of that happening.

I wasn't wrong.

January went by, then February. Nothing. No shiny new cards arrived in the post. Which wouldn't have been such a bad thing, except for the looming fact that Brexit was fast approaching, with an initial deadline of the 31st March 2019. Which was by then only about six weeks away. We needed to exchange our driving licences, which required us to prove our address—and our residency. We checked online, and some people had been to the IMTT office to begin the same process of exchanging their driving licence. They had been turned away because they only had the same temporary stamped piece of paper from the SEF office that we had, and not their actual residency card. We were stuck.

I went back to the SEF office on spec to see if they could let us know what was happening. A small word of advice. Don't go there on the day public sector workers decide to have a lightning strike. It was not the best time to arrive. Although, with hindsight, perhaps it was the perfect day. I talked to the nice security guard, who obviously doesn't get the day off when the rest of the staff down tools, and he was sympathetic to our problems.

"Hang on a minute," he said, "there are a few staff still working in the back office. I'll see if someone can come out and help you."

He disappeared and returned a few minutes later with a member of staff, who beckoned me over to a computer. I have never seen the SEF office empty before, it was almost eerie.

The lady tapped away for ages on her keyboard, then explained that something had not been entered correctly on the system. She then brightly told me our cards would be with us soon.

"How soon?" I asked, explaining the problem we had with our driving licences and the March 31st deadline.

"I'm not sure exactly," she replied, "but you should be ok at the IMTT office with your stamped forms. They provide all the information they need to know."

Well, I'll save you all the details of the driving licence story for another chapter; suffice to say the magic cards didn't arrive in time for us.

✿ﻬ✿ও✿

And then, one day in April, the doorbell rang, and it was the postman on his moped, delivering an item that required a signature. It was my residency card. I eagerly took the envelope, then asked him if he had another one for Dave. No, just the one envelope. Oh well, I thought, Dave's will probably come soon.

I opened it up, and there it was, my shiny new residency card. It had the smallest typed information I have ever seen, I literally had to reach for my reading glasses to see what it said on the front. Then I turned it over, and my heart sank. After all those weeks, there was a mistake on the card. Where it should have listed the *numero do utente* I had gone back to the car specifically to collect, it simply said N/A.

With Brexit approaching, I knew I needed to have my health centre entitlement listed on the card. In an emergency, that might be an extremely important number if I was in an accident. With a sinking heart, I turned to Dave and said,

"I've got my card, but it is missing my health number. I'm going to have to go back to the SEF office again."

He looked at me in horror.

"I'm not going back there again. I almost lost the will to live last time," he spluttered.

It was decided. Off I went, on my own, back to the delightful SEF office. I didn't have an appointment, but that didn't deter me. I was ushered in and given a ticket by the security man. By this time, I knew his name and asked him how his family was doing. I sat down, expecting a long wait, but the security guard must have given me a golden ticket. I was the next person called. To desk number seven and Mrs Happy. Oh dear.

To my great surprise, she was smiling and cheerful. That threw me a bit. I thought back to our previous encounters with her. For those of you that remember the TV series called *Bread* in the eighties in the UK, you may recall the lady behind the counter in the DHSS office that the family were all afraid of. She shouted 'Next!' at the top of her voice and rarely smiled. That was who Mrs Happy always reminded me of.

She took my card, stuck it to a piece of paper with Sellotape, added my *numero do utente* details to the paperwork, scanned it, and filed it away on her desk. She handed me a printed copy of the document, stamped and dated, and told me my card would be with me in two weeks.

My nice new card. I had held it in my hands for a whole day, and now it was gone.

I walked out muttering to myself, two weeks... more like two months.

I wasn't holding my breath.

Two weeks later, to the day, the doorbell went. Our friendly postman was back again, clutching a familiar envelope. It was for me. I opened it, and there it was, my residency card, this time complete with my health number. The only thing absent, I noted this time, was that the card didn't have our address written on it. The old tri-fold card had our address on it. The new card didn't. It wasn't actually missing, there wasn't a space allocated on the new card design for them to write it. The irony was not lost on me. We had gone through all that bureaucracy to update our new address; only to be sent an ID card that no longer had an address written on it.

"So, how can it be an all-in-one card, if it doesn't have an address on it?" I said to Dave.

"Never mind about that," he said, "where's my card?"

Oh yes. We still had the small matter of Dave's missing card to solve.

"You'll have to go back to the SEF office," I smirked, "they won't speak to me about your card. You must go there in person."

I heard him muttering all the way up the stairs.

Dave had to go past Portimão for a photo shoot the following week, so I pulled out the scanned copy of his application form from January. I made him promise me he would drop into the SEF office on his way to the shoot. He came back home that evening and waved the piece of paper at me.

"You'll never guess what they said!" he spluttered incredulously. "They couldn't process my application because—wait for it—my height was missing from the form."

"What, the height you gave them when they set up the machine to take the photo? How could it be omitted when you told her what it was?" I replied, remembering the fun we had translating five feet, ten inches into metres, as the computer wouldn't accept anything other than metric measurements.

"I know, don't ask me, I don't know why it was missing."

Dave said he had asked the lady why someone in Lisbon hadn't called him and asked him his height, or at least written to the SEF office to let them know the information was missing. It seems they had just shelved his application as it was incomplete.

"Anyway, it's all done now, they said it will be with me in two weeks."

The infamous two-week deadline again.

Miraculously, to the day, two weeks later, our postman was back ringing the bell, and this time the envelope was for Dave. He eagerly tore it open, looked at the card, turned it over, and then I saw his face drop.

"They've missed off the *numero do utente* haven't they?" I asked him, desperately hoping he was winding me up. He wasn't.

"You'll have to go back to the SEF office again. You need that number on there."

I was sure I heard a whimpering sound coming from Dave.

"It was easy last time. I took the card in, with my *utente* certificate, she copied the certificate, got out her roll of Sellotape, and two weeks later, I had my card back. It took me less than ten minutes, in and out. It will be fine."

Dave went off to Portimão the next morning, muttering rude things under his breath about what he would like to do to the SEF office and Mrs Happy. Oh dear. I was glad I was 'busy' and couldn't go with him.

He rang me just before lunchtime, and I could instantly tell by his voice that things hadn't gone well. I've edited the following sentence to delete all the swear words…

"That ****** woman! I nearly walked out and told her where she could put my ******* residency card."

"Why, what happened?" I asked tentatively, dreading the reply.

"I waited ages then when I saw Mrs Happy, she told me she couldn't help me."

"But I went there with the same problem, and ten minutes later it was all fixed."

"I sat at her desk for forty-five minutes arguing with her. I reminded her she had sorted your card out and asked her repeatedly why she was not able to do the same with my card."

Dave said he got so frustrated as he sat there at desk number seven that he had banged his head forward onto the desk in front of her. He turned around to find the security guard had moved over to stand behind him, thinking he had damaged something, and was bemused to discover it was only Dave's head that was slightly dented.

After much discussion, and Dave refusing to leave until they sorted it out, Mrs Happy eventually conceded defeat and scanned

Dave's details, sellotaped it all together, and handed Dave his copied paperwork.

Two weeks later, Dave finally had his residency card, complete with his health number.

"Just think, only eight more years until we have to apply to have them renewed," I said cheerfully.

"She'd better have retired by then," I heard Dave mutter from the office.

12

Freelancing, Families, and Fish

I recently enjoyed interviewing friends Kyle and Yayeri about their experiences of moving here to live in the Algarve. They have a young daughter and a bouncy rescue dog, and live and work quietly hidden in the countryside. It was interesting to ask a younger couple about their life here, as so many people think the Algarve is just a retirement destination. But we know lots of young adults who move here to enjoy a quieter or slightly alternative lifestyle. Most work remotely, or for themselves, and strive for a more balanced way of life. Many come to the Algarve to bring up a family in a place that feels safe and welcoming. With the rise in home working, this is becoming a viable option for more and more people.

Yayeri is originally from the Netherlands, where she studied journalism. She did her internship in the UK, where she met Kyle. Before that she had worked all over Europe as a ski teacher, receptionist and kids rep. Kyle is from Germany. He studied business administration and has worked in digital publishing in both Germany and the UK.

They have been living in the Algarve for about five years, and they were originally drawn here by the sun. Their favourite things are the Atlantic Ocean, the fact their dog enjoys complete freedom here, and that the weather allows them to spend a lot of time outdoors.

When I asked them if there was anything they missed about home, Kyle gave an unexpected answer,

"Proper forests in which you can lose yourself and that bad weather can actually be nice. Here in the Algarve, rain just feels depressing. But in the Netherlands, Germany, or the UK it's a consistent part of the weather and can even be sort of romantic."

Yayeri added,

"I also miss *gevulde speculaas*, a typically Dutch type of cookie. And Marktplaats, an online second-hand marketplace. There are Portuguese sites like OLX and CustoJusto, but they aren't as good."

They were both honest about the reality of living in a beautiful place, but still having to work every day, albeit from home.

"We expected to spend a lot of time outside, especially at the beach or on the water. However, most of the time we only explore the Portuguese seaside when we have friends from other countries over for a visit. In reality, we spend many hours sat in front of our computers."

I asked them about how easy it is to make friends here and to feel settled. Their reply was typical of what many people find when they move here to live permanently, rather than simply holiday here.

"There are lots of expats here from many countries, and it's easy to make friends with most of them. However, it sometimes seems different with the Portuguese people. It can take ages before they warm to you. Raising a baby definitely helps to accelerate that process, though."

We talked about ways that people can get out and make new friends here. They reminded me that the local dog shelters are always looking for volunteers to help walk and look after the animals. They also recommended finding out if you have a local Casa de Povo nearby which is a great way to get involved in local activities. I had heard about these but wanted to find out more.

Casa do Povo means House of the People, and they are community centres that are set up in towns and villages. They host events where local people can come together to socialise and learn new skills.

The Casa do Povo's mission is to "contribute to the development of the community in the social, educational, sports, cultural, and leisure areas guided by an integrated service of quality and proximity." They aim to "… be recognised as a dynamic and reliable institution that provides a quality service, capable of promoting the global and harmonious development of individuals through an integrated and innovative intervention in their different responses."[1]

The first Casa do Povo was inaugurated in the village of Barbacena, in 1934, by dictator António Salazar. They became community meeting houses for villagers and were a social institution, run by an organisation of rural workers, offering economic and cultural support for the local population. They also provided healthcare and education, with women being taught homemaking skills, and the men, agricultural skills. Both were also taught handicrafts. Casas dos Pescadores (Fishermen's Houses) were created to provide the same services for local fishing communities.

From 1982, the Casas do Povo became a public entity for social and cultural development, working with the authorities to resolve problems that affected the local population. Nowadays, they are linked to Portugal's social security system and there is even a national Casa do Povo Day celebrated on September 11th.

The Casa do Povo in the town of São Bartolomeu de Messines is an incredible example of the power of community spirit and local fund-raising. They organise community parties and holiday camps, theatre shows, dance and music lessons. They have a choir, offer bureaucratic help, and host activities for the elderly.

They have sixteen different sports taking place, with teams and classes covering all ages and abilities. They also have adapted classes for disabled participants, such as wheelchair handball. There is a nursery (for children aged 0-3), an infant school (for 3 to 6-year-olds) and after-school clubs to support working parents. They have even raised enough funds to create a sensory room for children and adults with communication and mobility difficulties.[1]

I asked Yayeri and Kyle about how their Portuguese language is coming along and felt reassured they seemed to be in a similar position to me.

"It should be better than it actually is after five years. The Portuguese offer integration lessons for foreigners and we attended one of these courses with a nice mix of nationalities. That's definitely something we'd recommend. Apart from that, you should speak Portuguese as often as possible. The problem is many Portuguese are pretty good at speaking English and if you're lazy or shy, you stay in your comfort zone and use English instead of learning to speak Portuguese properly."

Bringing up a family in the Algarve can seem idyllic, although as Yayeri joked, it is probably the same as anywhere else, with lots of work and no sleep. She continued,

"Joking aside, that's one of the main advantages of being here. You can count the number of days you have to stay inside almost on one hand. In other words: no screen time, but spending the whole day exploring flora and fauna outside. Add to that, the Portuguese are super child-friendly and offer you priority whenever you carry a child on your arm."

I have always been impressed by this fact. Here in Portugal, shops, supermarkets, and other establishments give priority to those with babies and youngsters. There are specific checkouts at most major supermarkets for the elderly, the disabled and those with young children. They are invited to step forward to the front of the queue to be served. The first time it happened to me I was surprised, but quite happy to let someone older than me jump the queue. Then I looked up and saw the sign above the till and realised why. I did wonder to myself how old I would have to be before I could do the same thing.

Kyle and Yayeri both agreed they love to fly or drive back home to see family and friends. It was interesting asking them what differences they noticed when they returned home as opposed to being in Portugal. As Kyle explained,

"We mostly work from home here. When we travel to Germany and Holland and get caught in one of the ever-present massive traffic jams there, we ask ourselves why do all these people commute, what's the idea behind it?"

Probably because they live in the countryside here, Yayeri added she appreciates the hustle and bustle, city life, and especially the shops back in Holland. Shopping here in the Algarve, they enjoy the local markets, which offer plenty of fresh produce. They have found that coffee, wine, beer, fish, and restaurants here are much cheaper than in either Holland or Germany. Cars or electronics are more expensive. They explained they import natural cosmetics and some electronic goods from Germany, as these things are either non-existent here in Portugal or just more costly.

I must agree with them at this point. Much as we like to shop locally whenever we can, there are some things we instinctively turn to Amazon for. I have recently swopped to shopping via the Spanish Amazon site. I had one of those 'd'oh!' moments when I suddenly realised my UK Amazon account was still valid on the Spanish site. For some reason, I thought I had to set up a new account there, until I googled it, and found out all I had to do was log on as normal. All my account information, including my credit card for payment, was already there, waiting to be used. They usually offer free delivery from Spain across to Portugal, and far from being more expensive, I have found some things to be cheaper there than from the UK site.

I asked Yayeri and Kyle if they had a secret place they could recommend, and they both said Armona Island.

"Even though there are many tourists there in summer, it's still easy to find your own spot to escape the crowds."

Their ideal day would start with a *galão* and a *pastel de nata* or two. I love a *galão*, which is made from espresso and hot milk. It is like a latte without as much froth, made with a quarter coffee and three-quarters foamed milk, and served in a tall glass. The glasses don't always come with a handle on them, so you end up either waiting for your drink to cool down, or you do a juggling act with a napkin, or three, wrapped around the glass. I particularly enjoy ordering two of them together at a café as you have to ask for *dois galãos* which sounds as if you are saying 'doish galoish'. It is a fabulous phrase to rattle over your tongue.

Readers of my first book will know how much Dave and I love *pastel de nata*. These delicious small pastries are irresistible, especially if they are still fresh and warm from the oven. So far, so good, for Yayeri and Kyle's perfect day out. They would then spend the entire day on Bordeira beach, where dogs are welcome, and where their daughter can play in the shallow lagoon. They would finish their day by finding a place that does nice grilled fish for dinner.

They are both big fans of eating fish, and they have quite a few favourite restaurants. What they all have in common is the absence of tablecloths. We are quite alike, as we also gravitate to places that are not fancy or posh. And, as they both explained, in a local restaurant they can "see the food before it gets barbecued."

Living in a different country has taught them both to stay flexible and keep an open mind. I asked them what advice they would give to someone considering a move to live abroad, and apart from the obvious cheeky answer of "get a passport", Kyle advised that,

"For us, we've moved abroad two times already, and it was (both times) way easier than we initially thought. But it really depends on the type of person you are. Definitely have a look around, take your time, and speak to others in the country you'd like to live in. For most Europeans, Portugal isn't too far away from their home country. It's a short flight or a nice road trip in case you need to visit friends or family at home. So moving here is not like leaving the planet."

Their three top tips for relocating to Portugal are as follows:

Spend some time here on holiday before committing—also, if you can, stay in the low season.

Learn the language—you don't have to be fluent; a little goes a long way.

Be patient—bureaucratic things can take quite a long time here.

I asked them where they thought they might be in five years' time. They gave me two options, and their answers amused me, as Yayeri said,

"Travelling through Mongolia on horseback."

And Kyle replied,

"Travelling through Mongolia in our VW campervan."

It looks like they are off to Mongolia then. They just need to decide on what form of transport to choose. My advice would be, with a young child and a rescued dog, I'd go for the campervan option. I'm not sure their dog would sit still long enough to enjoy horse-riding.

They finished on an interesting note,

"Did you know the longest train connection in the world goes from Portugal to Vietnam? We'd say that's option three."

Now there's an idea for a travel book.

---

1. Portugal Resident (25.03.2020). Website article by Isobel Costa *Casa do Povo*. Accessed 30th July through https://www.portugalresident.com/casa-do-povo/

13

The Driving Licence Debacle

The 31st March 2019 was looming. The newspapers were full of alarming headlines regarding Brexit and the 'will we - won't we?' crash out of Europe scenario that had been forecast. In early 2019, it seemed likely things would not be sorted out in time before the end of March deadline.

The one thing outstanding for us was the need to exchange our British driving licences. They were European Union licences, and, therefore, valid in Portugal. Years before, we had been to the IMTT office in Faro and recorded our driving licences with them. We carried a separate piece of paper with us in the car that registered our UK address on the licence alongside our Portuguese address. It was rarely, if ever, requested by the police on any random stop checks. It covered us—that is—until Brexit.

If Brexit went ahead as planned, we would have a transition period for sorting out the paperwork. But if we crashed out on the 31st March without a deal, then we would hopefully have a grace period of ninety days to exchange our licences. In a worst-case scenario, we would have to apply for a new Portuguese licence. This would involve taking a driving test as a new driver in Portugal. I shuddered at the thought of that. I wasn't sure which would be worse, re-taking a driving test after all these years, or having to do it all in Portuguese. One thing was certain, I wanted to avoid that at all costs.

There were two problems we were facing, and the first was that we were still waiting for our residency cards to arrive in the post. Lots of people told us the IMTT office would not accept the piece of paper the SEF office had issued us with. The IMTT insisted that they required the full residency card or papers. We were in a classic catch-22 situation. We had wanted to do the licence exchange before this time, but we knew we were moving to a new house. We had to wait until we had moved and had a new address. The residency application had to take priority. Without the residency paperwork, we couldn't apply for the driving licence. Our SEF appointment had not been until January, after our moving date in September. And we were still waiting for our residency cards to arrive two months later.

The second problem was that virtually every British person we knew had come to the same hurried conclusion as us. They needed to exchange their licence before the Brexit deadline. Facebook was full of horror stories about how long people had queued outside the IMTT office in Faro to get an appointment. By early March, people were arriving at 6.30 a.m. and finding that a queue had already formed outside the building. The office opened at 9 a.m. and was only issuing a maximum of fifty driving licence exchange tickets each day from the ever-present ticket machine. If you didn't have a ticket below number 50, the security staff turned you away and told you to return another day.

We panicked. We live almost ninety minutes' drive away from Faro with a beautiful dog that needs a morning walk. You must be there in person to exchange your licence as they take your photograph and you must sign a form. Previously, you could use an agency to do the work for you, but they changed the rules on that, and you cannot do it through a third party any longer. We calculated we would need to get up at 4.30 a.m. if we wanted to be sure of a ticket, which was totally unrealistic.

We worked through the paperwork required and found out we each needed a medical certificate. Dave wears glasses all the time, including when he drives. This meant he also needed to have an up-to-date eye test. I bundled him off to the local opticians in town, and he came back the same day twenty-five euros lighter with his completed eye test. Our paper trail had begun.

Next up was a medical. The advice was limited on this, other than we knew some health centres would do them for you and others wouldn't. Of course, our local health centre didn't. Great! A retired doctor, who has a private practice in town, was the nearest option. We rang his mobile phone number - five times. Each time, he advised me he was busy. He said if I called him the following morning then he could tell me if he could fit us in that afternoon. It was ridiculous, and we gave up trying to book him.

That left us, in the second week of March, with no medical completed and no licences exchanged. Luckily for us, our good friends Jan and Chris were in the same boat, two weeks ahead of us. They told us about the International Health Centre in Albufeira, where you could book in and get the medical completed for thirty euros. That sounded a lot better than the seventy euros each we had been quoted for going the private practice route.

Off we went for an afternoon out in Albufeira, taking Kat along with us. They were great in the health centre and let her inside the reception area, so we sat and waited our turn. I went in first; the doctor asked me about five simple health questions and took my blood pressure. Then came the eye test, which was hilarious. The doctor asked me to stand about ten feet away from the chart on the wall, and then said to me,

"Which line of letters can you read?"

"Well, the bottom row is enormous, shall I read those for you?" I replied, rattling them off for her.

"That's fine," she said, ticking something on her paperwork, then inputting it all onto the computer.

She printed off a form for me and told me the IMTT office would access my information from the computer records. She also advised me to keep the piece of paper and take it with me to the IMTT office 'just in case'.

Dave was next up, his medical was even simpler as he had

already done his eye test, then the doctor jokingly asked us if Kat needed an examination too!

We were all set; our medicals were completed. Next step, the dreaded IMTT office.

Jan and Chris were one step ahead of us again. They said they had arrived at Faro at 8 a.m. and queued until 9 a.m. for them to open. They had taken a ticket each, then waited over five hours to be seen. This was not what we wanted to hear. They said the woman behind the counter looked exhausted and fed up. I am sure she had not expected that Brexit would cause this much stress and extra work for her.

There had to be another way. We searched through our favourite Facebook groups and discovered we could, in fact, attend any IMTT office. Beja, on the map, was only two hours away and reported to be less busy than Faro. We decided we would get up early and drive there. I printed off maps and set the sat-nav to choose the more scenic coastal route. With a picnic and Kat in the car, we headed off for our day out 'up north'. We travelled via the N120 to Odemira, which then led onto the N263 to Beja, as it looked a prettier route. It was also preferable than driving to Albufeira and joining the IP2 motorway.

✿ﻬ✿ღ✿

What I hadn't bargained for was my photography-loving husband sneaking one of his camera bags into the boot of the car. It was the 26th of March, a Tuesday, and the deadline for a possible no-deal Brexit was Friday 29th March, as the 31st fell on a Sunday. Nothing like cutting it fine. We also still had our SEF temporary papers with us for our residency. There was nothing else we could do but travel up there with them and hope they were in a good mood at the IMTT office.

The route was spectacular. On every side we passed fields of crops, grasses, and stunning red poppies, stretching far into the distance.

"I'm just going to stop and take a few shots," said Dave, with a gleam in his eye.

"OK," I replied, "but we must get there this morning, it's our only chance, and we have no idea how big the queue will be."

"I won't be five minutes."

I have heard that phrase so many times. Five minutes to Dave is an ever-expandable vague notion of time. It can inflate in direct correlation to the number of shots he wants to take, and how long his camera takes to set up.

I drew the line after the fifth 'five-minute' stop, as we were now seriously behind schedule. We rolled into Beja at 11.30 a.m. and parked opposite a café, almost next to the building we needed to locate.

We got out of the car, sorted out Kat, and went to cross the road. Immediately we heard a loud voice calling,

"Yoo-hoo! Dave, Aly… over here!"

We looked over at the café and couldn't believe it. There were eight people sat at the tables, and we knew five of them. Two were friends from the Alentejo area who run a yurt business, and the other three were people we knew from Carvoeiro. We started chatting, but I interrupted Dave and reminded him we hadn't even reached the IMTT office yet, and we needed to get our tickets. I hurried off, leaving him talking, and returned with the requisite pieces of paper numbered 51 and 52. The machine displayed inside the office showed they were only on number 26. It was going to be a long day.

Our yurt friends said they had numbers 44 and 45, so we agreed they would let us know when they were called. That would give us time to saunter over to the building ready for our turn. We settled down at the café and prepared ourselves for a lengthy wait.

The street was pretty, lined with ornamental orange trees, which made the area nice and shady. The IMTT was opposite a public park. We set off for a walk with Kat, but sadly there was a 'no dogs' sign on the entrance. After taking it in turns to look around, we both agreed that Beja was somewhere we would like to return to in the future.

After a lazy lunch, finally at about 3 p.m. our yurt friends told us they had completed their paperwork, so we walked to the IMTT building. We sauntered in with Kat, thinking the worst that could happen is someone would ask us to take her back outside, but no-one stopped us. It was an impressive high-ceilinged hallway, with comfy sofas. Tiny signs on the walls showed the offices present inside. The IMTT was around to the right, then left down a dark unlit corridor. At the end was the standard government office set-up you would expect. Lots of seats, a ticket machine, and a big red-numbered computerised screen that displayed how far along the staff had reached dealing with customers. It showed that ticket 'T'; which was our category, was showing number 53.

"Help, Dave, we've got ticket numbers 51 and 52. How can we have missed our turn?" I said, panicking a little.

This was not good. We had driven all that way, sat for almost four hours waiting at the café, and we had not been there when our numbers were called out. And the Brexit deadline was potentially only three days away.

I scampered over to a desk and explained we had just missed our numbers; we were very sorry and please could they still fit us in. I must have looked desperate enough, as the lady told me not to worry, to take a seat and they would call us next.

It transpired that a group of five people had come in together before I had taken our tickets; they each had a ticket but got bored waiting. The machine called their numbers, the assistant waited about thirty seconds for each one to respond, then moved on to the next numbers.

We were lucky. Whilst we were sitting there, another woman came in looking hassled. She was clutching ticket number 42, and she was told unceremoniously, "sorry, come back tomorrow." Ouch.

We gratefully sank into the chairs in front of a friendly lady who dealt with us quickly and efficiently. Luckily, the photocopy of our residency paperwork from SEF was sufficient. We handed her copies of our passports, our medical forms, and Dave's eye test, and our original UK driving licences.

The camera they had linked up to the computer fascinated Dave, and he asked the operator far too many questions. They were very proficient in setting this up and taking a reasonably acceptable headshot with the equipment they had. Then it was just a quick signature, a pat on the head for a well-behaved Kat, and the lady handed over a copy of our application forms. She assured us that would be sufficient should the police ask for our documents.

The only downside was that the form had an expiry date on it— the 25th May 2019. We only had two months.

"What happens at the end of this time period if we haven't had our driving licences through?" I asked.

"You come back here and have the paperwork stamped again."

Well, that would be fun, I thought.

We set off for home, tired but elated that we had done it.

The next day we checked on a few Facebook forums. To our dismay some people had been waiting months, sometimes, almost a year, before they received their new driving licence in the post. And every two months you had to return to the IMTT office to renew the temporary form.

"Why don't they issue something that lasts until the new licence arrives? Why does it need an expiry date?" I asked Dave, a little bemused.

"No idea, it just does," came his helpful reply.

Jan and Chris, who, by this time, were ahead of us by about six weeks, had to renew their forms in April. They had decided they couldn't face the queues at Faro again. Even though the infamous 31st March had passed without a Brexit murmur, the need to exchange UK licences was still there, and the Faro office was busy every day. Our friends travelled to Beja, based on our recommendation, however, they hit a snag when they reached the front of the queue. Faro did not have the modern camera equipment that Beja had, and our friends had supplied passport photos for their licences. Faro had stapled the photos to their application forms. Their temporary forms did not have a copy of their images attached, and Beja were initially unwilling to stamp and endorse their papers for them.

They must have taken one look at our friend's face and quickly changed their minds! Jan said she was fit to burst by this stage of the proceedings, and the staff agreed to endorse their forms for them. They even gave them six months instead of the usual two before the next renewal date. There is obviously a positive side to looking like you are about to explode in a small office space.

Our two months were almost up. Friends from Carvoeiro said they had checked and found out you did not need to go in person to the IMTT office to renew. If someone took the paperwork up there, they would stamp it. One of the group offered to be the courier for everyone, including us, and they went up there armed with a bundle of forms. They returned with them all stamped and reissued, no problem. It cost us a bottle of wine and a thank-you card, and we were most grateful.

And then, only two weeks later, the postman knocked on our door holding two official-looking envelopes. Both our licences had arrived on the same day. It had taken less than three months. The first thing we did was ring our friends Jan and Chris, and say,

"Guess what we got in the post today? Our driving licences have come! Have you had yours yet?"

I cannot print their reply.

We took photos of us holding our shiny new cards and gleefully sent the pictures off to them via messenger.

Our friends waited almost six months for their licences to arrive.

14

Kat the Dog at the Vets

W e adopted our little rescue dog six years ago. Kat is a much-loved and important part of our family. She is a beautiful, sweet-natured girl who captured our hearts the minute we met her and is now a constant shadow by my side.

She has a genuine character and personality all her own, and she is a delight to have around. It doesn't need me to tell you how much we love her. The locals here call her *ovelha* which is a female sheep or *macaquinha* (little monkey). With her fluffy black curly coat and her cheeky ways, both those names seem appropriate.

We had used the same vets here in the Algarve since we adopted Kat. Almost four years ago we noticed a lump appear on her back and mentioned it to the vet.

"Oh, that's ok, it's only a fatty lump, just keep an eye on it," we were told.

Fast forward another year to when her annual jabs were due, and a different vet at the practice glanced at the lump again but didn't seem at all bothered by it. She even joked that as Kat was a little overweight, that was where the extra fat had come from.

We continued to observe it. Over the winter months her longer curly coat covered up the lump, but underneath all the curls we could see it seemed to have changed shape. We went off to the groomers for a spring trim so we could have a closer look at what she had growing on her back. It looked to have grown a little larger, although Kat was unconcerned by it.

We mentioned it to a friend who has dogs, and they highly recommended a veterinary hospital in Portimão, and gave me their details. I called the reception and explained my concerns, and Dr Carolina Rocha was duly booked for an appointment the very next day, which was a Tuesday. That evening we had a call from Dr Rocha to introduce herself. She wanted to find out a little more about Kat and what the problem was. She also reassured us that Kat would be in expert hands. We were happy we had followed our instincts and hunted down a different vet's practice for a second opinion, and that was before we had even met them.

We drove to the vet hospital on the Tuesday morning, and apart from having fun trying to find somewhere to park, as they are on a busy main road, we were on time. On entering the building, I was impressed by the reception area and staff. Dr Rocha was friendly and patient and asked all the usual questions whilst taking time to reassure us. She seemed surprised the previous vets had not been concerned about the lump. Kat trotted off into the back medical room to have samples taken for testing. She was perfectly at ease with the staff who were lovely with her; they were very gentle and friendly. Our first surprise was the fact they said they would have the results by the end of that week. We discovered they have a laboratory on site and do basic tests in-house, which was splendid news.

We had a nervous few days; then on the Friday we received a call from the vets who said that Dr Rocha had requested us to come in and see her to talk about the results. That was not what we wanted to hear. Dear Kat, she is so precious to us, but we were also realistic that if it wasn't good news, it was better to know and do something about it quickly. The receptionist then said,

"Can you come in on Sunday morning at 10 a.m. when Kat's doctor is next working?" and continued, "that will be Easter Sunday, is that ok?"

Of course, we said that was fine.

The practice is open 24/7 all year round with an out-of-hours emergency set up, for which we were incredibly grateful. The sooner we knew what the problem was, and what we could do about it, the better.

Sunday morning we returned to the vet hospital and discovered it is much easier to park outside there at the weekend. Dr Rocha was most efficient; she had all the results laid out ready, and she explained everything to us. We agreed the best way forward was for Kat to have surgery to remove the lump which had signs of 'turning into a cancerous growth'. She explained they would run tests beforehand to make sure Kat was fit enough for the anaesthetic and the resulting surgery. As she was about nine years old—it's hard to tell exactly with a rescue dog—they were pleased her heart was strong. All her other test results were in her favour too. They were confident she would survive the surgery with no complications or other problems. Her appointment was booked immediately for the following Tuesday morning.

It was scary, but they reassured us that Kat would be well looked-after. It was also great to know we only had to wait until the Tuesday; I am not sure we could have waited a long while once we had made the decision. They gave us advice on what to do and not do on the day of the surgery, which included not feeding Kat any breakfast. We had a quiet couple of days with her and tried not to show her we were worried. She is a sensitive soul, she always knows when I am not feeling well or I am upset, and she will snuggle in close to comfort me. I think she might have had a few extra biscuits and even more cuddles than usual, though.

☼ફ☼ભ☼

On the Tuesday morning I took her over there early at 8.30 a.m. I hugged her and told her I would return to get her in time for tea. They promised to ring us once they had completed the surgery. I had to fight back a few tears as they led her away. She trotted off with them, no problem, but glanced back at me as she went through the doors to the treatment area. I held it together until I reached my car, then I sat for a while trying to steady myself. I kept telling myself she would be fine, that she was a tough old girl, and I would be hugging her again very soon.

Needless to say; I was a bag of nerves all morning. I had planned a 'busy day' to get through the hours ahead, which included doing the weekly shop at our local Continente supermarket to keep me occupied. I was at the trolley bay about to enter the store when my phone went—it was the vets! My heart was in my mouth, it was only 11.30 a.m. Surely it couldn't be good news, that early?

They were quick to reassure me all was fine.

"The surgery is over. It went well. Kat is fine, she is sleeping," they said. "You can pick her up at 4.30 p.m. today."

I must admit I broke down and blubbed in front of all the trolleys and shoppers. The sheer relief of knowing she was ok was too much for me to contain. I wanted to run straight over to the vets and hold her in my arms. I counted how many hours I had to wait until I could bring her home.

As a strange coincidence, the friend that had recommended the vet hospital to us, had one of her dogs in there at the same time. She did the sweetest thing that day as she visited her own dog. She knows Kat well and went to find her in the recovery room to give her some fuss and attention. She then came round to our house to tell us what she had done and to reassure us that Kat looked well; she was just sleepy. There are some lovely people in the world, and that really meant a lot to me.

I was there early, of course, to collect our little monkey. She trotted out looking fine, albeit wearing a plastic collar around her head to protect the wound. The greeting she gave me was monumental. She whirled round, bumping into me with the awkward collar on and cuddled in close, nuzzling me. It was as if she wanted to tell me everything that had happened to her. The assistant smiled at us, saying,

"She sure is glad to see you again."

That was nothing to how delighted I was to be back with Kat. The plastic collar lasted about ten minutes as she bounced into every wall and car as I walked her to where I had parked. Bless her; she couldn't get her head around it (literally). She is such a star though; she didn't need it anyway and was content to leave the bandage and stitches alone.

She had a big plaster over the wound, and they had shaved her back, which did look rather impressive. She had also had her teeth cleaned and two teeth removed, although that didn't seem to bother her at all. We were told she must have ten days of rest, with only short walks allowed. Strictly no jumping up or down until the next appointment in ten days' time. The lump was being sent to Lisbon for analysis, and the results would be back within a week.

Kat was an absolute star. She was obviously tired, but none the worse for her adventures, and she was determined to trot around as normal. We were so relieved to have her home again, and ruined her with a dinner of roast chicken, a new brand of softer food because of her tooth extractions, and heaps of love and time. She did not leave my side for the next ten days.

She seemed to heal well and was none the worse for her adventures. I had fun trying to remove the thick sticking-plaster from her back on the second day as recommended, but Kat didn't even flinch.

The vets were great. As soon as the results were back from Lisbon; they contacted us early and emailed us the reports. Our new favourite Portuguese word was now *benigno*. It was a benign tumour. Oh, the relief!! We really appreciated that they did not make us wait until the planned day of our next appointment to let us know the results. So then it was simply a case of going back to have her checked over as the stitches were all dissolvable inside her.

Less than two weeks later, Kat was back to her old self. The wound was healing nicely, and her fur was already growing over the scar. She was soon rolling on her back to have her tummy rubbed and grinning broadly at us.

The staff at the vet hospital were brilliant. They were professional, calm, and knowledgeable, and very patient with us and Kat. Their set-up was impressive, with the latest equipment and training in place. We were delighted to have found them.

Their prices were also reasonable too. The total cost of the initial consultation visit and tests was only forty-four euros. The surgery itself and aftercare totalled three hundred euros.

Our pet insurance company were excellent when we contacted them to explain what was happening. That is, once I managed to get through to them. Their published number begins with the digits 96, and I didn't realise I was supposed to be ringing a Spanish number. 96 is the start of a landline number in Spain, so I should have dialled +34 first. In Portugal, however, 96 are the first digits of a mobile phone number, so I ended up calling an irate and none too happy old Portuguese woman. Her number was identical to the insurance company's Spanish landline number. I am sure she must have been fed up with people ringing her mobile and asking for pet insurance. I think they have since amended their website to clarify that you should be dialling a Spanish, and not a Portuguese, number.

They recorded everything and gave me advice over the phone and made it extremely easy to complete the claim form and paperwork. Only one week later we had full reimbursement (minus the excess) paid into our bank account.

We have spoken to several friends with dogs after this happened, and two of them admitted that their pets also each had a lump they had been told was 'fatty and not to worry'. They have both since booked appointments with their vet (or a new vet) to get a second opinion.

Our little Kat is so precious and special to us. We are just delighted she is fine now and can go back to enjoying her long walks with me each morning. And every time I look at her when her coat is trimmed, and I see the impressive eight centimetre scar on her back; I take a deep breath and remember how lucky we are to have her with us, fit and healthy.

15

Sweet Potatoes, Events, and Fairs

The humble sweet potato. It is not a normal potato, or nightshade; the sweet potato is a member of the morning glory family. It is a tuberous root that is both nutritious and delicious. Sweet potatoes, or *Ipomoea batatas*, have been cultivated since somewhere between 2500 BC and 1850 BC. The sweet potato was native to the tropical Americas, where the Incan, Mayan and Aztec peoples all consumed it. The history books debate who first introduced them to Europe. Some say it was Christopher Columbus who took the sweet potato back with him to Spain. Others report that the 15th century Portuguese explorers brought it home with them.

Seen as a delicacy in parts of Europe in the 16th and 17th centuries, legend has it that King Henry VIII of England loved eating sweet potatoes. Maybe he had heard the rumour they were an aphrodisiac. In the 18th century, during the reign of King John V, the sweet potato entered the Portuguese royal cookbooks. Before that, in Portugal, it was food fed only to animals and slaves.

According to Maori legend, there is a wonderful love-triangle story attached to how we came to have sweet potatoes here on our planet. Whanui was the brightest star in the Lyra constellation in the northern hemisphere. One night, Whanui met Pani, who was the wife of Rango-Maui. Whanui fell in love with Pani and seduced her, even though he knew it was wrong. She subsequently gave birth to sweet potato children. Rango-Maui was so disturbed by their presence he sent the sweet potato children down to earth to live. Whanui was so angry about this, he retaliated, throwing three types of caterpillar after them, designed specifically to feed on the sweet potatoes.[1] Maybe that explains why the local people look after their sweet potatoes so carefully, to keep them away from greedy caterpillars and other tuber-eating animals.

The Aljezur region is famous for its *lyra* variety of sweet potato, which is grown only in this region. I wonder if it was named after the constellation in the story above. It has a characteristic yellow pulp and red skin. The parishes of São Teotónio, São Salvador, Zambujeira do Mar, Longueira/Almograve and Vila Nova de Milfontes grow an incredible 8,000 tonnes of the *lyra* potato annually. The climate and soil in these areas produce the most wonderful potato, which has a much sweeter and softer centre. If you eat it raw, it tastes like chestnuts, and it also makes the most amazing mashed potato. The *lyra* is harvested only between September and mid-November each year. The best quality potatoes are then available until about April. My favourite variety, however, is not the *lyra*, but the *batata doce roxa*, which has an unusual purple-coloured flesh. It stays purple even after you have cooked it and makes a brightly coloured mash which almost looks too good to eat. (Only kidding; it doesn't last five seconds on my plate. I love it).

The humble tuber even makes it into another historical tale. Christians seized the town of Aljezur from its Moorish occupation in 1249. The Knights of the Order of St James of the Sword, led by the Santiago knight, Paio Peres Correia, were instrumental in this epic moment in local history. According to legend, the knights drank a special potion made from sweet potatoes before every important battle. [Although this clashes with the generally accepted date of introducing this vegetable into Europe]. The force of the invasion and the speed with which they took the castle of Aljezur stunned the Moors, who could not react to such a sudden charge. The knights decided it was their sweet potato potion that was the determining factor in the victory. Time, and a liberal dose of creative marketing, then turns this elixir into what is now the locally famous *feijoada de batata doce de Aljezur* (the Aljezur sweet-potato bean stew).[2] I'd love to get the recipe if it can give you that much strength and speed!

Whatever the truth of such legend, the fact stands that Aljezur is the true home of the sweet potato. Given a protected geographical status under European Union law, the tubers from Aljezur have an IGP seal (Indicação Geográfica Protegida), which makes them rather special. They are one of sixty IGP products registered in Portugal, and one of only three items listed in the fruit and vegetables category.

And every year, at the end of November, there is an entire festival dedicated to the humble sweet potato in Aljezur. Described as the biggest autumn gastronomic festival in the south of Portugal; it draws crowds of over forty thousand people each year. They serve an amazing thirty-five tonnes of sweet potatoes in one weekend. They are the chief ingredient in a whole range of different products and foods. They are sold in cakes and sweets, as fried slices or chips, or served with sugar and cinnamon. You can even sample sweet potato liquor or taste them roasted in a wood-fired oven.

Well, we had to go along to see what all the fuss was about. Aljezur has a large events hall on the edge of town. There is usually ample space to park on a normal day; however, we left the car behind and walked up to the building and we were glad we did. Even the overflow parking area was full, there were so many cars and vehicles trying to park. Inside was a wonderful mix of local people and tourists enjoying live music, stalls, and exhibitions. Several restaurants and cafés had set up home in the main eatery area, and all the menus included sweet potatoes as the star of the show. We tried a delicious sweet potato stew, followed by sweet potato cake for dessert.

The stalls were a lovely mix of handicrafts, fresh produce, confectionery, and locally produced traditional goods. The programme had several chefs lined up to give live cooking demonstrations, all showcasing the humble sweet potato. One stand even had some eco-bikes that made fruit and vegetable juice. You pedalled away as fast as you could, and the gear system on the bike transferred energy from the pedals directly to an attached blender and juice extractor. At the end of the allotted time, you were given a glass of juice to drink that you had just pressed.

The sweet potato fair was great fun, and we are proud of our little town hosting such a prestigious and popular celebration. The event has been running for over twenty years and shows no signs of slowing down. In fact, it seems to get bigger and better every year.

✿ฬ✿ଋ✿

There are some smaller villages around the Aljezur area that are worth exploring and Odeceixe is right up there amongst our favourites.

Drive out of Aljezur, keep going through Rogil, and then watch out for some eye-watering hairpin bends immediately prior to the left-hand turning to Odeceixe. This stretch of road is not for the faint-hearted. Follow the signs to the free car park and then meander down into the centre past the local market building.

There are lots of nice cafés and restaurants to enjoy in this village, mostly serving traditional Portuguese fare. Then, after lunch, have a stroll around and wear off some calories. The church is easy to find, but the doors are always locked whenever we pass by. The gardens have a lovely old-fashioned country cottage feel to them, full of plants and flowers. And the view from the end of the church path is wonderful.

Many of the houses have been sympathetically restored and there are lots of pretty holiday cottages with colourful doors and windows. There are some nice authentic craft and gift shops to explore too. And all roads will eventually lead you to the top of the village and its impressive *moinho* or windmill. If you go up there on a windy day, it is quite eerie as the wind blows through the sail masts. It makes a loud, almost haunting musical sound; something I have never heard before.

There are plans afoot by Aljezur Council to further renovate the windmill to make it more of a tourist attraction and allow easier access up the hill. The views from the top are spectacular, so I hope they keep the natural beauty of the area if they do the work.

Back in the main square there are some wooden benches, and this is a tranquil spot to sit and watch the world go by. You get the feeling that nothing would happen quickly here. The village gets busier in the summer months as it is a haven for surfers and people looking for a relaxed holiday.

The highlight of the village's calendar is the month of June. Every town and village in Portugal seem to have their own adopted saint (or three), but Odeceixe really knows how to celebrate in style. The popular saints of Saint Anthony, Saint John and Saint Peter all have their special days in June and Odeceixe pulls out all the stops to welcome them.

One year we happened upon this by chance on the way to somewhere else. We arrived in time for lunch to find the streets lined with an amazing display of paper flowers. They were hung above the pavements and strewn from every available outside surface or pole.

Everyone seemed to have played their part in decorating the village, with what looked like thousands of these flowers, all handmade and stunningly pretty. The streets were also full of wonderful sculptures and statues made from recycled materials.

One lovely feature was a series of dolls fashioned from old bottles and paper that depicted brides and grooms. Displayed on each of the steps that led up to the church, they were fabulous. I think children from the local school created them, and they added something special to the occasion.

The day we arrived there, the preparations were in full flow for the music, dancing, and street barbecues planned for that evening. Sadly, even though several people asked us to stay, we had another appointment and couldn't make it back there in time. But every year since then, we try to stop by and see the displays and enjoy the festivities.

We also love the drive along to the river Seixe, which meanders down to the beach and the sea. It is stunningly beautiful and leads across to Odeceixe beach. Beware the signs from the village marked *praia* though—don't be fooled into thinking you can walk there in five minutes. My advice is to take the car as it's a lot further than it seems.

Once you arrive there, Odeceixe beach village itself is a quiet little place. It has a handful of streets, a few houses, and a café or two, and a tourist gift shop. The view from the bench at the top of the hill though is spectacular. And the beach itself is glorious.

For such a small area there is so much going on, with good food, a friendly welcome, excellent artisan shops, and the most beautiful beach imaginable. If you want a day out with a difference, then head west and make sure Odeceixe is on your route. Preferably in time for the annual festival of the saints.

The summer patronal festival in Aljezur, by comparison, is a quieter affair. Well, it is until the live music starts up in the market car park in the evening. Called the Festa de Nossa Senhora d'Alva, the event takes place on the 29th August each year. It translates roughly as The Festival of Our Lady of the Dawn. She is the patroness of the town, and the Igreja Nova church is dedicated to her. The day begins with an early swim at Odeceixe beach. The participants recreate the typical pilgrimage that families in the past would have made to spend the bank holiday at the beach. Many people dress up in traditional costume to recreate the history of the day. Live music played at the beach brings the period costumes and occasion to life.

At 3 p.m. religious ceremonies begin with the celebration of the Eucharist in the Church of Nossa Senhora D'Alva, followed by a procession that travels through the streets. They used to set up trestle tables outside the Igreja Nova church in the afternoon, and the locals feasted on free sardines. Sadly, the event became too popular and successful, and the council moved it to the large multi-purpose building on the edge of town. It has undoubtedly lost some charm and authenticity because of this decision.

We prefer to stay around the market area in the old town, where traditional live music and food is available. Participants and visitors alike wear at least one piece of white clothing to the evening's celebrations, and it is an eye-catching and enjoyable event.

For a more lavish colour-themed experience though, you need to head to Carvoeiro, which hosts an annual Black and White Night to celebrate the summer solstice. First started in 2014, the event attracts over thirty thousand people. Entrance is free, there are live music acts and bands scattered all around the town, with the main stage situated right by the beach.

The numbers are topped only by the epic bi-annual Noite Branca (White Night) spectacular that happens at the end of August in Loulé. This is possibly the biggest event on the Algarve calendar, with over eighty thousand people attending this free gathering. They paint the city white, everyone wears white clothes, and it is a riot of celebrations.

In 2019, the White Night began precisely at 8.03 p.m. which was the exact time of the sunset, on the last Saturday in August. The streets were filled with music, animation, live acts, and cultural events. The shops even offer you a discount for wearing white clothing.

If you would rather see twelve thousand white candles than eighty thousand people dressed in white, then head for the annual Mercado de Culturas à Luz das Velas (Cultural Market by Candlelight). Held in Lagoa near the pretty Convent São José and the surrounding streets, this is another not-to-be-missed entry in the calendar. It is free to wander around and enjoy the sights and stalls and street entertainment.

There is a programme of live music, with exhibitions, workshops, and performances for all the family. The dominant feature are the candles – twelve thousand of them, all lit by hand and sat nestled in individual glass jars. Lighting starts at 8.30 p.m. and requires a small army of young volunteers. Arranged into intricate patterns on the streets and pavements, each year these sparkling votives celebrate a different theme.

There is a great selection of food on offer. Try to get there early, about 7 or 7.30 p.m. if you want to eat, as it is much quieter then, and you will be able to find a seat. There are also lots of stalls selling a range of foods, including herbs, seeds, and dried fruit. It is not a huge event, you can walk round it all in under an hour, but you end up doubling back and re-visiting the stands again. There are some lovely handmade and original products for sale, alongside more commercial items.

And once it is dark, the place is transformed with all the candles twinkling and shining. It is magical to witness all the lights, although you need to watch where you are walking as they are all arranged around your feet. The convent's chapel opens its doors and is lit simply with a row of candles on each side of the aisle. It is not often you get to see inside this revered place of worship. Next door, the main convent building is also open and usually hosts an art exhibition alongside the main stands. The town gets busy once night-time approaches, with families, locals, and tourists all filling the streets with noise and bustle. Watch out for the street entertainers that creep up behind you too.

There are so many fairs and festivals held across the Algarve all year round. In my previous book, I concentrated on describing the annual Silves Medieval Fair, and the carnival at Loulé. But everywhere you go you can find a local patronal festival, a fiesta that is celebrating a saint, potato or fruit, or a music event. The Portuguese like to dress up, commemorate their history and celebrate life, and we are always delighted to enjoy these events with them.

---

1. Heifetz, Milton D. and Tirion, W. (2004). *A Walk through the Heavens: A Guide to Stars and Constellations and their Legends*. Cambridge University Press.
2. Portuguese Tradicional Products (s.d.). Website article *Batata Doce de Aljezur PGI*. Accessed 26th June 2020 through https://tradicional.dgadr.gov.pt/en/categories/vegetables-and-cereals/638-batata-doce-de-aljezur-pgi

16

It's Not All Sunshine and Roses

Sometimes you can find the grass isn't always greener when you move here to live in the Algarve. In fact, unless you are looking at a plush, landscaped, and well-watered golf course, the grass here in the summer is often parched and dry. I wanted to interview our friends, Gerty and Raymond, as I know they have struggled with relocating here, and I was interested to find out why.

As they readily admit, some people might see their viewpoint as negative, and they realise not everyone will see things the same way as they do. They describe themselves as 'sceptically realistic'. They have been living abroad now for fourteen-and-a-half years and have struggled with both their health and settling here. They have been very honest in their answers.

"We have met so many people and listened to so many different stories. We find that someone also needs to tell the other side of the story sometimes. Moving to another country is not always for everyone, it's not all sunshine and roses."

Gerty is fifty-six years old and Raymond is seventy-four years old. They both finished high school in Belgium and became sales representatives in different companies. They were independent, responsible for selling and promoting products in Belgium in retail shops. They were able to meet lots of different people, which made their jobs fascinating. They then moved to the Far East, but after nine years living in Asia (seven years in Bali and two years in Penang, Malaysia), Raymond decided they had to look for a more secure place to live.

The fact they could not get health insurance in Asia, above the age of sixty, made him realise it was not the best place to stay. Although they loved both Bali and Malaysia, Raymond wanted to move back to Europe, but certainly not back to Belgium, because of the high cost of living. It was a friend of theirs that came up with the idea of Portugal, although they know most Belgian people move to Spain or France.

They have been living here in the Algarve now for five years, based in the town of Portimão. This is the biggest town in the western Algarve, with a population of over fifty-five thousand people living in a densely populated area. It is mostly known for its shops and retail centres, with pedestrianised streets with small independent shops, and a large purpose-built indoor shopping arena.

The cafés and restaurants are frequented by local people, and there are historic buildings and churches to explore in the older part of town. It is not a pretty destination, and not on the tourist map, but it is a busy and interesting place that has everything you could need.

Gerty and Raymond enjoy the availability of good healthcare and the more relaxed way of life that Portugal offers them. The fact the weather over here is much better than in Belgium is important to them. In wintertime (although it is considerably colder than they thought it would be) they find it is still pleasant during the day, when the sun is shining. They both enjoy going for a nice walk, though they admitted they tend to stay at home more in the summer to avoid the busier crowds of people.

They said they both sometimes miss good food from Belgium, concerts and the theatre, cosy tea-rooms, and restaurants, but certainly not the grey and rainy weather!

Reminiscing about Asia, Gerty added,

"I miss the heat and also the kindness of the Balinese people, and the social life we had in Penang."

They hoped to have the same kind of social life here in the Algarve they had in Belgium, Bali, and Penang, but this has proven difficult for them to find. Everything is more spaced out here, and most of the people they know play golf and only stay for the golf season or wintertime.

"We have not found it easy making friends over here, a lot of people don't live here full time, and there is a lot of coming and going. Making friends with Portuguese people over here in Portimão is almost impossible. They are very closed, and most of them don't speak, or pretend not to speak, a second language. Also, the fact that most of the Portuguese have never travelled abroad makes it difficult to find a topic to talk about, except talking about the weather. They don't read books, watch different TV channels, or listen to different music."

They have found it much easier to make friends (or acquaintances) from other countries. They have friends from the UK, Holland, France, Germany, Sweden, Finland, and the USA, as most of them speak English. This was the reason Gerty became an event organiser for AFPOP (the Association of Foreign Property Owners in Portugal) because she recognised there are many people feeling lonely and in need of some company.

They initially joined AFPOP, which is one of the largest expat community organisations here in the Algarve, to meet more people. When they were looking for a new co-ordinator for the Portimão-Monchique area; Gerty volunteered for two years, arranging forty events with brilliant success. As it took up too much of her time and energy she had to stop, but in the meantime, she started organising events for her own friends. She was perceptive in recognising there is a big need for such activities amongst older people who feel very lonely over here.

They are also members of NCA (Netherlands Club Algarve), which is a group formed for the Dutch community, and some other smaller expat groups that meet regularly.

I asked Gerty if there was anything that surprised them when they moved here.

"We expected better insulated housing with central heating

because the winters over here can be very cold and humid. Air-conditioning can be comfortable in the summer, but it is not the best way of heating your house."

They rent an apartment in a condominium, which was not easy to find. They visited about seventy apartments before they found a suitable one, describing one of the problems as follows,

"Most of the Portuguese like to rent out their property at crazy prices for just a few months during the summer. Also, all these apartments are furnished and because we like to live with our own furniture, it was not so easy to find a nice place unfurnished. But we did, with the help of some Swedish friends."

I asked her if she had any tips for people relocating out here to help them settle quickly.

"It seems to depend on which part of the country you are moving to, but we did not feel very welcome at the official offices, for example, the Freguesia or Finances, over here in Portimão. At the Finances they did not even want to help us get a NIF number without having a lawyer because we came from Malaysia. They also refused to talk English or French, although we know that for the last twenty-five years, they have had to learn a second language in school. We had to speak Portuguese or have a translator with us. We found this unacceptable as you can't expect people arriving in the country to speak the Portuguese language within a few days!

Also, the bureaucracy over here is a nightmare. They send you back home at least two or three times for another paper or copy of a document that they supposedly needed but never asked for in the first place. It also seems there are no fixed rules, and it depends on who you have in front of you."

Gerty agreed with me that Portuguese is a difficult language to learn.

"I can understand most of the small talk, I can read messages in shops and bills, but I still can't talk Portuguese. As I mentioned before, we can't practise the language as the local people don't talk to us, and we don't watch Portuguese television. And for Raymond, who has short-term memory loss, it's completely impossible. Now we only go to the shops where we feel welcome and can speak English or French."

I asked Gerty if they still go back to Belgium to visit friends and family. She replied honestly,

"Raymond does not want to go to Belgium anymore. I like to see my family once in a while, but as Raymond says, they can come over here as well if they like. I went to Belgium for the wedding of my half-brother after being away for ten years. I liked the feeling of being 'home' again, but the traffic and the stress everywhere kept me wanting to return to Portugal as soon as possible."

☼ﻬ☼ﻬ☼

Gerty was keen to tell me what she thought of the shops here in the Algarve.

"Because we both love shopping, we were very disappointed in the local Aqua shopping mall, where you've finished looking around in about twenty minutes. As we mentioned, we came from Penang, where you have shopping malls that almost take you the whole day to walk around! Now, with the arrival of Mar shopping in Loulé, we have a little more choice available. Grocery shops, however, are plentiful over here. It is almost unbelievable how they can manage to survive. Prices are comparable with Belgium, sometimes even more expensive because of the tax difference. In general, the choice of what is available over here is extremely limited and mostly low quality."

Gerty explained they find it is still affordable to live here because they need less money for heating, fewer winter clothes, and the restaurants are cheaper. They find that fuel, electricity, and the internet, are the same price as in Belgium.

I asked them what they thought about Portuguese food and their favourite restaurants. Gerty replied,

"We don't really like the Portuguese food because it's very salty and oily (fatty). Almost all the fish is cooked on a charcoal grill, the meat is chewy, and everywhere we find the same problem of overcooked fish or meat, which is not how we like to eat it. It's also too expensive for what you get. As Raymond always says, I am the best cook in town, so we eat at home most of the time. But if we can, we go to Indian, Italian, Chinese, Japanese, or French-Mediterranean restaurants. Our favourites are Vau Wine & Diner or Tokyo at Praia da Rocha, for sushi."

I asked her what had surprised her about Portuguese culture. Her reply was intriguing.

"The fact that a lot of them still live like during the Salazar regime. Nobody dares to take responsibility. They are very sad people. Although the Muslims were only over here for about two hundred years, all the historical events are still about that period (i.e. Medieval)."

Continuing the same theme, I enquired whether they had a funny story to share about life in the Algarve. They obviously find the bureaucracy here rather amusing.

"Spending four hours of our time at Finances to declare our 0% NHR tax, which we then found out would take us only five minutes to do online!"

With their love of travel and the Far East, I wondered what living in a different country had taught them. Gerty felt she had gained 'wisdom of life', and Raymond replied,

"The fact that you are very welcome in some countries and not welcome at all in others."

They lived for seven years in Bali (which they happily admit was Gerty's dream home, and still is), where it is much warmer and more humid, which was better for her health. She explained that,

"We miss the kindness of the people, it's priceless! We also miss the food and our four staff members. For Raymond, the summer over here is already warm enough, although the winter is much colder than he thought it would be. He is missing his sailing boats. Being on the water made him very relaxed.

We loved Penang for seven months of the year, we attended lots of social events, also different cultural events. Malay, Chinese, Japanese, Indian, there was always some kind of festival going on, and everyone was always welcome.

Unfortunately, for almost five months of the year, we had a haze over the island, from the burning of the Sumatra woods for the cultivation of cheap palm oil. This made breathing and living outside very difficult."

Health concerns are obviously important when you consider a move to live abroad. Gerty and Raymond immediately took out private health insurance when they arrived here, and they could not be happier with that decision. Raymond has already had prostate cancer treatment, and Gerty has been treated for her allergies and finally found out she has two autoimmune system problems. Raymond has had the first of two planned eye operations. As Gerty said,

"We could not have afforded all this in Asia on our savings."

I wondered where they thought they would see themselves in five years' time. Gerty replied,

"Let's hope we can stay together for a long time, but if Raymond dies first, I think I would go back to Bali for my health."

Gerty described their perfect day for me here in the Algarve, complete with timings.

They would wake up around 7 a.m. and read the news and Facebook in their pyjamas until 8 a.m. They would shower, etc. and have breakfast at about 9 a.m.

Afterwards they would do some shopping or go on an excursion (exploring a new place) or stay at home being creative. Gerty would be busy with her photos or organising new events, and Raymond with his paintings and reading on his iPad.

They would have lunch around 2 p.m.

Sometimes in the late afternoon they would go for a walk or visit a friend's home.

In the evening they would have dinner at about 7.30 p.m. They would watch television until 10.30 p.m. and be in bed by 11.00 p.m.

For people considering a move to live abroad, I asked Gerty what she would recommend they do first?

"Take a long holiday and travel from one place to another to find the place that suits you the best. Everyone has their own priorities (close to shops, close to the beach, far away from noise etc...) so don't let anyone else decide where to live for you."

I asked her what advice she would give to someone who is thinking about moving to Portugal. She replied,

1/ Don't be selfish and come over here with young children. Don't pull them away from their friends and school. Let them enjoy life, their friends, and grandparents, and once they are grown up and out of the house, then you can decide to move over here.

2/ You can love Portugal but find out if your partner feels the same way. Women (especially mothers) are not always very happy over here when they have to miss their family, children, and grandchildren. That's also the reason why so many couples travel back and forth to their family and keep a second home or apartment in their country of origin.

3/ If you decide to move over here with children, give them the chance for a good education; keeping in mind the question, will they ever want to go back home?!

4/ If you decide to buy a property, be aware of the quality of the build, the insulation, heating, and the location. Ask someone to assist you with an evaluation of the property. And try to visit the place in winter as well as summer. We know a lot of people who made the wrong decision because they did not have enough time to think about all of this. They were fooled by the agents who told them there were other people that also wanted to buy.

5/ Be sure you have a hobby; you can't fill your day with only going to restaurants and shops.

I was glad that Gerty and Raymond knew they could be honest with me about how they felt about their life here in the Algarve. The transition from one culture to another can be hard to manage and is not always easy. Pangs of homesickness, and/or missing a previous way of life, can make even an exciting move more difficult to cope with. Moving to a country with a completely new language to learn is also a challenge, alongside trying to navigate the choppy waters of bureaucracy.

Their recognition of the loneliness you can feel, even in a bigger town surrounded by people, was illuminating, and something I have heard expressed before. Having to go out and find new friends in an alien environment is daunting for many people, which is where clubs and societies like AFPOP can be real lifesavers. Leaving family and friends behind can also be hard, although with modern forms of communication now, keeping in touch with everyone back home is much easier. Lots of people say the only time they really miss someone is straight after they have finished chatting to them on a video call. This is when they remember how far away they are.

I think being honest and realistic about a move abroad is always important. Dave and I love our life here, and we have been extremely lucky that we have always felt we made the right decision in moving here. I know not everyone feels the same way about the Algarve. I hope Gerty and Raymond's honesty will be a cautionary word of warning to anyone contemplating the same move. Being forewarned of some of the issues, and seeing things from several different perspectives, can only be a good thing.

17

The Life-Altering Illness

It began before we even moved house. On one of my morning walks with Kat, I tripped up a step and hurt my foot. Nothing unusual there, I am eternally clumsy. Several days later, a searing pain started in one of my toes and spread to three of the other toes. By this time, I thought my foot should be starting to heal, but I was in agony and could hardly walk. The next morning, stubborn to the end, I hobbled out to walk Kat along the beach. I hoped walking barefoot in the sea might ease the pain a bit. A week later, and still struggling, one of my fellow dog-walker friends, Dagmar, asked me why I was limping. I explained what had happened, and she said,

"Take your shoe and sock off then and let me have a look. I was a physiotherapist in Germany for many years, I'll see what I can do to help."

We sat at a deserted café early in the morning before anywhere was open and I showed her my foot. I wish I could tell you the ensuing pain made all the difference, as she stretched, pulled, and kneaded my strange-shaped toes. It eased the discomfort a little, and she told me to rest as much as I could. I reminded her we were moving house in just over a week's time. She strapped two of my toes together and suggested I kept them bound together for a couple of weeks, during all the upheaval.

Several weeks later, having unpacked half a hundredweight in boxes, my toes finally eased up enough to remove the tape that had become a permanent fixture around two of them. Over the next few weeks, other odd joints in my body started to hurt and swell for no apparent reason. One of my knees kept playing up, then an elbow, then my thumb joints were swollen, but only for a day. The next day they were back to normal. It was as if I had a mini alien inside me that was pushing joints out of kilter, only to move on to another joint a few days later. I felt like a human version of the fairground game 'whack-a-mole'.

I had also begun the dubious pleasure of the menopause. For several months, every time something went wrong, I blamed it on that. My fiftieth birthday came, and I hid the fact I was in a lot of pain, and felt tired all day. The birthday party in our favourite local restaurant that evening was a lovely surprise. I enjoyed their finest chocolate mousse, and a fabulous cake cooked for me by dear friends. But even the double desserts could not take the edge off the heavy feeling I had that something was not quite right.

I carried on until February, from the previous August, before I could no longer deny there was a problem. My fingers had swollen to the size of sausages and were like concrete. I am not a fan of the medical profession at the best of times, but I duly contacted the health centre here in Aljezur and booked an appointment to see a doctor.

I am so grateful they were short-staffed because of long-term illness, and they had a locum doctor from Norway working there. Dr Victoria spoke five languages, including English, and she patiently listened as I described my symptoms. She was both sympathetic and professional. She ordered a series of blood tests, and X-rays on my hands, and explained where I needed to go to get them all done. She booked another appointment with me for the end of the month to review the results.

The first fun part was finding out I needed to book a consultation at the local opticians to get my blood tests done. The health service uses a vacant room at the back of the opticians to conduct the tests, bringing someone in from Lagos twice a week to cover the local area. I had never had a blood test before, and it was strange to be surrounded by pairs of glasses and comfy sofas whilst the examination was being done. I was told to return in ten days for the results. The tests were all individually priced at around seventy cents to one euro each. I had so many tests printed out that the total came to twenty-two euros.

Next up were the X-rays. I was in luck as I rang the local clinic in Lagoa the next morning. They said if I could get there on the Saturday morning (it was now Wednesday) they could fit me in. It was a busy clinic, but well organised, and I was in and out in twenty minutes, X-rays on both hands completed. They cost me five euros in total.

Then it was a waiting game until I could see Dr Victoria again. Dave came with me for this appointment and we sat patiently as she read through the results. She turned to me and said,

"Well, there's no doubt from the blood tests. We know what it is from your markers. You have Rheumatoid Arthritis."

Initially, I just felt relieved. Now I knew what was wrong with me, I thought, and we could fix it.

Dr Victoria looked sympathetic and sussed me out very quickly.

"It's no good me telling you about the drugs I can prescribe you, is it?"

I'm not a fan of conventional medicine, and she was right about what my response would be to that question.

"Well," she continued, "I want you to go away and get a copy of this book from Amazon and start there."

She printed out the details for me and handed me the piece of paper.

"The book is written by a doctor who had MS. She got herself out of her wheelchair and returned to riding her horse with a strict diet plan. Have a look and see what you think."

Dr Victoria turned out to be a Functional Medicine doctor in private practice, and she could not have been more helpful. The beauty of the health system here means that although they give you a time and date for an appointment, the timings are fluid. If a patient needs a little longer than their allocated twenty minutes, then everyone waits. I think we used up half her lunchtime too, as we were with her for almost an hour.

By the time we left the health centre, I had a much better idea of what RA, as it is often abbreviated, was. I had an auto-immune condition, and no-one knew what caused it. There was no cure for it, but I could help relieve the symptoms through diet and supplements. Dr Victoria also said she would add me to the waiting list to see a specialist rheumatologist at Faro hospital. She warned me that the only treatment they would recommend would be anti-inflammatory drugs and/or steroids. I think she could tell by my expression what I thought of that idea.

We went home, and I sank into a chair, exhausted by all the information I had received. Several days, and lots of Google searches later, my head was spinning. I downloaded the book Dr Victoria had recommended and took a deep breath before starting to read it. Somehow, I knew that my life was about to change drastically.

❀ℬ❀ℭ❀

So began what turned out to be a long process of trial and error. What quickly became obvious to me was the need to alter my diet completely. Out went the chocolate, cakes, bread, pasta, processed foods, sugar, and dairy. No more pizzas, no more chocolate mousse. We joked that the profits at our favourite A Bica pizzeria were about to take a nose-dive. Dave was brilliant throughout all of this and declared he would eat the same food as me. There isn't a perfect word to describe this, it's not really a diet, in the sense that I am not trying to lose weight, although I found I lost a lot of weight in the ensuing months. I describe it as more like an eating plan, or a way of life. Certainly, it affected every aspect of our lives, as I battled through numerous research articles and websites all purporting to have the miracle cure for something that has no cure. From bizarre dietary supplements and recommended anti-inflammatory foods, to the faintly ridiculous rubber wristband that promised to fight off free radicals, I tried many things.

Eating out became a challenge, as there were so many foods on my banned list. Interestingly, local Portuguese restaurants are good as they usually have a basic menu. Fish or meat, plainly grilled, with salad (no tomatoes or peppers) or cooked vegetables. No rice or potatoes. But sweet potatoes, oddly enough, are fine, as they are not classed as nightshades. My Portuguese got better, as I rapidly learnt how to explain what I could, or in most cases, couldn't eat, to everyone. Oh, and no alcohol either. Only plain water, green tea, and luckily for me, I seem to be ok with an espresso here and there too.

I also discovered that CBD (cannabidiol) oil, and acupuncture, help enormously. The first time I went for an acupuncture treatment, I was pretty nervous. I'm not a fan of needles, so you can guess how desperate I was to relieve some of my pain and inflamed joints, without having to resort to taking drugs. I went into the treatment room, hobbling badly with one extremely swollen knee, and walked out forty-five minutes later almost normally. I could not believe what one session had achieved, and the best part of it was that my knee remained less swollen and sore in the days ahead. I spent several months, and a lot of money, on subsequent acupuncture treatments, to alleviate my problems. Fingers that were swollen, bent and crooked, gradually straightened. My knees were less inflamed, and my ankles almost returned to normal. But it was a slow process.

I have always been a positive person, and other than a few angry 'oh crap' moments when I could not open a jar of something—or even on one occasion open my bedroom door to get out of the room —I have tried to battle on as best I can with this illness. I admit to having some dark moments, of course, but I have always reasoned with myself that it could be a lot worse. We have lost friends to cancer at a ridiculously young age, and many people are born with illnesses that hold them back all their lives. I reached almost fifty years old whilst enjoying extremely good health all my life. RA might have come along to spoil the party a bit, but I doubt it will kill me, and I have just got to adapt to a different way of life.

It took me a long while before I could paint again. Staring at my empty studio, with my paints and brushes sat there waiting for me, was difficult, but I was sure I would return to them.

My one over-riding joy, which shapes my days for me, is my daily morning walk with Kat. I am determined to take her out every day, even if means that for the first ten minutes or so, I will hobble down the road like an old lady. The fresh air, the peace and quiet of the river, and the delight I have in watching our beautiful girl snuffling and darting along, are priceless to me. There is absolutely no way I am going to miss that morning walk. After the initial struggle to get moving, I always find walking seems to help me and my joints. I return home with a smile on my face, a happy muddy dog, and a readiness to tackle the day ahead.

One challenge I have found is that it is difficult to explain to others what is wrong with me. If I mention Rheumatoid Arthritis, most people only hear the word arthritis and immediately tell me they have arthritis in their thumb too. Although similar in words, osteoarthritis is vastly different to RA. The arthritis they know occurs in specific areas, often fingers, and is isolated to that particular part of their body. RA is more like an alien that is inhabiting your entire body. On any day of the week, it might move to a knee, or an elbow, finger, toe, shoulder... you name it, the alien might visit it. Swelling, concrete-like joints, constant pain, loud cracking and popping noises (most alarming until you get used to them) and strange-shaped joints ensue.

Other problems also resulted from the initial illness. I can no longer eat nuts as the skin around my eyes becomes red and angry, and in the winter, I now have the onset of Raynaud's disease to endure as well. Imagine one, or more, of the tips of your fingers turning a yellow-white colour and becoming completely numb to the touch. Add to that, the fact that you cannot use that finger for anything useful at all, and even the thickest pairs of thermal gloves don't warm your hands up when you are out on a walk, and you begin to get the idea. Not much fun. Thank goodness the winters here are short (although it can be very cold at night and in the early morning), and the summers are long and hot.

You also learn to adapt as best you can to something like this.

Jars are not tightened quite so severely, and kettles are only half-filled with water. The door from the kitchen to my art studio is never closed properly, as I cannot open it again if it is shut tight. The dog harness with the tricky clasp is pushed firmly to the back of the drawer. My morning routine is now less about jumping out of bed to greet the day, and more about waking up slowly and stretching everything gently. I discover which joints are not working so well and give them an extra five minutes to warm up before I can reach for my slippers to get up.

I have learnt to listen to my body and to rest when I feel tired, even sometimes going back to bed for a sleep after lunch. As we are living in a Mediterranean country, this siesta lark is acceptable, although I should probably have moved to Spain if I had wanted to embrace this tradition fully. The Spanish take their siesta much more seriously than the Portuguese, even closing shops for the afternoon and re-opening later in the day. The Portuguese might have an hour or more for lunch, but they tend to be open again by 3 p.m. at the latest. When I have mentioned having an afternoon nap to local friends, they usually pooh-pooh the idea. They just like to have a long, leisurely lunch hour—or two—before returning to work. It usually also involves a glass of red wine, too.

I thought I would miss alcohol more than I do. I haven't missed it at all. There is something different about not being able to drink, as opposed to just deciding not to drink anymore, that makes the decision much easier, for me at least. Understanding that even one drink, or one slice of chocolate cake, will result in my body flaring up and being in agony, means I have managed the mental side of this illness quite easily. It is just how it is.

The hardest part is not knowing what causes this in the first place. No-one seems to know why an immune system suddenly turns on itself and starts causing these problems. It is also hard not knowing whether this is a permanent thing, or whether it might suddenly go away as quickly as it arrived. Everyone seems to have a different view of this and reading other people's experiences shows just how individual this illness is.

What I am convinced of is that diet plays a huge part in helping

—or hindering—this alien creature that has invaded my body. The recommendations all state you should cut out all inflammatory foods for at least three months. Then you can slowly try to reintroduce one food type at a time, cautiously monitoring it for an effect. So far, this has been an unmitigated disaster for me. Eggs—nope. Plain yoghurt —no. Nuts—definitely not. I tried buckwheat, which despite the name, does not contain any wheat or gluten, and is related to rhubarb, so in theory, it should have been ok. I tried it by eating the smallest organic buckwheat cracker imaginable, and by the next morning I had swollen up like a balloon. It took four extra acupuncture sessions to get me back on track from that experiment.

❀ஐ❀ର❀

The specialist rheumatologist appointment at Faro hospital took fifteen months to come through. I had given up waiting, so it was with some surprise that I opened an envelope one day in the post and found they had scheduled my appointment. Thanks to Covid, we were in lockdown, so I called them and had the date deferred. Strangely enough, once they had contacted me, they suddenly seemed in a hurry to see me. They kept calling me with a new appointment, and each time I declined as I did not want to travel to a hospital location that had Covid patients inside. Eventually they agreed I could have the consultant specialist ring me at home instead, on the eventual allotted date and time allocated to me. This was almost four months after the original date of my appointment.

He was actually very nice. We exchanged a couple of emails in advance of the day, and he concurred that my symptoms were consistent with Rheumatoid Arthritis. Well, if it hadn't been that; I'd like to have heard what he thought it was that had ravaged my joints and body for almost two years. Unsurprisingly, he then offered his solution, which was an intensive course of drug treatments, with no actual end date in sight. Just a long list of rather unpleasant side-effects, including the potential for liver damage. I politely asked him what would happen if I decided not to follow the strategy proposed. I was at least reassured by his answer,

"Well, you will stay with me. I am your doctor for life now with this chronic condition, as there is no cure for it. But the sooner you start on the treatment, the better."

He gave me the details of the drugs, and I went away and researched them more thoroughly. It is hardly encouraging when you find out that the main procedure consists of a drug that is prescribed in a much higher dose as a treatment for cancer. And that all the side-effects mean you are given a prescription for another set of drugs used to counteract the original drug's effects.

I wrote back to him, thanking him for his time, but declined the medication plan. I figured it had been almost two years, and contrary to his entreaty that I would only be getting worse without the drugs, I actually felt I was in a much better place with managing it all. And my most recent blood test results had shown that I had halved my RA score from fifty-two to twenty-six. The two years had given me plenty of time to research, experiment, and discover a simple, clean-eating plan that gives me respite from the worst of the illness. I still have bad days, but I can usually trace them back to something I have tried to re-introduce into my diet. Chickpeas—no can do. So now I just stick to the plain food that seems to work for me. I often need to have a rest in the afternoon, but I am back painting, and writing, and walking Kat every day. Life could be a lot worse than that.

18

The Portuguese Way of Doing Things

Some things just work differently in Portugal. Take banking for example. The Portuguese have an excellent Multibanco cash machine system. Unlike at a basic ATM, at a Multibanco you can do so much more than simply withdraw money. You can pay bills online, authorise payment of your property tax or social security bill, transfer money and even buy concert tickets. It is a sophisticated system, and worthy of the 21st century.

In the branch, however, things are a little less modern. I do like the fact that the bank teller sits behind an impressive desk and there is just a line marked discretely on the floor for you to queue behind. There are no plastic screens or booths here, it is more like entering the office of a solicitor. Our local branch has a polished, if rather austere, and deathly quiet interior, with acres of empty floor space.

Nothing happens very quickly inside this particular world of banking. Once you are buzzed in—you have to remember to press the 'let me in' button before you are allowed to enter—you can easily wait ten minutes for the person ahead of you to finish being served. The bank teller is a happy chap that likes to talk to each customer about their day, and the weather, and the new car he bought last weekend. And then some more conversation about the weather. You can be in a hurry, and even tap the floor with your foot, or sigh deeply; nothing will register with him or induce him to speed up.

I had the fun of standing in line behind a dapper-dressed Portuguese man who had stepped up to the counter carrying a briefcase one morning. Oh dear, I thought to myself, this is going to take a while. I was not disappointed. Almost twenty minutes later, the teller got up from behind his desk and walked over to the safe at the back of the main office area, jangling a set of keys. He returned about five minutes later holding a great wad of bank notes, all taped up with rolls of paper. He sauntered across the main area and back to his desk, whereupon he started counting it all out using his electronic machine. No security concerns, no worries at all. I had no idea how much it was all adding up to; that is, until he handed it over to the man stood waiting with his briefcase and said loudly in Portuguese,

"Nine thousand euros today for you. No problem."

The man packed it all in his briefcase and departed.

It's not something you would see in the UK, that's for sure.

The teller loves to wind Dave up. Whenever we have been in the bank, and our transaction requires a signature—which is almost every time we are in there—the teller passes over a piece of paper and says,

"Signature, please."

He always seems to smirk a little, then glances at the afore-mentioned piece of paper, now complete with Dave's scrawl, and says,

"That's not your signature."

"Yes, it is," replies Dave wearily, "you say that to me every time."

"Ah yes, but how do I know it is you, without the correct signature?" he replies obstinately.

I've never really got my head round this brand of logic. The teller knows us; he greets us by name when we arrive. Dave has a passport with his photograph on it, and now his shiny new *residência* card—also with a photograph on it. And yet still, Mr Teller is not happy.

"Well, if my signature doesn't match the one you have, let me see what you have on your records then," says Dave helpfully.

"Oh no, I cannot show you that one," comes the reply.

"But it's my signature - why can't I see it?" asks Dave.

We usually give up at that point, Mr Teller hands over the money or paperwork he owes us, and we depart listening to him say,

"Thank you for coming in today, see you again soon."

✿ℬ✿ℰ✿

Dave had the delight of receiving his latest bank card in the post last week. As I am chief finance officer for the household, and Dave hates anything to do with money, he looked at it blankly and squeaked at me,

"I've got to get the card authorised. Last time it said I could go into the branch and do it, but this letter doesn't mention that option."

Thoughts of going to visit our friendly, laid-back-to-horizontal Mr Teller sprung to mind. I smiled as I thought about the fact that authorising a card would definitely require a signature.

"Well, it says that you can do it online, or you have to ring this number here," I said to him, "I'll try to do it on the computer for you."

The online system is very efficient; however, sadly for Dave, it wouldn't let me authorise his card as the programme knew I had logged in as me and not Dave. And Dave doesn't do online banking. At all. Ever.

So the only option was to ring the number. Of course, he put it off to the last minute, and of course, I nagged him until he did it. I sat in the background when he made the call, which he put on speaker phone for my enjoyment. The problem is that you must not have anyone else there with you when you ring the bank under such circumstances, so I had to be extra-quiet. Which proved to be exceedingly difficult listening to the phone conversation that followed:

"Hello, good afternoon, can I help you?"

So far, so good. The man was reasonably proficient in English.

"Yes, I'm calling to get my bank card authorised so that I can use it before my old card expires."

"Yes, I can help you with that," said the bank man confidently. "Do you have the letter there that we sent you with the card?"

Now at this point you must remember our shared police officer background. It would be fair to say we might be considered a little prone to assuming the worst in a situation. I immediately thought about how easy it would be to steal someone's post from their mailbox. Or to open mail delivered to your address that belonged to the previous occupant. Perhaps that would only occur to me and my warped, slightly cynical mind.

"Yes," replied Dave, "I have the letter here."

"Good, can you tell me the address on the letter, please? Your address."

(Seriously?)

Dave rattled off the address on the letter. Which is, of course, our address. It is; however, written slightly differently on every single bill and statement that comes to us from a range of different companies. One version even has our house number inserted at the end of the address after our postcode, and just before the word Portugal.

The bank man on the other end of the phone congratulated Dave on getting his address correct. Except sadly, he was a little too excited in his enthusiasm to thank Dave for answering the first question correctly, and replied,

"Thank you, Mr David Sheldrake for your answer."

I had to stuff my hand in my mouth to stop myself from laughing. Ah-ha, I thought to myself, you've blown it already, you've told the customer what his name is on the account. That's one less question you can ask in a minute.

The bank man seemed unperturbed by this, and continued gamely on,

"Now can you tell me the last eight digits on the card you have in front of you, please."

I was trying not to chuckle. What, the card you have stolen, that is attached to the piece of paper that you have also stolen?

Dave manfully read out the numbers.

Then there was a pause — a long pause.

"Thank you, Mr Sheldrake. Now can you, erm, can you hold on a minute please?"

I was almost going red in the face, trying not to laugh. The phone call went on hold and the tinny background music loved by all Portuguese departments started to play.

It seemed as if they don't really get many people that ring up to authorise a card anymore. The poor man sounded as if he was desperately hunting around for more questions to ask Dave.

"In a minute, he is going to ask you what colour T-shirt you are wearing today," I said, trying not to chortle.

Bank man returned, and at last asked Dave something he couldn't possibly know from the letter that came with the card. Although it is a question that is easily answered if you had one of Dave's till receipts handy.

"Can you tell me your fiscal number, please?"

This is a unique tax identification number issued in Portugal to anyone and everyone. The number is known in Portugal as a Número de Identificação Fiscal, or fiscal number. It can be added to any receipt for tax purposes.

Dave duly obliged with his magic number, was placed back on hold, then bank man returned on the line again.

"Your card is now authorised. Thank you for your call."

I was still wiping the tears of laughter from my cheeks several minutes later.

At least the card is valid for the next two years, before Dave has to make that phone call again.

ꙮꙮꙮꙮꙮ

Our bank is not the only company to cause us equal amounts of desperation and mirth. The following story left me helpless with laughter. I've changed the names to protect the guilty.

It started with an innocent phone call I received one afternoon.

"Hello, could I speak to Mary Jones please?"

"I'm sorry, I'm not Mary Jones," I replied, thinking to myself, I do know a Mary Jones, though.

"Who is calling, please?" I asked.

"Oh, I'm sorry this is Pixie Mobile. I need to speak to Mary Jones."

"Well, I'm not Mary, sorry."

"Ok, don't worry, I will contact her another way."

I thought no more about it. Until I received another call about two weeks later. From a man that sounded suspiciously like the same man as last time.

"Hello, could I speak to Mary Jones please?"

"I'm sorry, I'm not Mary Jones," I replied, thinking, here we go again.

"This is Pixie Mobile. I need to speak to Mary Jones."

"I know, you called me about two weeks ago."

"Yes, I did, I am sorry. But this is the number I have for Mary Jones."

"I know, but I am not Mary. Do you not have another number for her?"

"No," came the sheepish reply, "I do not have another number for her."

My light-bulb moment came. Mary had asked us if we could pop over to her holiday apartment one afternoon and let Pixie Mobile in so they could install the internet and a phone line for them. Mary was back in the UK; we had their keys, and it was no trouble for us. That was about three years ago, and Mary gave Pixie Mobile my phone number so they could make the arrangements directly with us.

"Well, I know Mary. I can get her home number for her; she lives in the UK. What is your number and I will call you back with her details?"

"Thank you, but I cannot call a UK phone number."

"Sorry, did you say that you cannot call a UK number? You cannot make international calls?"

"Yes, that is correct. I cannot call the UK. When will she next be in Portugal?"

"I have no idea, thanks to Covid," I replied, baffled by the way the conversation was going. "I'll get her to contact you."

"Thank you, yes that would be helpful."

I messaged Mary and explained what had happened. Her reply came back. She was somewhat horrified to realise that as they had not been out here in quite a while, their Portuguese bank account was low on funds. They had forgotten to transfer money across to cover any bills, including their Pixie Mobile account's standing order.

She assured me they had transferred over some money, and hopefully that would solve the problem.

About four weeks later, I received another phone call.

"Hello, I work for Pixie Mobile. I need to speak to Mary Jones."

I patiently explained the situation to them again,

"No, I'm not Mary Jones. Yes, I do know who she is. No, she lives in the UK."

All the while thinking, don't they ever update their records?

"I need to speak to Mary Jones," came the reply.

"Yes, I appreciate that. But she is not here. And apparently you cannot call her in the UK."

I explained to them what had happened with her bank account. I appreciated that under the Data Protection Act, they could not tell me anything about Mary's account, and I did not ask them. But I figured if they knew the circumstances, they would be able to sort everything out for her.

"Thank you for letting me know. Sorry for troubling you."

I thought that would be the end of the matter. Oh, I should have known better.

Two weeks later, whilst I was out walking Kat peacefully along the river, the silence was shattered by my phone ringing.

"Hello, could I speak to Mary Jones please?"

"I'm sorry, I'm not Mary Jones," I replied.

"I work for Pixie Mobile. I need to speak to Mary Jones."

"I know, but I am not Mary. I have had several conversations about this already."

"Yes, but I need to arrange to collect the equipment from her address."

"Sorry, why do you need to do that?"

"Because her account has been closed. I am ringing to tell you I need to collect the internet box from her house."

I explained again about the mix-up with her bank account.

"Can you not simply continue with her account? She has deposited money in her bank now. If she owes you anything, can you not just take it out? She does not want to close her account."

"Her account has been closed. It is my job to collect everything."

I realised I was talking to a debt-collecting agency, not Pixie Mobile.

"Do you have a number Mary can call you on? Then she can clear everything up directly with you?" I asked hopefully.

"No, I do not have a number she can call me on."

"Sorry, did you say you don't have a number she can call you back on?" I asked, slightly amazed. "Can you call her then; she is in the UK at the moment?"

"No, I cannot call the UK. When will she next be in Portugal?"

I was starting to get dizzy.

"Well, not this year, that is for sure. Not with Covid and the problem with flights."

"Oh," came the dejected reply.

"Well, how are you going to sort this out then? You cannot call her in the UK, and she cannot call you. And she is not coming back here anytime soon."

"Yes, that is a problem. But I need to collect the equipment."

We were going round in ridiculously small circles.

"I need to speak to Mary, then call you back. I will need a number to call you back on."

"Oh, ok. I can give you a special number. Please hold the line for a moment."

Off he went, I have no idea why. Presumably to find out what his phone number was.

"Ok, I have a number you can call. Can you take it down, please?"

"Well, no, not at the moment. I am out walking my dog. I do not have a pen on me. Please, text me the number, and I'll call you back in about half-an-hour."

"I am sorry. I cannot send you a text."

"You are joking, right? You work for Pixie Mobile. One of the biggest telecommunication providers in Portugal. And you cannot phone an international number? Or send a text message?"

If only he could have seen my face at that moment.

"No, that is correct. I will call you again in thirty minutes."

He rang off, and I called Dave and asked him to contact Mary for me. I relayed what had happened and suggested he check with her what she wanted us to do.

I got home, and Dave said Mary had tried everywhere to find a phone number or email address for Pixie Mobile, without success.

Sure enough, thirty minutes later, my phone rang again.

Dave answered it. I sat in the background, chortling with laughter.

The man on the other end was very helpful. Well, he tried to be.

Dave said to him,

"Mary has been trying to find a phone number or email for Pixie Mobile to contact them. You must have a number for them if you work for them?"

"I will check the internet for you and find a number," he replied, and proceeded to tap away on his keyboard.

Dave logged in at the same time and found Pixie Mobile's internet page. Five minutes later, the man on the phone gave up. He had clicked on every link on their page to find their contact information, and each time he clicked somewhere and opened another page; he came up blank. We were following his every move online, clicking through the same website — nothing.

"So, what are we going to do, then?" asked Dave.

"Well, I need to remove the equipment."

We were at a stalemate. And equipment-removing man wasn't budging. Even though Mary did not want to lose her internet package and had added funds to their bank account over here, Pixie Mobile could not take out the money she owed them. They said they could not reinstate her account, as the contract had been terminated.

Dave then offered a solution,

"I can go over to the apartment, but I am not waiting there all day for you to turn up. I can go there and remove the equipment and bring it back to my home here. You can collect it from here."

"Yes, we can do that. Thank you."

Dave asked him exactly what equipment they needed, and the man described the internet box, remote control and the gateway that plugs into the phone line.

"And I cannot call you, so what happens after that?"

The man agreed he would call Dave again in one week's time to arrange to collect everything from our house.

We let Mary know the news. She was philosophical about it all, and then brightly messaged us back.

"Did they mention the phone? We had a telephone installed too."

No, they had not mentioned a phone. This is the company that provides internet and phone packages to homes and businesses. That cannot call international numbers and does not have a phone number or email address you can contact them on. And cannot send text messages. And also does not keep a record of what equipment it has installed in a property.

They come highly recommended.

19

Tick Fever

I t started with a terrible headache and a sore neck which I put down to a batch of computer work that had left me sitting at my desk for too long the day before. I went to bed after taking two painkillers, thinking I would feel better in the morning, but if anything the pain was worse. I took Kat out for her usual walk first thing; it was July, and the early morning air seemed to help a little. But by lunchtime, I crawled back upstairs to lie on the bed, feeling pretty rough.

By that evening, I had a high temperature and the start of a fever; I felt awful and knew something was wrong. I changed into my pyjamas, intending to go to bed, and noticed a bright-red mark on my thigh.

I looked it up, already thinking I knew what it was. A tick bite. Kat wears a collar to stop her getting ticks and other nice crawly creatures. The collar, however, can take a while to work, and we sometimes see these horrors still alive and vainly scrambling across the sofa or bed before they finally die. The collar is not a foolproof method of protection by any means, but it seems to be the best option out here.

I guessed that one of these ticks had found me instead of Kat on our walk. Dave came upstairs concerned to see how I was feeling and smiled at Kat who was curled up beside me and seemed to know something was wrong. I had a poor night. I did not sleep very well, and felt uncomfortable all night. Our house is cool, and I had the window open slightly, but I still felt hot and horrible.

In the morning, Dave walked Kat (much to my disgust as I adore my morning walks with her), but I could not even get out of bed, let alone go out. Dave then went out shopping, leaving me sleeping upstairs.

He came back clutching a bag from the pharmacy, and the instructions to take me to the health centre to see a doctor if I didn't feel any better.

"Look what I've bought," he said, waving a packet in front of me, "it's a thermometer. I thought it would be fun to see what your temperature is!"

I'm not sure I considered it 'fun' at that moment, but settled back with the thermometer under my tongue to wait for the results.

"Mmm," said Dave, as he looked at the red line, "that's not good."

"Why, what is it?"

"102.4 on the dial."

"Is that high?" came my reply. You can tell I'm no medic.

"Yes, I think that's bad," said Dave, scurrying off downstairs to look it up on the computer.

"It says here you should call an ambulance if it reaches 103," he shouted up to me a few minutes later. "We'll check it again in a while."

I drifted off to sleep.

"102.3 now," said Dave, as he checked my temperature a few hours later. I didn't care, I was simply trying to drink some water, eat a tiny amount of food, and go back to sleep.

I checked the bite on my leg, trying to discover if the tick was still in there. I couldn't see anything, and the red mark was a little less angry by the second day. I researched it more thoroughly—it didn't have the telltale bullseye red ring that signifies Lyme disease— but it certainly looked like a tick bite.

My whole body ached, my joints were inflamed, no doubt thanks to my Rheumatoid Arthritis as well, which was probably going mad under the fever and pains I was experiencing all over. My head and neck were the worst affected areas, and all I wanted to do was curl up and sleep, as I felt giddy every time I tried to sit up.

By the third day, which was a Friday, I was a little better when I woke in the morning. I decided I was just about well enough to drag myself off to the local health centre. They run an appointment system, but they also let you turn up first thing in the morning, take a ticket, and wait. The receptionist asks you a few questions, determines how serious your problem is, and decides whether to give you an appointment for that day or not. Often this requires you to sit and wait for an hour or two, or come back in the afternoon. It does at least mean if you need a doctor, you can usually see one the same day.

Dave and I arrived at about 9 a.m. which is later than they like to assess people, but it was the best I could do. I had printed out my symptoms in Portuguese, including learning that I needed to say I thought I had *febre da carraça* — tick fever.

The receptionist took one look at me, didn't even ask me what was wrong, and hurriedly gave me an appointment for 10.15 a.m. She ushered us both round to sit in the waiting area in the corridor. Blimey, I thought to myself, I must look rough.

I didn't have to wait that long. At about 9.45 a.m. the doctor called me in. Dr Victoria must have been on holiday, and I sat down in front of a different male doctor and handed him my typed-out note. I was too exhausted to manage to speak much Portuguese, and luckily, he spoke a little English, so we managed ok.

He checked the bite to make sure the tick had departed, asked me how I felt, took my temperature, then prescribed a course of antibiotics and anti-inflammatories. He was extremely specific about telling me I must finish the treatment, and if I was any worse over the weekend, I had to call an ambulance or go to the hospital. He wanted to hear from me again on the Monday morning if I was no better.

Off we went to the chemists, then home, where I took the first of the tablets, and crawled back to bed. Over the next couple of days, I tried to eat, but I could only manage small forkfuls of mashed sweet potato, and sips of water. By the Sunday, I started to hallucinate, and felt giddy every time I moved. My arms and legs were aching terribly. The fever appeared to have lessened though, and I was in no hurry to go off to hospital, so Dave and I agreed I would see how I was over the next few hours. I slept, woke feeling a little better, and ate some more mashed potato.

Dave took my medicine packs and looked them up on the internet. He came back upstairs, waving the pack of antibiotics at me, and saying,

"I think I know why you are feeling so rough again," he said, "these tablets are for treating typhoid amongst other things. The side-effects are bad, and include hallucinating, nausea, and vomiting. I think you are in for a tough few days, kiddo."

He wasn't wrong. I can honestly say I have never been so ill in my life, and it was a full ten days before I started getting better. I lay in bed every morning listening to Dave take Kat out for her walk and felt awful. Kat would return and come back to bed, curl up asleep beside me, and I would do my best to stay positive.

Eventually I was well enough to go downstairs, shower, dress, and walk around our little garden. It was a slow process, and I didn't start to recover until a couple of days after I had finished the course of tablets.

Once I was back on my feet, and able to walk Kat again in the morning, albeit it a bit slow for the first few days, I started to improve, and finally, after about three weeks, I was more like my old self.

When I talked to English friends about what had happened, the conversation usually went along these lines:

"I had tick fever, I felt pretty rough."

"Oh, are you ok now?"

"Yes, fine, thanks. I've got the scar from the bite to remind me, though."

The same conversation with my local Portuguese friends was a whole different story.

"Where have you been, we have not seen you?"

"I had tick fever, but I am ok now."

"Tick fever?" came the reply. This was always accompanied by a horrified expression, followed by,

"I knew someone that had tick fever. They went to the hospital in Lisbon, and they died."

My English friends were interested but not too bothered. My Portuguese friends were far more vocal and concerned, and without exception, every single one of them had known someone that had had tick fever — and had died.

✿ℬ✿ℛ✿

Ticks are blood-feeding parasites that love to hang around on tall grass and shrubs waiting for their prey. Although I have always thought they were an insect, they are related to the arachnid family, so they are closer to a spider than anything else. They have an ambush strategy in play, they wait for an animal like Kat to walk past, and then they extend their forelegs and climb aboard. I've seen them crawling along the ground too, but they are small enough to pass by undetected, especially in Kat's curly fur.

Kat has her special collar from the vets, which does the trick most of the time, so if we find a tick in the house it will usually be lying dead. The premise behind such a device has always mystified me. The collar slowly releases chemicals, principally the pesticide Deltamethrin, that deters the blood-sucking insects like mosquitoes, ticks, and sand flies from biting and hopefully kills them quickly too. Deltamethrin is derived from a natural pesticide called Pyrethrin, which was discovered in chrysanthemum flowers over one hundred years ago. They consider it to be one of the safest insecticides. I am not a big fan of using chemicals on a dog, but this seems to be the least dangerous method of tick and flea prevention we can use here.

One evening, last spring, Kat must have disturbed a nest of ticks. We came home from her late-night walk and she jumped onto the bed, ready to settle down for the night. Suddenly I saw one, then two, then more of the little blighters crawling across the duvet. I usually have a roll of masking tape handy; it has been the best thing I have found for dealing with them swiftly and mercilessly. Plonk the tape on top of them and then fold it over tightly, shutting the critter in the middle. Job done. Except on this occasion, they just kept coming! After counting twenty-seven, I gave up and hauled her off into the bath and showered her. At 11.30 p.m. Needless to say, she wasn't overly impressed. Come to that, neither was I.

I have had several people ask me since my tick fever episode if my Rheumatoid Arthritis is actually Lyme disease. I had my RA diagnosis long before the tick fever came along. I also had no sign of the bulls-eye red ring around the site of my tick bite, which is the usual indicator for this illness. It's funny what you can become an expert on living here in the Algarve. Portugal is a low-risk country for Lyme disease. We are a high-risk area though for three diseases that all end in -osis (Ehrlichiosis, Anaplasmosis and Babesiosis if you are interested) which are carried by dog ticks.

I am constantly checking Kat for any creatures that might be lurking, and we always maintain her fur trimmed short in the spring and summer months. This is mostly to keep her cool, but also because it is much easier to check her over when we can see her skin under her curls. She has what I call a 'kit check' after every walk, but I am still surprised by a crawling creature now and then. Having been so ill myself, it is not something I would like repeated, for myself, Dave, or Kat, and I pounce on them as quickly as I can with my masking tape.

20

Shopping and Cooking
Sheldrake-style

The Algarve has a lot of shopping malls or forums. They usually have a large supermarket placed alongside smaller boutique shops and children's play areas. Many even have a multi-screen cinema complex hidden away on the top floor. What they all have in common is a host of restaurants, cafés, snack bars and seating areas. I am convinced that the Portuguese like the idea of shopping far more than they actually shop. You can see entire families wandering around, sitting eating, or at least grabbing a coffee and a pastry. Few of them seem to carry any shopping bags.

I'm not impressed by the latest spa treatment on offer at many of the forums, the one where you sit with your feet in a tank full of small fish. They cosily swarm up and start nibbling on your toes whilst you sit there, usually in full view of everyone walking by. You get a nice close-up view of someone's hairy toes or gnarled feet as they sit in the window and try to look nonchalant. No thanks—not for me!

For a better shopping experience, with no sign of swimming and nibbling fish, I like to head for the large retail zone known as Aqua Shopping in Portimão. This is a multi-storey shopper's delight. It also houses two of my favourite shops, Natura, for excellent quality well-priced clothes and Tiger, for fun. Natura also sells fabulous incense sticks and quirky jewellery and accessories.

But Tiger wins hands-down as the best place to wander around, picking up cheaply priced things you didn't know you needed until you saw them in the shop. They have unusual stationery and toys, gifts and sweets, small household items, and the weirdest card selection I have ever seen. It's the type of shop you wish had been round the corner when you were a youngster growing up. And as I am just a larger version of a small child, I can never resist a quick look around when I am passing.

Aqua is also home to a large Primark clothing store. There was great excitement on the Algarve when people heard they were arriving. Well, I was happy. I know there are ethical conversations to be had about the sweat-shop labour that allegedly surrounds such stores, and it is a difficult debate to begin. My problem stems from the fact I am unusually tall for a woman over here. The height of a good percentage of the male population only reaches my shoulders, and women are even shorter than that. Trying to acquire any clothes with arms or legs long enough for me was a real challenge before Primark arrived. The only two places I could buy trousers were Decathlon or Sports Direct. Both are sports shops where I would aim straight for the men's section.

Dave didn't fare much better, as for some reason best known only to Portugal, most men's trousers come in a standard thirty-two inches (or sometimes even longer) inside leg measurement. It has always baffled me why this is the case, but I'm sure it keeps local seamstresses (or probably wives) busy shortening all the legs on the trousers purchased. No wonder you see most of the older female population wearing skirts or dresses. One set of trousers to take up must be enough work for one day.

Poor Dave, although he is a reasonably tall 5'10" (or almost 1.8 metres in new money), his inside leg measurement is very short. This was beautifully illustrated when he bought some chino trousers and had to have them taken up. We know a lovely seamstress locally, and he duly dispatched them off to her to have the legs shortened. When they came back, they were still a little on the long side.

"What length did you tell her to shorten them to?" I asked him.

"Thirty inches" he replied, looking sheepish.

"But your inside leg is twenty-nine. Why did you say thirty?"

"Well, I thought that sounded like I had really short legs, so I said thirty instead," he replied.

Dave's logic never fails to amuse me.

When I told her what Dave had done, Heidi, the seamstress, made me laugh with her reply.

"He should have given me his measurements in metric instead. That would have been about seventy-five centimetres, which sounds much better."

One challenge we repeatedly face is whether to shop in the Iceland Overseas Supermarket that opened in Portimão. They sell English foods from both Iceland (the frozen food supermarket, not the country) and bizarrely, Waitrose. Now I have always wondered how those two would get on if they met at a party. They are not exactly known as having much in common in the UK. One of them sells cheap frozen food and ready meals; the other prides itself on selling high-quality (for that, read expensive) fresh foods and fancy products. But they sit together in a store that for some expats is the highlight of their shopping week.

I love spotting the British customers in there. You can usually find them pushing a large trolley laden with food, exclaiming over an open freezer door, "Oh look! They've got proper sausages."

The Portuguese that wander in there always seem to be slightly bemused, and they tend to only carry a small shopping basket around the store. You'll have to be quick to catch me in there, I'll be the one scurrying round, holding at most about three items in my hands. I will sigh deeply as I reach the only till that is open, and then have to queue up behind expats John and Shirley, who are emptying enough frozen food onto the conveyor belt to feed a family of eight for a fortnight.

✿ఞ✿ఞ✿

Shopping for food has become slightly more of a challenge since my RA diagnosis. I have a list of staples I rely on each week that make up the bulk of our meal planning. Any new item requires me to scrabble around for a pair of glasses so I can read the inordinately small print on the back of the packet. Usually there is an ingredient in there somewhere that I cannot eat, and I return the item to the shelf. It can be frustrating. Gluten-free is a given, and the bio and organic ranges, which are, of course, more expensive, have become commonplace in our shopping trolley.

One thing that I still miss, as I have such a sweet tooth, is anything you would remotely classify as a cake or biscuit. I have got used to having a green tea or herbal concoction instead of my favoured British cup of tea; however, the ubiquitous biscuit to accompany this has been sadly missing. I have a dear friend in the UK who is an absolute whizz with recipes and cooking, and she offered to help me in my quest. I sent Tiffany my admittedly rather short list of things I can eat. It was much easier than trying to explain all the foods I have to avoid. She set to work and soon replied with a couple of easy recipes for me to experiment with.

It should be noted at this point that anyone that knows me will know that the words 'Alyson', 'kitchen', and 'recipe' have probably never been uttered together in the same sentence before. I am, it is fair to say, an absolute disaster when it comes to culinary matters. I can just about operate a kettle and a toaster. Anything else is very hit-and-miss.

Luckily for me, Dave loves cooking. It is a good job, really. If it was down to my ability to create anything even remotely edible in the kitchen, I doubt he would have married me. On one of our early dates, you know, the ones where you are still trying to vaguely impress the other person… I attempted to roast a chicken in the oven. I'm not sure the oven had actually seen much action before this moment in my newly single, living in a rented flat, still young and haven't got a clue what to do stage of existence. I happily invited Dave round to dinner, and fiendishly chopped vegetables and peeled potatoes whilst the chicken was, I hoped, merrily roasting away. The table, of course, looked lovely. I'm happy making everything look nice when it comes to decoration. It's the artist in me. When I was born, the scientific part of my brain was deleted, in favour of all things right-brain and creative.

Time for the big reveal and out came the chicken. Off came the tinfoil, and all looked well. Slightly brown on top, with a crispy skin. There's nothing to this cooking lark, I thought to myself. That is, until I came to carve. The bird was still frozen in the middle. Arctic solid. Frozen. We ate out that night. And Dave took over the cooking soon afterwards. Almost twenty-five years later, he is still the one wearing the apron and brandishing the oven gloves.

Naturally, I enlisted his help in creating the delicious-sounding recipe ideas from Tiffany. After the first batch of goodies were created, I was allowed to be left unsupervised in the kitchen, as there was no actual cooking involved. I just had to use the whizzy, blendy, sharp-bladed mix-it-all-up machine. And I can now create a flapjack-like cake that tastes amazing, and some 'power balls' that are divine. My sweet tooth is finally satisfied.

The cake consists of gluten-free oats, which I can eat. (They are my go-to breakfast every morning — porridge with bananas, blueberries and red fruits liberally scattered on top.) Add some blanched almonds to the oats, coconut flakes, coconut oil, and chopped fresh dates from the market, and a generous scoop of organic carob powder, and you are away. I have found that although I cannot eat chocolate, raw carob powder is fine and tastes sweet and earthy.

The power balls are even more fun to make, and very easy. They must be, even I can make them! Twenty chopped dates, a cup of almonds, carob powder, and coconut oil. Add a dash of hot water (my secret ingredient), whizz them up, roll the sticky mixture into balls, and skid them around a bowl scattered with desiccated coconut. Ta-da! You have chocolate balls. With coconut flakes stuck to them. Delicious. They are about three centimetres in diameter, so the perfect size for a small treat. They might keep for up to a week in the fridge, I wouldn't know. I make about twenty-eight at a time, and they generally last for three or four days. Possibly that long. Although in fairness, Dave and I don't eat all of them.

I have discovered that several friends and neighbours enjoy nibbling on my chocolate balls. Especially my friend Petra from the market. She enquired one day what I was making with all the fresh dates I was buying, and why I was religiously counting them individually as I put them into a paper bag. I explained my new recipes and the next time I went to the market I took her a couple of chocolate balls to try. All nicely wrapped up in a cellophane bag with a 'home-made with love' sticker on the front. She chortled when she saw them and was delighted. She was also rather rude about them. Most of our friends have a naughty sense of humour. Petra is Dutch, but speaks perfect English and fluent Portuguese. We tend to stick to English when we see each other.

The next time we needed food from the market, Dave went, and I handed him another packet, all neatly wrapped up with two more balls inside for Petra. As soon as she saw them, and in a loud voice, she exclaimed,

"Oh Dave, I do love your balls!"

It became a standing joke. Last week, as I left the market, I gave her the now-famous culinary treat and gleefully (and loudly) said to her,

"Have fun licking my balls."

Several people turned round in amazement. I forget sometimes that most Portuguese people speak at least a smattering of English.

Another recipe that became a success, until I sadly realised that chickpeas were causing me some problems, was a home-made hummus dip I perfected. I was gutted when I discovered it was creating more inflammation, as it was so tasty. The secret was the spoonful of honey I added to the mixture. It was a lovely lunchtime treat, especially once I discovered you could make a type of toast by thinly slicing a sweet potato and placing it in the toaster to 'grill'. Hummus on top of sweet potato 'toast' was delicious.

Hey, I can actually make food we can eat, I thought to myself. Without needing to know the phone number of the accident and emergency department. Or the fire brigade. My culinary prowess reached its dizziest heights yet last month. There is a new foodie magazine that has been launched here in Portugal, called *Relish*

Portugal. It is a sumptuous affair, full of gastronomic delights, recipes from Michelin-starred chefs, reviews of top eateries, and features on local delicacies. You get the idea. They also feature an artist in each edition, and the lovely editor contacted me and asked if she could showcase my artwork. I was, of course, delighted to accept.

Then she said to me,

"We like to include a recipe from each of our featured contributors. Can you send me over your favourite recipe?"

Well, once I had finished laughing, I emailed her my hummus and sweet potato extravaganza. I wrote it with my usual panache and it was, it would be fair to say, slightly tongue-in-cheek. The 'recipe' included the instructions:

"Toast the sweet potato slices in the toaster on full-heat setting, at least twice, until they are cooked."

"Plonk the hummus on the 'toast' and scoff."

At this point, the editor kindly added the following translation:

"Put a spoonful of hummus atop the toasted sweet potatoes and enjoy."[1]

I literally cried with laughter when I saw they had printed this verbatim in the magazine. Of course, I now swagger round the kitchen reminding Dave that I am now a recognised gourmet chef and I have had one of my recipes included in a top food magazine. Oh, the irony. I wonder if they would like my recipe for char-grilled frozen chicken for the next edition?

---

1. Relish Portugal Magazine (09.10.2020). Online Magazine *Relish Portugal Oct Nov Dec 2020 Edition*. Accessed 10th October 2020 through https://relishportugal. com/wp-content/uploads/2020/10/RelishPortugalOctNovDec2020.pdf?fbclid= IwAR2lVUIqAYqq1TMG_264ZQpB3v3EV_bVD66VSk4Vhmnnd1MVT-OBLJq8k3s

21

You're Making Me Hungry

I have been surprised and delighted by how welcoming and friendly all our Portuguese neighbours have been. Barely a week passes that someone does not arrive at our door with home-grown fruit or vegetables for us to enjoy. I have experienced new foods and flavours I have never seen before, like the local speciality called *percebes*. It is a mollusc, known as the gooseneck barnacle in the UK. This is a real delicacy. It is similar to a mussel, with the texture and flavour of a clam. Our friend, Paulo, at our local café, insisted on offering us a plate of *percebes* one afternoon. He was amazed we had never tasted them before and gave us some to try 'on the house'. They were delicious.

A neighbour handed me a bundle of leaves one morning from their garden and told me to make a herbal drink with it. I had never heard of *Chá Bela Luísa* or *Lúcia Lima* (*Aloysia triphylla*) before, although it smelt of wonderfully fresh lemons. The Portuguese use it to season desserts and fruit salads, and they add it to jam, oils and vinegar. But mostly they simply brew a sweet tea from it. Lemon verbena, as we know it in English, also calms the nerves, relieves an upset stomach, and reduces a fever. It is even a mosquito repellent. Rural living has so many wonderful surprises.

Sadly for Kat, I have had to ask lots of locals not to feed her. They all delight in fussing her and sneaking her the odd biscuit, chunk of bread or slice of ham. Individually each item is only a small morsel, in her eyes anyway, but the total of all these treats builds up. Both our local cafés are regular haunts for her and her chocolate-brown 'please feed me' eyes. She has perfected the art of sitting patiently, usually handily right next to the fridge that holds the ham and cheese supplies, and sits looking cute and adorable until someone feeds her.

We have never given her 'human' food from the table when we are eating. This has resulted in us being able to take her anywhere with us without fear of any problems. We have lots of local restaurants that welcome her in and let her tuck herself away under the table, whilst we dine there. I love seeing the faces of the other people sat in the restaurant when we get up to leave and she quietly trots out from underneath our table.

One place we won't be taking her to, as it has closed down since we visited it, was a Chinese restaurant in Lagoa. We went there one summer evening, to try something different. The waitress was obviously having a problem with mosquitoes, and as we sat and perused the menu, she came over to us and grinned.

"I will sort out the flies for you," she said, brandishing an over-sized tennis racket.

We found out what it could do when she arrived with our starters, and I had ordered soup. She placed my bowl in front of me, then spied a mosquito flying overhead. With a lightning speed Rafa Nadal would have been proud of, she grabbed the tennis racket, whizzed it over our heads and clouted the mozzie. The racket was battery-powered and had a small electric shock that ran through it when you pressed a button. The result was a loud cracking sound, a spark of blue light, one dead mosquito, and an acrid smell of burned flesh. I looked down and found the hapless creature floating in my soup.

She apologised, whisked my bowl back to the kitchen and came back with it less than a minute later. No doubt she had merely scooped the critter out with a spoon and returned my soup to me, 'sans protein'. The debacle continued whenever she spotted a mozzie; the racket would fly into action and we heard the unmistakable sound of flesh meeting death at a high voltage. We jumped and cringed—and checked our plates—every time she sparked another unfortunate mozzie into an early grave. Needless to say, we left as quickly as we could and never went back there again.

۞ෲ۞ൽ۞

We do like a decent-sized portion of food when we go out to eat. An experience I will never forget is the night we went to one of the poshest hotels here on the Algarve. I had better not name them. Dave had been asked to photograph a charity event that was being held there. He needed some assistance, as it was quite a prestigious occasion with many people attending, so I offered to go along to help. I'm not a professional photographer by any stretch of the imagination, but I know one end of a camera from the other, and I am good at fetching things. We were working for free, as we liked the charity the event was in aid of, and they had kindly agreed to feed us both during the evening.

We arrived to find almost 150 people, all dressed up in their finery, milling around the exhibition area. Inside the main room, the tables had been laid out and everything looked very appealing. Flowers adorned each table, the candles were lit, and the wine flowed freely.

"I'm looking forward to dinner," I said to Dave, "I'm starving. This photography lark makes you hungry."

We were eventually guided to a table and sat with other guests who had each paid over one hundred euros for a ticket to the event. Our starters arrived, and I looked down in amazement at the smallest plate I had ever seen. On it lay two pieces of lettuce, a tiny assortment of miniature hors d'oeuvres, and a toothpick. I scoffed it all in about three seconds flat.

I glanced over at Dave, who raised his eyebrows at me and made me giggle. I waggled my toothpick at him and we tried to stifle our laughter.

"Oh well, let's hope the main course is a bit bigger," I said to him.

I should have kept the toothpick handy. The main course arrived, admittedly on a slightly larger plate. It was also accompanied by cutlery, which was a good sign. The problem was that the plate might have been a decent size, but there was a vast expanse of emptiness around the edge, with what appeared to be some decoration in the middle. Closer inspection revealed three small slivers of beef, two (yes, just two) piped mini swirls of mashed potato, and a smattering of little baby vegetables. A swirly pattern of an unidentifiable sauce completed the proceedings. The food covered about a third of the plate.

I stared down in amazement. Seriously, was that it? I couldn't even drink some wine to lessen the horror if I had wanted to, as we were working. I sat in silence, finished eating and glanced around to see if anyone else was thinking the same as me. Everyone seemed happy, chatting away and drinking copious amounts of wine. Perhaps that is how posh people stay thin, I thought to myself. They merely eat miniscule portions of fancy food and drink lots. Oh dear.

Dessert was another disappointment. It was so uninspiring I can't even remember what it was. A quick coffee, and then it was time for the auction and the speeches and we were back to work.

We arrived home about 1 a.m. both feeling very hungry. We scuttled into the kitchen and made two large rounds of sandwiches each. A giant mug of tea, a few biscuits, and we were finally sated. So much for fine dining in a fancy hotel. Give me an unpretentious restaurant with a decent portion of simple food any day.

One thing that was guaranteed to fill me up is a local bread, called *pão de Deus*, which literally translates as 'bread of God'. Sadly, no longer on my wish list thanks to my RA, this was one of my favourite morning treats. It is made with a soft, fluffy, almost brioche-like bread, with a wonderful centre comprising a creamy filling with coconut, egg white and sugar. Add to that a piece of ham and a slice of cheese, ask the staff in the café to warm it all slightly for you, so the cheese is just melting, and you have heaven on a plate. Dave used to look on in disgust as I groaned with pleasure as I ate every morsel. It was too sweet for him. For me, it was as close to perfection as a snack can get.

Another good filling option are *bifanas*. This is a steak sandwich, specifically a pork steak, which is seasoned with garlic and spices and served in a bread roll. Each establishment seems to have their own slight spin on the particular spices and sauce they cook it with, and the soft bread soaks up the juices. Tradition states it should be accompanied by a small beer. They are an inexpensive way of grabbing a quick bite to eat for lunch.

Pork is a staple meat here in Portugal. One of our favourite places is a local restaurant in the square that serves an excellent *porco preto*. The Iberian black pig is found in central and southern Spain and Portugal and has a propensity to obesity. Perfect for creating a fatty, marbled meat that cooks beautifully either in the oven or on a grill.

The traditional way of farming these special pigs is to allow them to graze in total freedom around the cork and holm oaks and open pasture of the countryside. They will consume around seven to ten kilogrammes of acorns a day, gaining about one kilogramme of weight each day until they reach a maximum weight of around one-hundred-and-sixty kilogrammes. A hefty beast. The meat is then prepared, and hams are also cured, creating the famous *presunto* ham known throughout the region.

✿❦✿❧✿

Forget the Seven Wonders of the World, here in Portugal the hotly contested award ceremony was the intriguingly titled Seven Wonders of the Portuguese Gastronomy. I had to find out more and see how many of the winners I had eaten and enjoyed. A shortlist of twenty-one traditional dishes was chosen by a panel of experts, covering six different categories – starters/appetisers, soups, seafood, fish, meat, and sweets. The Portuguese general public were then asked to vote, and the organisers announced the seven winners with much fanfare.

They stated that the heroes were the recipes that reflected

genuine and traditional Portuguese values and defined the Portuguese culture and identity as a nation. That is a lot to ask of a bowl of soup or a humble sausage.

The prize-winning *alheira de Mirandela* is no ordinary sausage though. It is actually more of a sausage look-a-like, on account of its history. It is mainly produced in the north, and is not something I have had the pleasure of tasting.

It is a smoked sausage made with bread, several kinds of meat (usually poultry), olive oil, lard, garlic and spicy paprika. It can be fried in olive oil and served with cooked vegetables as a main course. It can also be wrapped in cabbage and stewed.

The history of this humble delight is fascinating. At the time of the Spanish Inquisition, the Jews here were persecuted and killed for their religious beliefs. They created a sausage made mostly out of chicken meat and bread, fashioned to look like a traditional pork sausage—an ingredient prohibited by the Jewish faith. They managed to pass themselves off as Christians (presumably by waving their sausages around) and, therefore, escaped death.

The *queijo Serra da Estrela* cheese comes from the region with the highest mountain in Portugal, of the same name. This is a ripened cheese made with sheep's milk, and the flowers of the thistle plants which grow locally. Creamy-white or yellow in colour, it is described as a semi-soft cheese. I prefer to call it a stinky runny cheese – and is one that I leave for Dave to devour. I'm a plain cheddar kind of girl. Dave considers me a heathen when it comes to cheese, as I grew up eating Dairylea cheese triangles. Dave likes his cheese to be as smelly as possible and preferably crawling off the edge of his plate. I'm sure he would have voted for this cheese if he had been asked. Certainly enough Portuguese people selected it to win the award.

Next on the podium is *caldo verde* soup. I have to confess this is one soup I can happily pass over on a menu. It is made with potato and shredded kale, with chicken stock and garlic thrown in for good measure. A slice of Portuguese chouriço sausage is added for extra flavour. This is a traditional, simple, winter-warming soup, but it just doesn't do it for me. I'm always put off by the pieces of kale swirling around, and it invariably seems to be too 'thin' for me. I like big chunks of meat and vegetables in my soup.

I'm much happier with the winner in the seafood category. *Arroz de marisco* (seafood rice) is a traditional dish you can find served all along the Portuguese coast. It includes rice, tomatoes, peppers, onion, garlic, chilli, and a selection of local fresh seafood such as shrimp, clams, mussels, lobster, and crab, as the principal ingredients. It is often labelled as a *cataplana* on the menu which is the name of the dish they cook it in. It is like a Spanish paella, but they do not reduce it down as much, making it more akin to a fish stew. The aroma when the server brings it to your table, and the lid is first lifted off the bowl is stupendously good.

Staying with fish, next up are the ubiquitous *sardinha assada* (grilled sardines). These are synonymous with the Portuguese cuisine and you will find them everywhere. The best ones are eaten in the summer, served with a simple salad, boiled potatoes and fresh bread. They are always grilled and seasoned heavily with sea salt. The smell as they are cooking is amazing.

If you are feeling brave, fill your plate with sardines and eat them the Portuguese way. Place a fish between two pieces of bread and chew the lot—including the head of the fish!

Just as a tip, if you are shopping for sardines at the market look out for the difference between the fresh fish and the frozen imposters. The fresh ones have a shine to them, their gills are intact and their eyes are perfectly clear. They are also nice and firm to the touch, and don't smell too fishy. Older fish lose their shine, start to pong a bit and turn flabby. That could almost be a piscine metaphor for life and ageing.

Leitão da Bairrada or roasted suckling pig, from the famed Bairrada area, won the award in the meat category. The first known recipe for suckling pig in Bairrada is from 1743 from a monastery in the region. Prepared in the traditional way, this is no quick meal. It can take three days to cook, including letting your pig joint soak in brine for twenty-four hours. Then it gets hung for another twenty-four hours, before you can begin the cooking process. Or you can simply order it in a restaurant. The result is meat that is crispy and crunchy on the outside, and extremely tender inside. Delicious!

I've saved the best until last, of course. The dessert that claimed top prize is the humble *pastel de Belém*. Or the *pastel de nata* for those of us that cannot travel to Lisbon for a quick pastry. This delight dates back to the nineteenth century, and follows an ancient secret recipe made in the Jerónimos monastery. After the 1820 Revolution, all Portuguese convents and monasteries were closed down and the workers and clergy were expelled. In an attempt to survive, someone from the monastery placed sweet pastries for sale in a small shop. The cakes were extremely popular and quickly became known as *pastéis de Belém*.

There are only a few renowned pastry masters who know the authentic recipe that has remained unchanged to the present day. The owners of the famous Belém pastry shop proudly describe themselves as the original source of this delightful sweet indulgence. They estimate that they produce and sell around twenty thousand pastries every day, and the queues outside the shop are legendary.

An old Portuguese proverb states that, "A bride who eats a pastry will never take off her ring", and so it is fairly common to see newlywed couples at the Belém bakery. Portugal is a country of traditions so, before the reception, the bride and groom visit the bakery to indulge in a sweet pastry. It sounds like the perfect wedding cake to me.[1]

---

1. Lisboa Cool blog (s.d.). Website article *5 Facts About the Belém Pastries*. Accessed 14th October 2020 through https://lisboacool.com/en/blog/5-facts-about-the-belem-pastries

22

New Year's Eve

N ew Year's Eve in our old house was always a noisy affair. We lived above the site of the firework display that covered the whole Portimão area. We could also see fireworks from as far away as Vilamoura and Albufeira from our balcony. Our neighbours enjoyed banging on their pots and pans with metal spoons at midnight. The first year it happened, it frightened the life out of us. You can begin to understand why we longed for a quiet night in on New Year's Eve.

Except this year was different. It was our twentieth wedding anniversary. It seemed impossible to believe all that time had passed and we were about to celebrate such a milestone. We both agreed we wanted to celebrate quietly, rather than have a big party, so we decided to treat ourselves, dress up, and go out for a special meal together. We thought it would be difficult to find somewhere that would let us take our precious Kat with us inside their restaurant on such a busy evening. It would be too cold to sit outside, so we would have to leave her behind. We needed to find somewhere that didn't have a stretched-out set menu. I would never leave Kat alone at midnight with fireworks and loud bangs happening all around her. From the previous year, we knew it would be quieter in our new home than in our old house. There would still be the possibility of fireworks at Igreja Nova, though. I wanted to be home in time to be with her to reassure her.

I mentioned our dilemma to Petra, when I met her one morning at our local café.

"Where can I go that doesn't have a special menu for New Year's Eve?" I asked her.

"Oh, that's easy, you must come to Paulo's. We gave up on the set menu idea a few years ago. We only have our regular dishes. Come early and Paulo will look after you. I'll be there too."

Well, that was an easy decision to make. O Paulo's is one of the locally famous eateries here in the Aljezur area. It overlooks the beautiful bay of Arrifana, and the food is renowned for its quality and rich flavours. It is also somewhere we kept promising ourselves we would visit for an evening meal, and just happens to be owned and run by Paulo, Petra's husband.

"Will Paulo be able to cope with me and my crazy diet?" I asked Petra.

"Of course. You tell him what you can and can't eat and he will supervise it all in the kitchen."

I grinned back at her.

"Well, that was easy. Two reservations for New Year's Eve for 7.30 p.m. please."

It was exciting to think we were finally going to experience Paulo's famous cuisine. We had been to the restaurant in the afternoon a few times. The view from the outside terrace area is magnificent, and it is a lovely spot to sit and watch the sunset. Accompanied by a nice warming cup of green tea for me, and an espresso and a large slice of cheesecake for Dave. But we had never been there in the evening, despite our best intentions. Our plan was perfect. Celebrate our special anniversary in a posh restaurant with exquisite food. And home again in time for Kat.

New Year's Eve dawned bright and cold. I wrapped up to take Kat on her morning walk and returned to find Dave already up and making our breakfast. We exchanged small gifts, having agreed that our main present to each other would be our meal out that evening.

I teased Dave about how long we had been together and reminded him of his hilarious antics when he proposed to me all those years ago.

❄☙❄❧❄

Millennium Eve was approaching. The only thing we had decided was that we didn't want to end up at a boring party on the night when the calendar tipped us into the new millennium.

"Let's get married then—on New Year's Eve," Dave said to me one day in July that year. "That way, we can celebrate the New Year in style in our own way. And I'll never forget the date of our anniversary."

"That sounds like a plan!" I replied.

We had been together for almost three years; we were settled and happy. Both of us had been married before and had done the traditional wedding route the first time around. I had even worn a dress that, glancing back at the photographs, had looked suspiciously like a small meringue. I blamed Princess Diana. This time it would be about us, and our love for each other. And less about the expected traditions.

We started to plan and soon had our wedding venue booked, and friends invited.

I began to tease Dave.

"Well, I will 'probably' be there. I'll put the date in my diary and let you know. I might get a better offer, of course, but I'll pencil it in."

The teasing was because, as I kept reminding him, he hadn't actually proposed to me. Not properly. Simply saying, let's get married then, wasn't going to cut it.

And then he surprised me one day with two tickets to Venice, leaving the following week. Five days of sheer bliss, in a place I had always wanted to visit. I was stunned and extremely excited.

We arrived and took a water taxi to our hotel, right on the waterfront. It was the smallest bedroom I had ever seen, but I didn't care. We were in Venice, in September, and I couldn't wait to explore.

We spent the whole time wandering the streets, enjoying the sights, and taking hundreds of photos. We ate at little cafés and bistros and visited the main attractions. We fell in love with the sheer thrill of meandering through the back streets and experiencing the joy of a different culture.

And then, on the final night, as we were walking across St. Mark's Square, Dave dropped down on one knee, took out a small package from his pocket, and proposed to me. I squealed with delight, and said to him,

"Is this it? Is this my 'real' proposal?" Well, he deserved a bit of teasing.

"Yes, this is it. Will you marry me?"

Of course, I said yes. The ring fitted perfectly, and we were grinning as people around us clapped.

"And now, off to dinner. I have a table booked."

We sat at a local restaurant watching the sights and chatting about our upcoming special day. We must have been infectious in our enthusiasm as the next table joined in and started talking to us. Five loud and chatty women from Chile all exclaimed in delight as we told them we had just got engaged. It became a little party as we all talked, drank champagne and shared stories.

I got up to visit the bathroom, and upon my return, I laughed in delight as I saw that the Chilean women were all brandishing roses. One lady had a flower held in her teeth.

"Your man is a very nice man. He buy us all roses." [sic]

I sat down and smiled at Dave.

"Where's my rose then?" I asked him.

"Oh no, I forgot yours. I forgot to buy you one."

He was off like a shot down the road after the flower seller before I could even reply to that one.

He returned looking rather sheepish a few minutes later, carrying an armful of roses.

"I bought everything he had left. I am sorry!"

I shook my head at him in amusement.

"You do realise I will never let you live this down, don't you?" I said to him.

"Oh yes, I know. I'm dead."

I reached over and kissed him.

✧☙✧◖✧

We spent the afternoon of our anniversary walking along our favourite beach at Monte Clérigo with Kat. It was a beautiful sunny day, with a few clouds scuttling across the blue sky. Kat was in her element; it was low tide and she could snuffle in and out of the rock pools. We returned home tired and happy, and I sat quietly for a while in our little courtyard garden. We had plenty of time before we had to get ready to go out for our meal.

I started thinking back to our wedding day. We knew we wanted something special and intimate, surrounded by close friends and family. We were lucky enough to secure a slot in a Gothic Folly in Devon called Haldon Tower. When we booked it, they told us we could get married at 11 a.m. but we had to be away by 12 noon as the tower was booked for a private overnight party. We discovered later that Noel Edmonds had reserved it, but we were not bothered by that. An hour would give us the time we needed to have a simple registry service. We had planned to have two poems read out, and then a quick set of photographs afterwards.

The tower was stunning, a beautiful slab of white that juts up out of the forest surrounding it. You could see for miles all around, and as our friends arrived, we had surprised them with some live music to enjoy. One of Dave's colleagues, Jez, was a cellist. He had played at the Royal Albert Hall in London and was good enough to turn professional. We had no idea why he was wearing a police uniform instead of pursuing a career in music. He came with his mom, who was a celebrated pianist. As we entered the ground floor of the tower and climbed the ornate wrought-iron staircase, the elegant sounds of his cello swept up the stairs. It was the perfect accompaniment.

The service was as simple and beautiful as we hoped it would be. We were both so excited to be finally getting married, and I grinned all the way through the proceedings. We had arranged the chairs into two semi-circles and all we could hear around us was sniffing and crying. It was hilarious, loads of our friends were crying (with joy, I hope) as we said our vows to each other.

"Could you lot pack it in with the snuffling, please?" said Dave at one point, which set everyone laughing.

Soon it was over, the paperwork was signed, and we were married. We set off back downstairs to stand outside the tower for more photographs. I smiled to myself, thinking if only people knew that the man holding the camera was the main reporter and photographer who covered all the Exeter City football games. Trust Dave to get some football into our wedding day somehow. It was cold outside, but the sky was blue, and the sun even appeared right on time for our photos. Perfect.

And then it was time to head over to one of our favourite pub restaurants. We had it all planned. A champagne breakfast with smoked salmon and scrambled egg. It was exactly the relaxed, fun meal we hoped it would be.

Then it was off to Birmingham to a concert in the evening, followed by an early flight out to Cape Town the next morning. We had read so many horror stories about the new millennium, and how planes were going to fall out of the sky because of the change of year. We giggled as we boarded the plane as we realised we were the first flight to leave Birmingham airport that morning. If the planes really were going to mysteriously crash thanks to the calendar ticking over, we would be the first to know.

We were whisked away into business class, which was a lovely surprise. Being on honeymoon has its perks, I thought to myself, as we settled into the posh seats. They treated us like minor royalty all the way over on the flight, with champagne, and even a card signed by all the crew. It was a fabulous start to our three-week honeymoon in Cape Town, which exceeded all our expectations. We absolutely loved it there and were sorry to board the return flight back home.

❈૭❈ର❈

I dusted myself down and stood up. I had sat in the garden too long, and I scurried off indoors to get ready for our special meal. We arrived at exactly 7.30 p.m. at Paulo's restaurant in Arrifana, having settled Kat on the sofa in the lounge for the evening. We promised her we would be back soon, and before any fireworks were due to be set off.

The minute we arrived, we saw Paulo talking to another couple. He beamed at us and said,

"Where's Kat? Why didn't you bring her with you?"

Oh, after all that fuss, she could have come with us. Never mind, there's always next time.

We stood and chatted outside and met the other couple who spoke some English and a smattering of Portuguese. It was hard to tell their nationality. I decided they were Eastern European but couldn't put my finger on exactly where they were from. Little did I realise at that moment what a great source of entertainment they would become later in the evening.

Paulo showed us to our table and introduced us to our designated waiter. Paulo reassured me that Petra had told him all about my special diet.

"Do not worry about anything. You tell me exactly what you can —and cannot—eat, and I will prepare your food for you personally in the kitchen," Paulo said. "I have given you one of the best tables in the house. Enjoy your evening."

We really felt spoilt then. The restaurant was beautifully lit and decorated, and we had a view straight out of the glass windows onto the coast. We could see twinkling lights in the distance as we perused the fine menu and decided what to eat.

It was still early for a Portuguese restaurant, and the tables filled up slowly around us. The couple we had met outside came in and sat at a table diagonally opposite to us. I was facing them, but Dave had his back to them all evening. It was fascinating to watch them interact with each other, and I kept whispering to Dave what they were doing.

"She's feeding him!" I exclaimed in amazement.

"What do you mean, she's feeding him?"

"Well, they've got the starters on plates in the middle of the table. She's holding a fork and selecting things from the plates and reaching over to feed him off the fork. It's bizarre," I replied, trying not to giggle.

Dave and I are avid people-watchers, and luckily the restaurant was getting busier as more diners arrived. The background noise drowned out my stage-whispers to Dave.

"Now she's grabbed him round the throat with both hands. He looks petrified."

Dave was trying hard not to turn around to see what was happening.

"She looks half-mad. Her eyes are drilling a hole into his head."

It was fascinating. She didn't seem to be play-acting. The man looked petrified and sat stock still as her hands gripped tightly around his throat.

She let him go after about thirty seconds and busied herself tidying up the empty starter plates as if nothing was amiss.

"This is going to be a fun evening," I said to Dave.

A waiter appeared at their table, and at the same moment, the woman flung her arm forward, sending a glass of white wine spinning. It crashed onto the table and broke, scattering pieces of glass everywhere. The waiter shot off to get a cloth to clean up, as she picked up the shards of glass and purposefully piled them up neatly beside her plate.

They both went outside after the waiter had set everything straight on their table. I glanced over after about half-an-hour and watched as she returned to the table, sat down, and called the waiter over. He came back with a glass of red wine, which she calmly sat and sipped. There was no sign of the man she was with.

"He's missing," I said to Dave, "Where is he?"

"Perhaps she's pushed him off the edge of the cliff. It's dark outside, and it's quite a drop to the rocks below. No-one would know," he replied with a hint of a wicked grin.

"Stop it! That's not funny. She certainly looks mad enough to do something like that."

Another fifteen minutes passed until finally he returned to their table and sat down.

Our main course arrived then, and we tucked into one of the specials of the restaurant, rack of lamb with vegetables. Paulo had been marvellous, as he had promised. The meat usually comes cooked in a breadcrumb coating with a marinated sauce, neither of which I could eat. We said we would be happy with it served plain, but Paulo had split the rack in half, and cooked each half separately. Dave could enjoy the full experience, and I could eat some almost rare, tender, and succulent meat. Each mouthful was a delight.

I glanced over at the couple at the next table, but they had gone out again. They were missing almost an hour, by which time our desserts had arrived. We had finished our meal, and they had barely eaten their starters. It was going to be a long night for the staff at the restaurant. Dessert was sublime, and we savoured every mouthful.

I glanced over and our friends were back at their table, but they seemed subdued. I decided they must have been on something, apart from the wine, and left them to it.

Our waiter returned clutching small espresso coffees. The perfect end to the meal. Then, with excellent timing, as we finished, our friend Petra arrived. We cleared our table and moved over to the entrance area to chat to her. We thanked Paulo for a wonderful meal and evening. He tried to persuade us to stay. The live music had started, and some couples were already dancing between the tables in a slow and elegant waltz. We stayed for an extra half-an-hour, then left the revellers to their party and drove back home.

It had been a beautiful day and the perfect way for us to celebrate our twentieth wedding anniversary, and usher in the start of 2020 and a new decade. We had been living in Portugal full time for almost nine years. We were as excited and happy with our decision to live here as the day we left the UK and boarded the ferry to Santander to begin our new lives. We were still happily in love with each other after twenty years of marriage, which was also something to celebrate.

"Who knows what the next twenty years will bring," I said to Dave as he drove back home.

"Well, one thing is for certain, we will still be living here in Portugal," he replied. "And we will definitely be going back to Paulo's restaurant again. That meal was superb."

We returned home to an excited little dog who was very happy to see us return. And as the clock struck midnight, we toasted the decade ahead. A few fireworks went off in the distance, Kat was content, and we retired to bed.

23

Fique em Casa

The word Covid didn't even exist in most people's language until the year 2020. Initially, I remember hearing things in the news about the Corona Virus and thinking, that was the name of a fizzy drink from the 1970s. Suddenly there were stories about people dying, and it all turned serious rather quickly. Spain had reported cases, and the numbers from Italy were horrifying. This wasn't just a distant illness affecting people in a different continent, it had reached Europe. And then it arrived in Portugal. In the Algarve, a family had travelled to Italy to enjoy the pre-Lent celebrations that precede Ash Wednesday. Seven people were infected, and we heard one of them sadly later died in hospital.

After that, it seemed to be only a matter of days before we were in lockdown. The Portuguese government had the foresight to view other country's figures and actions, and to respond accordingly. The measures were all-encompassing. You were only allowed out to shop, walk your pet, go to the doctor's or other health appointments, and it was your civic duty to stay at home. You had to wear a mask when inside any official premises or the supermarket. All other shops and establishments were closed. No group gatherings, no visiting people, only two people from the same family in a car. The supermarkets all had strict timings; they invited in key workers for the first hour of opening. Then anyone aged over sixty-five for the second hour. After that, the public were allowed in, with everyone keeping two metres apart and hand-sanitising on entry and exit. They disinfected everything and everyone.

I continued to walk Kat along the river each morning. Our local café was closed. Everywhere was eerily silent, especially at 6.30 a.m. There were virtually no cars moving. One morning I watched with some trepidation from a distance as a team sanitised the car park and roads ahead of us. They wore boiler suits, protective masks, gloves, and breathing apparatus as they sprayed every surface with a fine chemical spray. Best not walk along there anymore, I thought to myself, as we turned around and backtracked our way home.

The river walk became my sanity. It was so peaceful, and the surrounding silence made the bird song I could hear even more beautiful. I couldn't believe there was anything wrong with the world as I walked along there in the early morning sunshine. Yet reality would creep back in as I arrived home and watched Dave grab a mask, gloves, and hand cleanser as he jumped into the car to go shopping. Initially, we had a job trying to buy any masks, resorting to spending twenty-five euros on a pack of five reusable masks from the local chemists. We even had to email them and wait until they had them in stock. Within a few weeks, there were large packs of disposable ones available in all the supermarkets.

The local Câmara were brilliant in Aljezur. They updated people regularly on Facebook with bulletins. They drove around the town with a loudspeaker attached to the roof of a car with a pre-recorded message: *Fique em Casa*. Stay at home, protect yourself, your family, and all of us. The message looped around in both Portuguese and English. It was so loud you couldn't miss it as it went past your house. We always smiled as we heard the Portuguese version as it sailed past us. They would turn around at the top of the road, come back, and sit parked outside our house as the English version played. As we are the only English people in the area; we thought they must do it especially for us.

For weeks, Aljezur was one of only three districts in the Algarve that had escaped the virus. Every week, fresh cases were reported, and the news worldwide was grim. We were incredulous at the reports we read, particularly from Britain and America. Here we were, in total lockdown, which was being observed remarkably well by everyone in Portugal, and yet other countries seemed to carry on as normal. In the UK, schools and shops were open, they even hosted football matches, sat on the beach in huge numbers, and blocked the main motorway routes down to the south-west with people travelling on holiday for Easter.

Then we had our first cases reported here in Aljezur. They isolated the family in question and two people were taken into hospital. They discovered that one person connected to the family worked for the local Câmara. Within days the entire staff of the council, over two hundred workers, were tested. All came back negative.

And then, slowly, the Portuguese government relaxed the restrictions. Ironically, just about the same time that Britain woke up and locked things down over there. Their numbers were astronomical, and their herd immunity plan, different to everywhere else in Europe, hadn't worked.

Portugal changed to a state of 'calamity' instead of being in a state of 'emergency'. It didn't translate well into English, and I smiled wryly at the definition of a calamity as something normally associated with catastrophes, tornadoes, and war.

A party near Lagos changed all that. It was a private function booked for twenty people, held in the local social club. Reports vary, but some articles reported almost two hundred partygoers in attendance. Whatever the numbers, the result was catastrophic for the local area, and the figures for the Algarve. Within two weeks, over one hundred people had tested positive for Covid, all linked to one party. People were shocked and began to heed the government's messages more. This was a virus that would not disappear anytime soon.

The numbers continued to rise in the Algarve, and although they were small in most areas; the Lagos party, and a retirement home for the elderly which had a large outbreak, skewed the overall percentages. Lisbon was battling its own large-scale outbreak, alongside Porto and the north. Portugal was not looking good on the international map. The region was despondent after all those weeks of enforced lockdown.

The British Government then declared that Portugal was not a safe enough destination to travel to. They changed the list of travel corridors but kept Portugal out. British holidaymakers who still travelled to Portugal would have to self-isolate for two weeks on their return home. They announced this right at the start of the main summer holiday season. It left many people angry, bewildered, or simply amazed. Spain had similar infection rates, and so did France, and yet Britain included them in their travel corridor.

✿ ❧ ✿ ❦ ✿

I wrote a piece for our Algarve Blog, which received thousands of views and comments online.

"The beaches are almost empty, the sand is soft underfoot, and the sky is a brilliant blue. A gentle breeze stirs the air as we walk along, enjoying the long stretch of sandy beach ahead of us, as the waves crash gently on the shoreline. It could be February in the Algarve, except for the temperature gauge, which is nudging thirty-five degrees.

Many people on social media say they feel safer here than in the UK. The cafés and restaurants are all complying with social distancing rules, tables are spread apart, and the wearing of a mask is compulsory unless you are sitting down eating. They disinfect all the tables and chairs after each customer. Hand sanitisers are everywhere, and you cannot enter a supermarket or shop without a mask. We have seen people turned away by the security guard at the door for not having a mask on."[1]

There were flights with only twenty people on them arriving at Faro airport. Many flights were cancelled, and people were concerned their travel insurance would be invalid if they travelled to Portugal. An enterprising Portuguese company set up an alternative travel insurance company that targeted British holidaymakers, allowing them coverage if they travelled to Portugal. There is always a way.

According to the Portuguese Economic Journal, they stated in July that Reuters had reported that to date, "only ninety-two Britons have arrived in the region, a figure far from what was recorded in previous years, when close to two million Britons filled the Algarve's restaurants, hotels and sands."

They continued, "To date, hotels in the Algarve have an occupancy rate close to forty percent, and without the effects of the pandemic, they should already be full. The number of unemployed in the region also grew 231 percent compared to the same period last year, increasing from eight thousand to more than twenty-six thousand unemployed, since many depended on seasonal jobs."[2]

We knew of lots of restaurants, bars, hotels, and guest accommodation businesses that were struggling. Without a busy summer season, many people and their families are facing a long bleak winter ahead. It is not only the frontline tourist industries that are suffering, wedding photographers and planners have found their entire season's bookings cancelled; or postponed until next summer. Musicians cannot perform, hair and beauty treatments, yoga, massage, and spa days out, are all luxury items that are being shelved. Boat tours and day trips, taxis, and theme parks are empty.

According to the figures in July, the United Kingdom "has so far recorded over 297,000 people infected with coronavirus and 45,545 deaths due to the disease. It is currently the country with the third highest number of cases of infection in Europe and the tenth largest in the world. Meanwhile, Portugal has 49,379 infected people and registered 1,705 deaths."[3]

These figures belied the problem facing the Algarve. Almost seventy-five percent of Portugal's cases were in Lisbon and the north, as seen from data issued in July by the Directorate General for Health (DGS):

"In line with what has been happening in recent months, most cases are in Lisbon and the Tagus Valley [LVT]. In the capital region and its surroundings, there were 172 [new] cases, that is, 75.1% of the total 229 cases announced today.

By regions, LVT remains the most affected area in the country, having so far accounted for 25,110 infected people and 582 fatalities. This is followed by the North with 18,441 and 828 deaths, and then the Central region with 4392 contagions and 252 deaths. In Alentejo, there [have been] 667 confirmed cases and 20 fatalities, and in the Algarve, 817 [have been] infected with 15 deaths.

In the autonomous regions, the Azores has had 160 contagions and 15 deaths and, in Madeira, 105 cases, with no fatal victims associated with the new virus since the beginning of the pandemic."[4]

The District Civil Protection Commission of Faro on the same day the DGS made that statement, based on data provided by the Health Authority, said there were only 242 active cases in the Algarve.

The list of countries exempt from UK quarantine was reviewed on the 27th July, and it was hoped the review may have included regional air bridges. This would have meant they could have included the Algarve; while areas such as Lisbon, with its higher infection rates, would still have been blacklisted. It was not to be, and the air bridge corridor continued to reject the Algarve and Portugal on its itinerary.

It was more than a little embarrassing to be British and living here in the Algarve during this time. There did not seem to be any logic at all to the UK Government's decision to leave Portugal off the safe air bridge list. And particularly the Algarve, with its low numbers of infections and safe procedures in place. Luckily for us, the Head of State, Marcelo Rebelo de Sousa, seemed to bear us no bad feeling.

"It is evident that we would prefer to have more British tourists, but that is not why we are going to treat badly [sic], on the contrary, we will treat even better, the forty thousand Britons who live in Portugal," he pointed out to the Portuguese Economic Journal.[5]

It seems to me that 2020 has become a lost year for tourism here in the Algarve. I can't help wondering how many businesses will survive this pandemic. How many cafés and restaurants will still be open next summer for both locals and tourists alike?

"It is more than a lost year," stated Elidérico Viegas, president of the Association of Hotels and Tourist Enterprises of the Algarve, in response to this problem. He emphasised that "...the truth is that the Algarve was practically out of the pandemic and was strongly affected by criteria that do not take into account other realities."[6]

Was it all too late, though? Even if the British Government had made an exception for the Algarve at the end of July or in early August, would people have already booked to go elsewhere for their summer holiday? We know some people came out here anyway and risked the fact that the air corridor might not be open to them on their return. But so many others could not afford to take the chance or could not add the two-week quarantine into their annual holiday entitlement from work.

The Algarve was a strange place over the summer period. We still had French (in smaller numbers than normal) and lots of Spanish holidaymakers here. Many of them had travelled down in their camper vans for their annual break. But everyone was reporting how much quieter the Algarve was than normal. The fear is that so many businesses will not have made enough over the summer to survive the ensuing long winter ahead.

The British government gave a small window of hope in late August, taking Portugal off its air corridor banned list, but only a few weeks later, the measures were reviewed, and Portugal was added to the list once again.

President of the Republic, Marcelo Rebelo de Sousa, made a point of visiting the Algarve for one day every week during the summer period. He vowed to show that the region is a safe destination and met with local people, mayors, and businesses. He said that the drawing up of a specific plan to support the region would be a national priority, recognising that an area so heavily reliant on tourism has taken a heavy blow:

"Now we have to look to the future. The Algarve deserves it because it has exceptional quality, it has a public health situation that is, even compared to other regions and countries, of quality, now it needs to be the choice of the Portuguese and also of foreigners who have to come here to allow the region to recover."[7]

This is a beautiful place to live and work, and Dave and I are delighted to call it home. We are proud to stand alongside local people and business owners who wear their face masks uncomplainingly, serving customers, and looking after their staff and clients, all through the heat of summer and on into the winter. Of course, I do not want to see infection rates rise here, or anywhere else, and I hope everybody who visits us here in the Algarve respects the rules that have been imposed. For their own safety, and everyone else's too.

The government has promised a package of measures, including injecting a sizeable amount of cash into the region. They have stated they will look at training programmes, investment opportunities, and the possibility of creating a more diverse range of industries that are not so dependent upon tourism.

As I sit here writing this, with winter on the horizon, and no hope of a vaccine soon, we cannot tell what the future will bring. We can only hope this dreadful virus can be defeated. And in the meantime, that people remain safe, behave sensibly, and the death rate continues to reduce.

Then maybe we can return to celebrating the beautiful beaches, scenery, food, and culture of this western European paradise, whilst also modernising its outlook and prospects for the future. The years ahead are going to be interesting.

---

1. Algarve Blog (25.07.2020). Website article by Alyson Sheldrake *The Algarve, Covid and the Air-Corridor.* Accessed 19th August 2020 through https://algarveblog.net/2020/07/25/algarve-covid-air-corridor/
2. O Jornal Económico (23.07.2020). Website article by Inês Pinto Miguel *'Reuters': Without Britons in high season, Algarve struggles for survival.* Accessed 19th August 2020 through https://jornaleconomico.sapo.pt/en/news/reuters-without-Britons-in-high-season-algarve-fight-for-survival-616911
3. ECO Portuguese Economy (24.07.2020). Website article by Luís Alexandre *UK maintains its travel ban on Portugal.* Accessed 19th August 2020 through https://econews.pt/2020/07/24/uk-maintains-its-travel-ban-on-portugal/
4. País A O Minuto (24.07.2020). Website article *Portugal regista mais sete mortos e 313 casos de Covid-19.* Accessed 28th August 2020 through https://www.noticiasaominuto.com/pais/1540341/portugal-regista-mais-sete-mortos-e-313-casos-de-covid-19?fbclid=IwAR1wzxdObINEIeJnuKq49v8Rg25M1Vo-PWm4YlBYF7j9aHg5GCIjgujdbhw

5. O Jornal Económico (23.07.2020). Website article *"If we would prefer to have more British tourists? It's evident". Marcelo comments on UK decision on air corridor.* Accessed 28th August 2020 through https://jornaleconomico.sapo.pt/en/news/if-we-would-prefer-to-have-more-british-tourists-and-evident-marcelo-comments-on-uk-decision-on-air-corridor-617744

6. Time 24 Story (24.07.2020). Website article *Portugal is again defeated by the United Kingdom. For the Algarve, it is "more than a lost year".* Accessed 28th August 2020 through https://www.time24.news/2020/07/portugal-is-again-defeated-by-the-united-kingdom-for-the-algarve-it-is-more-than-a-lost-year.html

7. The Portugal News (10.07.2020). Website article *It is necessary to "look forward and to fight" for Algarve tourism.* Accessed 28th August 2020 through https://www.theportugalnews.com/news/it-is-necessary-to-look-forward-and-to-fight-for-algarve-tourism/54771

24

The Future

"Life can only be understood backwards; but it must be lived forwards." —
Søren Kierkegaard

It has been twenty years since we fell in love with Ferragudo, on our first holiday in the Algarve. Fourteen years ago we bought our first house here, and almost ten years ago we moved out here to live permanently. Our plan was simple; to follow our dream of living abroad. To escape what felt like a suffocating and exhausting treadmill in the UK, and to embrace a more relaxed, simpler way of life.

Our dreams included the desire to pursue our creative instincts and passions. I had always wanted to have time to paint and see where that led me. Dave has had a camera since he was a young boy, and it has been wonderful to watch him grow into the professional photographer he is today.

I have painted and sold well over two hundred paintings and recently completed my hundredth commission. I have discovered and fine-tuned my own 'New Wave' style of modern paintings in acrylics. Every time I arrange my easel and paints, ready to start a new piece of work, I feel the same thrill and excitement as the first time I tentatively set up in my studio space at home. Could I — would I — be able to paint? Would anyone like it, or want to buy it? What on earth was I doing? And then later, what if I have lost my touch? I think the angst and pain of being creative never leaves you. You just learn to ignore the voices and keep working, regardless.

Sadly, for a while, my Rheumatoid Arthritis put paid to any painting endeavours. I spent several months walking past my studio, dusting off the tables and easel, and promising myself that one day I would return to my beloved paints and brushes. Of course, when I returned to work, I took on the biggest commission I have ever agreed to. Could I paint two 'New Wave' style pieces for a penthouse apartment in Lagos? The first painting was a mere eighty by one hundred and twenty centimetres. Large enough. The accompanying work was a triptych that measured eighty centimetres by two metres in total. It was an epic undertaking. Perhaps I should have eased myself back into things more gradually. Started with a smaller size. Taken on something slightly less complicated than two intricate street scenes, complete with all the trimmings.

But looking back on this, I am glad I went for it and really challenged myself. It was the perfect way back for me, to feel that buzz and slight tinge of fear as I set everything up and started painting. I felt an enormous sense of achievement when they were both finished, and the client arrived to collect them. I was back!

And then along came writing. Our Algarve Blog has always been successful, winning awards and exceeding over 100,000 views a year. Moving house gave me time to take stock of this, and to realise that the blog could rest a little easier for a while. I think we had covered so many events and locations that we had exhausted our options. Coming back to it again with fresh eyes means I can create original content as and when I feel it is necessary. Less pressure, no stress. My new motto, I think.

I continue to be a guest speaker and writer for the Live and Invest Overseas group and have the delightful title of 'western Algarve expert'. I now also write a monthly article for the Algarve-based Tomorrow Magazine.

But the real thrill for me was seeing my first publication in print.

I had always dreamed about writing a book that had my name on the cover. The response has been phenomenal and has left me astounded. And now, here I am, about to launch this, the sequel, with book three already in the planning stage. I am both excited and petrified too.

Relocating here to Aljezur was the best move we could have made. Dave has always adored the west coast beaches. He now spends as much free time as he can out there on the cliffs or at the water's edge, camera and tripod fixed in place. I can usually tell how successful a trip it has been when he returns home by how wet and soggy his boots and socks are.

Adopting our beautiful rescue dog, Kat, has been the best thing we have done since moving here. She has revolutionised our lives and made me realise how much of a 'dog person' I am. I absolutely adore her and treasure every walk along the river path we take together. She is the brightest, gentlest, and most loyal companion anyone could wish for. Time and love transformed her from the timid, skinny, and fearful little scrap that we brought home with us six years ago. She is now loving, affectionate, nosey, and loved by everyone that meets her.

I am a feisty, confident girl, born and raised in inner-city Birmingham at the time of the riots and pub-bombings. High-rise buildings, poverty, street-muggings, and a frantic sense of survival at all costs surrounded my early childhood. My parents never allowed me to play out in the street; it wasn't considered safe and travelling to school and back involved catching several buses each day, then looking behind me every time I walked home from the bus stop. Going away to University, then joining the Police, meant that life was always hectic and unpredictable. I revelled in the variety of the work, took the potential danger in my stride, and loved helping people, communities, and especially young people.

Leaving the Police and reaching the dizzy heights of a Director of Education might have seemed like the dream role for a working-class girl from Birmingham. The reality was a job that left me exhausted and critical of a church-based system of schooling that fell way short of the mark. I constantly worked over seventy hours a week, battling issues and problems both inside and outside of the office. It was no wonder I felt an enormous sense of relief when I finally handed in my notice; we packed up everything we owned and started our new life here.

Moving to the idyll that is the Algarve, and specifically Aljezur, has been incredible. We have had the luxury of time, and space in the diary, to rethink our lives and discover what is important to us. Decorating our current house has enabled us to embrace a style of minimalism that gives us a relaxing and welcoming home to live in. It also cuts down on the housework required as well—a real bonus.

My RA diagnosis was an undeniable shock to my system. I have always been rudely fit and healthy all my life, and I have had to learn to slow down and listen to my body. Most days I have a low-level of pain and discomfort that is manageable, and I am determined to avoid the medical prescription drug route for as long as I can. I am now in my early fifties and Dave has only a couple more years to go before he gets his old-age pension from the UK. It is strange to realise we have aged at all since we met almost twenty-five years ago, but our joints and bodies sadly tell a different story. In our heads at least, we are still very much youngsters, and that is what matters.

Dave is actually looking really good for his age; especially if you ask our Portuguese friends. On his sixtieth birthday, I got the Portuguese words for sixty and seventy mixed up. It is a simple mistake to make, *sessenta* (sixty) and *setenta* (seventy) sound remarkably similar. Well, they do to me anyway. With the outcome that I went round telling most of our Portuguese friends that Dave was seventy years old on his special day.

We have sadly lost several people recently, all of whom have died far too young, and many were a real shock when we heard the news. It makes you appreciate every day a little more. We have made several good friends out here, and ten years later, are still in contact with dear friends from our old haunts in England. Skype and social media make keeping in touch so easy, and for this I am very grateful.

✿❀✿❁✿

The laid-back, hippy, alternative-lifestyle inhabitants of Aljezur are a source of constant amusement. They inhabit a weird and wonderful parallel universe, and the courses and events they advertise on Facebook leave me chortling with laughter. Recent examples include the Cosmic Cacao Ceremony which invited you to 'experience your pure essence' whilst sharing stories, meditating, and joining in the intuitive dancing along with a freshly prepared cacao drink. All that for only twenty euros. So basically, prance around like a fairy with a cup of hot chocolate.

If chocolate isn't your thing, then how about the intriguingly named Agua de Florida ritual? This one was strictly for women. The advert described how they would gather together and collect herbs and flowers to make a healing water to drink. They would end the day with a ritual blossoming. Nope, nor me, no idea what that means. I have even seen an advert for a course on 'womb cleansing'. I decided not to look any closer at that one.

If you are a man, you are not left out. You can always join the No More Mr Nice Guy course. This one is for all men on their journey to 'auto-consciousness and authenticity'. By the conclusion of the week's course, whilst sleeping in a yurt, and presumably dancing around and shouting a lot, you would become an Integrated Man, committed to becoming an authentic Man-being. [sic]. Again—not a clue. But it costs 895.00 euros if you are interested. Hilariously, I discovered they host this retreat down the road from our house, hidden away in the woods. Dave has decided to change his afternoon walking route to avoid the area; just in case.

My pitiful grasp of Portuguese is slowly improving. I began having one-to-one tuition with a local lass, until the winter holidays, then Covid, cancelled everything. I was having lots of fun with my lessons with native speaker Maria (there you are, another Maria to add to my list). We progressed well, until one week the naughty child inside me came out to play, and we started learning rude words. Well, you can only take so many verb conjugations before your brain explodes. Our giggles reached fever pitch as we chatted.

"You do know that I have to smother my laughter every time you send me a text or email, don't you?" I said to her.

"Why, what do I write?" she replied.

"Well, I know that you mean *beijinhos*, which means little kisses."

It is a phrase commonly used out here, usually as a way of signing off a message.

"The problem is that you shorten it. As everyone does here. To the phrase BJ's."

"What is wrong with that?" Maria asked.

Oh dear, this was not going to be easy to explain.

"Do you know what a 'BJ' is in English slang?" I asked, thinking that would trigger her memory. Maria worked in England for a while, so I was hoping she might recall the literal meaning without me having to spell it out for her.

"No, no idea. Why, what does it mean? Is it rude?" she replied.

"Well, yes, it means blow-job in English."

It took us both about five minutes to stop laughing.

I have now started online classes with a new teacher from central Portugal. I've only had a few group lessons so far, and I am going to try to behave myself this time. I would love to get proficient enough to pass the required A2 level exam that you need to apply for citizenship. That is some way ahead for me, I think.

Brexit has meant that thinking about topics like citizenship and gaining an EU Portuguese passport has taken on new significance. I'm not a fan of talking politics at the best of times, but I have been distraught over how divisive this entire agenda has been. People that I thought I knew well surprised me by voting for Brexit. In some cases, they even live over here in Portugal, enjoying all the privileges and delights of this wonderful country, with free access to the entire Schengen area. And yet still they read the daily newspapers in the UK and believe the immigration headlines and voted to leave Europe. I do not think we have begun to witness what the consequences of this decision will mean for everyone concerned. I have felt saddened, outraged, and upset by the whole fiasco.

Being British and living here has not been a comfortable position for some time, but this has not been caused by anything the Portuguese have said or done. On the contrary, they have been most welcoming, reassuring, and as bemused by the proceedings as we have. It has been an embarrassment to be British over here, and I refuse to even begin to try to justify the decisions and behaviour of the UK Parliament. It is utterly ludicrous.

Add to that, the Covid disaster that rapidly seems to be eating away at an entire year on the calendar, with no end in sight. As I write this, we are about to enter late autumn, with winter approaching. Death rates continue unabated, schools and workplaces have tried to re-open and precautionary measures are still in place. No-one knows what the months ahead are going to look like.

And yet, through all these testing times, Dave and I feel extremely lucky to be here in our own little slice of heaven. The stresses and strains of our old working lives seem like a distant memory now. Our shared dream of living a relaxed, creative, simple life in the sun, has been more wonderful than we ever imagined it could be. My aim is to continue enjoying every single day of living here in the peaceful Aljezur countryside. I have no intention of ever going back to the UK to live, and Dave and I consider Portugal to be our home. Forever.

The Barlavento Guide

arlavento and sotavento are Portuguese terms of nautical origin
that refer to the side of the vessel facing towards, and away
from, where the wind blows, respectively. The barlavento is the
windward side of the boat that receives the wind, and the sotavento
is the leeward side of the boat that faces away from, and releases, the
wind.

The same terms are also used to describe the western and eastern
sides of the Algarve. The Barlavento Algarvio—literally the
windward Algarve region—gets its name from the Atlantic winds
that shoot across from the coast.

The Barlavento, depending on which parameters you choose,
includes the municipalities of Aljezur, Lagoa, Lagos, Monchique,
Portimão, Silves and Vila do Bispo. It may also include the town of
Albufeira. I described some of these towns in my first book, *Living the
Dream*. For this guide, I have covered the remaining towns and also
included a guide to the wonderful beaches of the western Algarve
coast.

Whether you are a tourist, part-time visitor, or full-time resident,
I hope the information here is of interest to you. If I can paint a

picture for you of the beautiful place we call home, then these guides have served their purpose.

25

The Land of Lagoa

Whenever I put Lagoa into the computer search engine, it changes the name to lagoon. The name Lagoa comes from the fact that the first settlements in the region were on swamp or marshland, as a result of the Arade river which runs nearby. The land was drained to create a fertile environment for housing and agriculture during the time of the Muslim empire. Lagoa was then geographically part of Silves, which was historically the capital of the Algarve.

In 1773, King Joseph I gave Lagoa its official status as a town. The region was an important area for wine, fruit, vegetables, and fish. Today it is known mostly for its shopping, leisure activities, and golf courses, but still, of course, its wine.

We have always enjoyed visiting Lagoa; it is a town that straddles many tourist areas but keeps a sense of normality, with its shops and busy centre. Although holidaymakers do find their way there, they don't tend to stay very long, which is a shame as the town itself has much to offer. It is also the central location for many large supermarkets and a travel hub for reaching a range of excellent tourist attractions. It hosts several annual large-scale events, and some smaller, but no less interesting, fairs and festivals.

Architecturally, it has a couple of outstanding ecclesiastical buildings that are worth visiting.

The parish church in Lagoa is the Igreja de Nossa Senhora da Luz or The Church of Our Lady of Light. It is in front of a pretty square called the Largo dos Combatantes da Grande Guerra. This translates as the Great War Fighters' Square, and it has an impressive war memorial surrounded by a small area of planted gardens and benches. It is a nice place to sit and enjoy the view of the church and avoid the bustle of the town.

The church was built in the 16th century, but, along with so many other buildings, it was completely destroyed by the earthquake in 1755. The new building dates back to the end of the 18th century. All that remains of the original church is a Manueline doorway integrated into the bell tower. The name Manueline denotes an ornate style of Portuguese architecture developed during the reign of Manuel I (1495–1521). Characterised by a mixture of elaborate Gothic and Renaissance styles—you can't miss it when you see it!

It is a typical Portuguese church with an impressive exterior, painted in white with large green doors. Inside it is cool and inviting, with wooden benches and stone arches. Plenty of gold paint surrounds the altar and there is a statue of Nossa Senhora da Luz which takes pride of place in the chancel. The church is open for visits during the day, and there are frequent masses taking place, although we have never yet managed to attend one. It is the sort of church that would be a remarkable setting for an Easter service or wedding ceremony.

Far less spectacular, but in my mind, more welcoming, is the Convent of São José situated almost around the corner from the church. The Carmelite Convent of Saint Joseph, with its beautiful cloister, chapel, and gazebo, was built in 1738 and survived the 1755 earthquake. In the convent's garden you can see a menhir from the Porches region, which originated between 5000 and 4000 BC. We adopted the word menhir from the French, with a combination of two words from the Breton language: *maen*, meaning stone, and *hir*, which translates as long. Literally a monumental, tall, upright stone. It is incredible to walk past this structure, touch its surface, and remember that it has existed for centuries.

The Carmelite convent was originally used to house and educate abandoned women and children. Today, the convent is the town's Cultural Centre and is home to a wide range of activities. It hosts art and photography exhibitions, concerts, musical events and plays, lectures and demonstrations, and a range of other cultural events. Upstairs, they have turned the original nuns' rooms into mini art galleries, and there is a small chapel from the 18th century which is used for worship and music concerts.

Dave has visited the convent several times for photo-shoots, with the proprietor's permission, and it is a fabulous setting for a portrait session. The cloisters and central garden area, with its deep well in the centre, is a peaceful place to sit and soak up the history of this magical space. Entrance is free, as are many of the events that happen here. We always pick up a leaflet when we are passing by to see what is planned.

From the convent you can head down into the centre of Lagoa, via the gaudily painted red pedestrian walkways etched into the edge of the road. I have no idea who thought this would be a good idea, but it certainly put Lagoa on the map when they were first painted. Luckily, the paint has faded a little now and doesn't jump out at you quite so much. The red path leads to the 19th century small municipal market. You can stock up on regional products, fruit and vegetables, fresh fish, and seafood here, and the market is open every day except Sunday. This is where the local people shop, and it is always worth stopping to have a look around inside.

The Lagoa region is the primary wine-growing area in the Algarve. The Adega Cooperativa de Lagoa building, which is on the main EN125 road, is the prime spot for wine experts and vineyard owners to congregate. I had no idea that the region produces almost two million litres of wine each year. It is mostly red wine, but they also create white wine, a rosé, a local liqueur and a dry apéritif wine.

For a real treat, we always visit the Quinta dos Vales Wine Estate, which is on the edge of Lagoa. This is a fascinating place as it uniquely combines a vineyard and winery with an outdoor art gallery. The grounds of the estate have a permanent exhibition of modern sculpture, with over one hundred large and impressive — and hard to miss — sculptures. Some of them are almost six metres high, with exaggerated fat hippopotamuses dancing in the air alongside Rubenesque women. The statues are brightly coloured and beautifully painted. They create a unique setting for the rows and rows of vines in the background.

You can book a wine tour in advance, where they will tell you all about the process of producing their wine. You also have the chance to taste the wine and to buy it. You can even make your own wine or purchase a section of the vineyard and own a little slice of wine-making heaven. The owner, Karl Heinz Stock, combines his love of wine and sculpture in an impressive location that is marketed as a wine estate with a difference. I can highly recommend a visit.

Back in Lagoa there are more artistic themes at the art gallery called the Lady in Red Galeria Arte do Algarve. It is located in the unused industrial space next door to the Adega Cooperativa de Lagoa building. The gallery mostly displays modern art, with regular featured-artist exhibitions. There is a café inside as well. The front section of the gallery is light and bright and a good space for art to be displayed. I have been asked several times to exhibit my work there, but sadly I always decline, as I have a genuine dislike of the rear of the premises. Dark, dank walls, often dripping with condensation or rain, are not exactly conducive to displaying expensive pieces of art. It is such a shame, as it is in a great location, with real potential. The work, and cost, involved in putting the structure of the building right, means that this is not likely to happen soon. My work will stay on my studio walls a little longer.

For more original artisan arts and crafts you should head to Porches, which is a small village in the municipality of Lagoa. The area is famous for its potteries and hand-painted colourful ceramics. The most famous of these, Porches Pottery, opened in 1968, the same year that I was born. I waited outside the shop one year on my birthday while Dave photographed me, stood in front of the ceramic sign proudly stating, 'established in 1968'. We have a beautiful hand-painted jug from the pottery given to us by dear friends which we treasure.

There is also a new initiative that has opened on the main road on the edge of town, called the Convent'bio. Their website describes the old convent building they house this in, which has been beautifully restored and brought back to life.

The space belonged to the Carmelitas Calçados d'Alagoa Convent, dedicated to Nossa Senhora do Socorro. It was founded in 1551 under the influence of Queen D. Catarina. As was common in the Portuguese Order of Carmo, the convent was located outside the environs the nearby village. The Carmelite brothers cultivated a vast area of agricultural land, in an area known for its fertility and for the quality of its vegetables, fruit and vineyards. The convent was an important place in the sixteenth and seventeenth centuries. The earthquake in 1755 caused serious damage to the building, resulting in its subsequent abandonment.[1]

We had driven past this old derelict building and land for years, and I was delighted to see that work had begun to renovate it. The resulting transformation is remarkable. Not only have they created an ambitious bio-organic farming project, with produce for sale, they have lovingly curated the cultural heritage of the original building. They have also created a wonderful open and well-lit gallery space for exhibitions. I have my eye on it; maybe one day I will have an exhibition of my paintings displayed there. The walls are certainly in an excellent state of repair—no damp or mould here!

✿❧✿❀✿

For those of you that love sport more than art, there are plenty of golf courses in the region between Lagoa and Carvoeiro. The Gramacho and Pinta regulation courses are part of the Pestana golf resort, and the Vale de Milho course is also nearby with nine holes.

One of the most popular leisure options for a fun day out is the Slide & Splash Water Park. This is one of the busiest aquashow parks in the Algarve, located between Lagoa and Estômbar. It is also one of the largest water parks in Europe, covering over seven hectares with a wide range of water entertainment for all ages. As well as the main rides, there are live animal shows, spa treatments, restaurants, and a shop where you can buy souvenirs.

The park opened in 1986 and was renovated in 2019. It is continually adding new and bigger slides and features and can cope with over four thousand visitors each day. It is worth buying your tickets in advance online if you are planning to go there. Often you can find a discount code in the local newspaper, and it also means you don't have to queue to buy a ticket before entering. It is quite expensive, currently priced at twenty-seven euros for adults and twenty euros for children. Children under the age of four get free entry. It is extremely busy in the summer, especially at the weekends.

I can recommend packing some food and chairs to take in with you. It might be a bit of a pain to carry, but it will be worth it when you arrive and find there is nothing to sit on. After a few hours, lying on the grass gets uncomfortable if you are not whizzing down all the slides. It is a well-laid out site, with rides and slides for all ages, but we found the restaurants to be uninspiring and expensive. (Especially if you have already spent the best part of one hundred euros on entry fees for a family of four.)

Lagoa has a large showground that hosts numerous annual events, the biggest of which is the annual FATACIL, which happens in August each year. You know when it is happening, as the traffic queues from about 5 p.m. each evening are horrendous in both directions around Lagoa. The parking is atrocious as walking to the entrance from the nearby designated car park is just too much for most people.

Before the council added their new central bollard system, the parking was even worse. The cars were abandoned in the middle of the road, with drivers utilising every available space to park, including the small central reservation area on the main road.

The event celebrated its fortieth year in 2020, and it has grown in size each year since the first small Regional Fair of Lagoa was hosted there in 1980. In 2019, they had seven hundred exhibitors and over 170,000 visitors over the ten days of the festival. For years we called it the FATACIL without knowing what the name meant. It is actually an acronym: FATACIL - the Feira de Artesanato, Turismo, Agricultura, Comércio e Indústria de Lagoa.

The themes are broad, from handicrafts, arts and crafts, to agriculture and tourism. Large businesses swamp the front area with luxury cars, boats, and swimming pools, whilst smaller ventures and artisans have booths displaying local goods for sale. If you like collecting leaflets and free samples, you will enjoy the event. There are lots of live demonstrations, and tons of food to eat and buy. You can find sweets and home-made cakes, dairy products, strings of sausages, fresh fruit, dried fruit, honey, canned fish and dried *bacalhau* codfish, piri-piri sauces and lots of wine. There is usually a livestock area, with sheep and goats, cattle, and horses. There are catering establishments set up, and the food is good, simple fare and plentiful. Live music and entertainment groups run all the time, although the best music and the headline names each night don't warm up until about 10 p.m.

It is always a dilemma with us as we like to get there early evening before the crowds arrive and wander round enjoying the stalls and the produce. Then we have something to eat, and usually by about 8 p.m. we have seen everything we want to. We can never decide whether to hang around until 10 p.m. and watch the main artists perform or give up and leave. We usually head home tired but happy, and think next year we'll stay for the music. We rarely do.

Another venue in Lagoa is the Sand City extravaganza. It used to be located down a side street near Guia and was quite hard to find. Two years ago they moved it to a new site, right on the N125 road near the International School. Every year more than sixty professional sand sculptors from all over the world come to the Algarve to craft the most amazing sand sculptures. Fifty thousand tonnes of sand are used to create the sculptures which are displayed over six hectares of land.

The themes change each year. One year it was all musical celebrities, then another year animals and iconic buildings were featured. It is the largest event of its kind in the world, which first started in 2003. This year you can see Pope Francis riding a Vespa, and Queen Elizabeth II having tea next to Big Ben. At night, the park is transformed as the sculptures are all lit up and the lights cast a magical glow over the features. Just remember to pack some mosquito spray in your bag if you are going to visit in the evening.

Eating out in Lagoa can be an interesting experience. We favour local Portuguese restaurants with simple menus, and there are several in and around the town that are great for popping into and grabbing a quick meal. A Paleta and Restaurante Lamim are both staples, and the Restaurante Barca Velha opposite the Fatacil ground, has an impressive set lunch menu. For posher dining, lots of people recommend Chrissy's in town, near the market.

❂ဆ❂ଓ❂

An entire book could be written about the beautiful beaches of the Algarve, and many of the best and most photographed are near Lagoa. The beaches here have limestone cliffs, with incredibly rich deep-ochre and sienna colours. The sand is soft and golden; the waves are often calmer, and there are hidden coves and caves to explore by land or boat. The rock formations and cliffs create an impressive backdrop, showing the centuries of sea erosion that have formed the landscape we enjoy today. A word of warning - these cliffs crumble easily. Please do not sit under them or walk too close to the edge of them.

The Algar de Benagil (Benagil Cave) is probably the most famous of all the sea caves in the Algarve. Many people take a boat trip out to witness this magnificent arched cathedral-like structure. There is a small and unique beach tucked away inside that can only be reached by boat. If you have viewed an iconic photograph of an Algarve beach with someone standing under a domed arch of softly coloured stone, you have most likely seen Benagil.

To the west of the arch, Benagil itself is still a working fishing village, and you can see prettily painted boats pulled up onto the main beach. This is a nice unspoilt beach, usually chosen by families or couples wanting some peace and quiet.

Praia da Marinha is known as one of the most beautiful beaches in the world and has won many awards. It is often used as an advertisement for the Algarve. The cliffs are impressive, and the sea really seems to be a brighter, more sparkling blue here. There is a long set of steps down to the beach, so take a moment to enjoy the fabulous views from the top before you descend. At low tide, you can walk around the sand and see the famous M-shaped arch of rocks that are slowly, but surely, crumbling. Who knows how much longer they will be there, but they are well worth viewing. If you stand at a certain point on the cliffs above and look down on the arch, add some fanciful editing with your eyes of the surrounding cliffs in front of you, and you have a perfect heart shape. Well, a little romance never hurt anyone.

Watch out for high tide, as the beach is all but immersed in water, and it does come in at a fast pace. (Yes, we've been caught before — well, Dave has, as he was so busy with his camera!)

Praia de Albandeira is a beautiful secluded beach and one of our favourites, probably because it is less well known than its nearby famous counterparts. Rocks on either side of the sand create a natural safe bay, and if it is windy elsewhere, you have a good chance of being protected from the elements on this beach. There are actually two beaches here, divided by a large rock, and it gets busy in the middle of summer. For the rest of the year, you can often enjoy your own private beach. There is another stunning arched rock formation here to enjoy, and you can even swim underneath and around this one.

The first time we walked along the cliffs, and out to the end of the arch, we didn't realise what we were standing above. I wasn't quite so impressed when we continued our walk and I looked back and realised what I had been perched on top of. It looks a lot more fragile and narrower from a distance.

From Lagoa travelling east, the walk above the cliffs is known as the Percurso dos Sete Vales Suspensos. The route stretches from Praia de Vale Centeanes in the west to Praia da Marinha in the east. It is so named because the route takes you past seven beautiful hanging valleys along this magnificent stretch of coastline. The round trip will take you almost twelve kilometres to walk.

Another option is to walk east from Marinha all the way to

Senhora da Rocha. There is a well-defined trail here which lasts for several kilometres. This path is much easier and will give you amazing views over the beaches below. It is hard not to be impressed by such magnificent scenery and the natural landscape along here.

There used to be a small fort called the Forte of Nossa Senhora da Rocha on top of the cliffs jutting out to sea. Inside the fort there was a tiny chapel, known as the Chapel of Nossa Senhora da Rocha, which may have pre-dated the stronghold structure built around it. The fort has long since fallen to ruins, but the chapel still exists today.

The view from the end of this promontory is fabulous. You can see all the way to Albufeira in the east and for miles along the west coast. It is the perfect place to catch the sunset or even have your wedding photographed.

The chapel itself is only open on certain days. Inside the chapel there is an image of Nossa Senhora (the Virgin Mary) and Christ. Even if the chapel is closed, you can still see the altar through the window. On the first Sunday of August every year, there is a religious procession when they take the image of Nossa Senhora from the chapel down to the beach.

Praia de Nossa Senhora da Rocha is a beautiful beach that has fishing boats drawn up on the sand and small fishermen's huts at the rear. You can go out on a boat tour from here and explore many of the cliffs and rock formations along the coast. This is a splendid region of the Algarve, full of character, amazing beaches, an incredible coastline, and interesting towns and villages to discover.

---

1. Convent'bio (s.d.). Website article *História Do Convento*. Accessed 20th August 2020 through http://www.conventbio.com/programs/ewpview.aspx?codigo=sobrenos

26

The Fishing Villages of Ferragudo and Carvoeiro

I s Ferragudo a town or a village? I think technically it is a town, but is has a quaint, unspoilt village-feel to it that so many other locations along the Algarve seem to have lost. This was our home for almost ten years, and I have fond memories of this charming place. It is also reputed to be one of the most photographed spots in the Algarve. You can probably blame Dave for that.

With its sloping hillside full of old fishermen's cottages, iconic white-and-yellow church, and the painted fishing boats bobbing in the sparkling water; it is easy to see why people reach for their camera when they arrive here.

The small harbour and walkway are lined with popular fish restaurants and all roads lead to the main square of Praça Rainha Dona Leonor. This is a lively place with several cafés and restaurants. It is a brilliant spot to sit with a coffee and a *pastel de nata* pastry and watch the world go by. My favourite thing is always to explore Ferragudo's narrow and cobbled streets. You walk past brightly painted traditional houses and wend your way to the top, where the church sits overlooking the river across to Portimão and Praia da Rocha marina.

Ferragudo is believed to have been first recognised as a

settlement in the 14th century, with fishermen finding rich pickings at the mouth of the Arade River.

There are several explanations on where the name Ferragudo comes from. There used to be an *agudo* (sharp) *engenho de ferro* (iron machine) on Praia da Angrinha for hoisting and landing fish. The easiest explanation is that the merger of the words *ferro* and *agudo* became Ferragudo. Others will tell of a Spanish nobleman called Johane Anes Ferro Agudo, who became the namesake.

Even the Roots of Ferragudo Facebook site cannot decide on the likely history of the name. The most far-fetched explanation is that in the battle to recapture the nearby town of Silves; the Moorish giant, Ferragut, was killed here, and they named the town after him. The giant is described in the *Song of Roland* that was popular with the crusaders who wanted to expel the Moors from Spain and Portugal. After a heroic battle, Crusader Roland killed the colossus who, according to tradition, "was not afraid of a spear and had the strength of 40 strong men."

The most logical reason for the name is that people found a safe place to anchor here. The old Portuguese verb *ferrar* is derived from the Latin *ferrāre* which means to throw an anchor, and the original Portuguese word *agudo* comes from the Latin *acūtus* which translates as urgent. The merger of *ferrar* and *agudo* led them to the name Ferragudo.[1]

According to several Portuguese historians, even before Ferragudo was founded in 1520, there was a watchtower built here. In 1918, the former occupant of the castle, Joaquim Coelho de Carvalho, wrote, "At the site of the fort, King João II, after the bay was attacked by Algerian pirates, ordered the construction of a watchtower."[sic] King João II reigned between 1481 and 1495, but the fort was only put into use almost 150 years later in 1644. Further documentary proof comes from a Dutch skipper called Lucas Janszoon Waghenaer from Enkhuizen. In 1584 he made a map of the Algarve coast to assist sailors in their travels. On the map you can see at the mouth of the Arade river at the place titled 'Fera gudo', there is an island with something red marked on it, which is referred to in the description as a tower.[2]

Today, the majestic Fort of São João do Arade is a stunning piece of history and architecture. Built around the original watchtower, the fortification was added in 1643. It is located on a strategic point on the river, partnered with the Fortaleza de Santa Catarina on the opposite bank at Praia da Rocha. These two imposing structures meant the area would have been well defended and protected from attacks. Sadly, by 1896, the Ferragudo fort was abandoned until the beginning of the 20th century when the poet, Coelho Carvalho, turned it into a home. It is still privately owned so you cannot go inside, but it is a magnificent landmark jutting out on the headland.

Above the village and on the top of the hill is Ferragudo's church, the Igreja Nossa Senhora da Conceição. Built in 1520, the church was destroyed in the great earthquake of 1755. It was rebuilt with the typical Baroque architecture and style seen in many local churches. Inside it is a pleasant mix of a bright interior with lots of gold and gilt and a 16th century image of São Sebastião. It is a nice cool interior to sit quietly for a few minutes when it is hot and busy outside, and the church is usually open.

✿✿✿✿✿

Ferragudo has several great beaches within walking distance of the village, including the smaller, local Praia da Angrinha, and the much larger and more popular Praia Grande. Angrinha is less developed and looks more like a river beach, complete with a series of old fishing huts scattered behind the main path. You can often see the fishermen fixing their nets here, all under the watchful eye of the Coastguard's office and launch. It also has a large free car park, and it is a lovely spot to walk along and watch the waves as they skid along the sand.

If Praia da Angrinha is known as the locals' beach, then Praia Grande is the bigger tourist destination around the corner. The sea here is a mix of estuary and ocean, but the man-made breakwaters for the lighthouses nearby ensure that the bay is protected and safe for swimming. It is a wide beach backed by the unmistakable gold and red cliffs of the local area. There are three or four bars and restaurants, and in summer you can hire sun loungers and parasols. There is a parking area, toilets, an outdoor shower, and a small play park for children. In the summer months there is also a marked-out court with beach volleyball competitions to watch, and a full lifeguard service.

Praia Grande has a wooden walkway which covers about half of the length of the beach which allows easy access for families or people with reduced mobility. It is the perfect beach to stroll along at sunset, or in the early morning in the winter months. Kat and I have spent many happy hours walking here and enjoying the fantastic view, fresh air, and gentle waves. At low tide, it is possible to walk through the rock pools all the way round to Praia de Molhe beach.

You can also reach Molhe via the main road to Carvoeiro. From the car park at the top, it is an easy climb down some steps to reach this small and pretty beach. The dominant feature is the long jetty which leads to the impressive Farol de Portimão Molhe Este. The lighthouse is painted green and white, and its counterpart on the other side of the water, the Farol da Praia da Rocha, has striking red and white stripes. They are both unmistakable features of the local area.

This is a much wilder stretch of coastline and the waves in the winter can tip right over the breakwater, crashing over the rocks, and spilling onto the pathway. We have witnessed some spectacular storms in winter from above the clifftop here.

Travelling east, the Ponta do Altar Lighthouse stands imperiously on the headland and is an impressive structure. Built in the mid-19th century, its location offers stunning views of the Algarve coastline. You can walk along the top of the cliffs here, although watch out for the blowholes where the sandstone has worn away. In some places, you can even see and hear the waves and water crashing below.

To the east of the lighthouse is Pintadinho beach, with its stunning limestone rock backdrop and soft gentle sand. The rocks have arches and caves—I have always been nervous of exploring too deep inside them—but they are fascinating structures. At dusk, the caverns are filled with nesting European swallows returning home for the night.

On the horizon line you can also see two prominent rocks in the middle of the sea, called *leixões*. The larger one is called the Leixão da Gaivotas, so named because sea gulls are its only inhabitants.

Further round the headland are a number of smaller coves and access to them is by boat, or when the tide is low, you can walk through from Praia dos Caneiros.

Caneiros is an absolute gem and is one of Dave's favourite beaches to photograph at low tide. It is a small sandy beach with imposing cliffs at either end, and it faces in the perfect direction for enjoying a spectacular winter sunset. There is a restaurant, the Rei das Praias, at the top of the car park, which has stunning views. It has an excellent fish menu too.

One event not to be missed in Ferragudo is the Festa da Nossa Senhora da Conceição. The village's patron saint is celebrated on the 15th August each year. Following a church service, the large and gaudily painted statue of Our Lady of Conception is carried through the streets. The parade reaches the harbourside, where the fishing boats are blessed. The statue is then transported onto a boat and travels around the harbour, with a flotilla of small boats behind her. They pass in front of both local beaches before returning to shore where the party begins in the square. At midnight, a loud volley of fireworks signals the end of this special day in the village's calendar.

Less spectacular, but just as garish, is the monthly flea market. The whole main square and surrounding streets are strewn with all manner of items, from dubious 'antiques' to second-hand clothing, toys and shoes, and handicrafts. I love to peruse the bric-à-brac stalls, displaying farm implements and tools, odd-shaped instruments of torture, and old pieces of furniture. The best pitches are hotly contested, with people arriving in the summer at about 5.30 a.m. to set up their stall. Kat loves walking past all these treasures, most of which are simply laid out on the floor on a blanket. I frequently have to buy a cuddly toy once she has sniffed it and picked it up!

When we lived in Ferragudo we would head to our favourite café every morning on our walks to say hello to Brun the owner and have a coffee for me and a biscuit for Kat. The Pastelaria Lanchonete was a regular haunt of ours. They also serve the best cheap lunches too. Brun's mom makes a hearty home-made soup, and if we are anywhere near there at lunchtime, we always go back to visit them. Next door, Brun has opened a new restaurant called Petiscos Capela which is a wonderful place to enjoy traditional Portuguese food.

Also recommended is the more international menu at Fim do Mundo with its giant steaks and convivial atmosphere. There are several excellent fish restaurants along the harbour front, the poshest (and most expensive) of which is Sueste which is in an old salt warehouse. You are spoilt for choice in the village, with a wide range of establishments that run from cheap snacks, Italian pizzas, and traditional fare, through to fine dining.

Leaving Ferragudo and heading east, you reach the small town of Estômbar, which has a history dating back to when the Moors occupied the Algarve. It was the home of the famous 11th century Arab poet, Ibn Ammar. Here lies the start of a land of legends and myth. There are even reported to be subterranean passages from here travelling inland for about twelve kilometres to the ancient Moorish capital of Silves.

Near to Estômbar is one of my favourite places in the Algarve, the Sítio das Fontes park. This is a wonderful place to walk or simply sit and take in the view. Two freshwater springs meet here and create a small lagoon prior to joining the Arade river. You can walk along beside the water, and spot wildlife and rare flowers at every turn. There is an old watermill, an amphitheatre, and a traditionally restored Algarvian house that sometimes has art exhibitions. It is a lovely location to relax and enjoy some peace and quiet. It is also a great place to go for a swim. The park has a picnic and barbeque area—just don't go there on the 18th of June and expect to find a space. This is the traditional Dia Internacional do Piquenique (the day of the picnic), when local people descend on the park in huge numbers. We went there with friends one year and had a marvellous time, with everyone sharing their food with each other and grilling their lunch together.

✧ⴵ✧ⴀ✧

If you keep travelling east, you will reach Carvoeiro, which is a much busier tourist destination, loved by holidaymakers and locals alike. The name of the village is believed to derive from *Caboiere*, which was an old moniker for a fishing village from the Medieval period.

Historically, this was a critical maritime location. The area where Vila de Carvoeiro is now located has a long history of military and pirate attacks. Nowadays things are a little calmer here, although it gets busy in the summer months. The main beach is quite small and gets packed with holidaymakers. The painted wooden boats hauled up on the beach are a reminder though that this is still a working fishing village. There are numerous restaurants, cafés, bars, shops, and ice cream parlours in front of the beach and all along the main roads leading in and out of town. Carvoeiro is well suited to families and tourists, as everything is within easy reach. The newer resorts are on the edge of town, and it has a stunning golden coastline with sandstone cliffs.

There are so many eateries here, you could choose a different restaurant every night of a two-week holiday, and still have places you hadn't explored. We like to go where the locals eat, so we often head to A Fonte, which is at the bottom of the 'in' road. The tables are covered with paper tablecloths, the menu is *prato do dia* (plate of the day) which is hand-written on a board, and the piri-piri chicken and fish are excellent. It is also great value too; you will have change from thirty euros for a meal for two.

There are only three roads in the main area of Carvoeiro, the 'in' road, the 'out' road and Lighthouse hill. The principal routes into and out of town are one-way, hence the names. The other is self-explanatory. Half-way up Lighthouse hill is a modern café, called the Earth Shop and Café. It is beautifully decorated and full of foody treasures to eat and purchase. They do a great healthy breakfast if you are up early, and their lunch menu is superb. We have also been there once in the evening, invited to a friend's private birthday party which was held there, and the food and atmosphere were perfect.

Just past the café is a turning on the left, the Rua das Moínhos, that leads to a tucked-away locals' restaurant called Ponto de Encontro. Their set menu changes every day, but for less than twelve euros you can enjoy a three-course lunch with wine or beer, and coffee. The plates of food have generous portions and the flavours are excellent, whatever you choose to eat. Be warned that the menu is different in the evening and is much more expensive. It gets busy at lunchtime, so arrive early!

If you travel out of town from the main square with the sea on your right, past the police station, you will climb up to the Forte e Capela de Nossa Senhora da Encarnação. The parish church already existed when, in 1675, this defensive military fort was added. Designed in the shape of an irregular polygon, it was situated in the spot where a watchtower would have been. Artillery pieces were placed to repel pirates attacking the village and its fishing port. In the 19th century, when piracy attacks disappeared, the fortress was de-activated. Parts of the original walls remain, and it is a great location to enjoy the fabulous views out to sea. It is also the perfect location to watch the sunset from.

From the church, I like to wander along the wooden boardwalk which takes you all the way across the clifftop to Algar Seco. This is a fun place to enjoy a drink or a meal at the Boneca Bar, which hides away in a secret spot overlooking the sea.

Algar Seco and its caves are also worth spending some time exploring. Rock formations created by the wind and waves have made natural pools and holes in the rocks. From here you can visit the Farol de Alfanzina. This lighthouse was built in 1920, and its beams guided ships along the coast. The light was also useful to local fishermen who used its rays to catch squid at night. It is possible to look inside the lighthouse on Wednesday afternoons when it is open to the public.

From here, heading east, are some stunning beaches, including Vale de Centeanes, which is surrounded by imposing and steep cliffs. The sea here is clear and bright, and the sand soft and welcoming. It is a lovely location to have a rest after all the dashing around, eating, and sight-seeing this chapter has covered.

1. Roots of Ferragudo (19.08.2020). Website article *Ferragudo a safe place to drop anchor*. Accessed 5th September 2020 through https://www.gloopla.com/PT/Ferragudo/111699970516486/Roots-of-Ferragudo

2. Roots of Ferragudo (s.d.). Website article *Castelo de São João do Arade*. Accessed 5th September 2020 through https://www.gloopla.com/PT/Ferragudo/111699970516486/Roots-of-Ferragudo

27

From Portimão to Alvor

Portimão is the second largest city in the Algarve, and its history stretches back to the Neolithic period, with the remains of settlements hinting at a prosperous past. Phoenicians, Greeks, and Carthaginians would all have passed through this port, trading with the Mediterranean and North Africa. The name Portimão is derived from its Roman name of Portus Magnus (Great Port) and it is a natural harbour at the base of the Arade river.

Initially, through five centuries of Arabian rule, Portimão was a small fishing village. Because of the constant raids by pirates, the coastal area of Portimão was not considered a safe place to live. In the 15th century, a new town called Vila Nova de Portimão was officially founded and a wall was built around the town to protect it. Until the 16th century, Portimão was often still the target of attacks from Moroccan, English, Dutch and French pirates. This led to the building of two fortresses to bolster the protection, one on each side of the harbour. One was in Ferragudo, the Fortaleza of São João do Arade, and the other was situated in Praia da Rocha, and named the Fortaleza of Santa Catarina. The Praia da Rocha fort was used until recently by the Maritime Police and the Fiscal Guard and is now open to visitors.[1]

During the second half of the period in history known as the Age of Discoveries; Vila Nova de Portimão developed at an alarming rate, growing beyond its walled perimeter. The thirst for adventure and exploration meant that seaports along the Algarve, and especially around the western area, were rising in popularity. The development of the fish canning industry further accelerated Portimão's prominence, and the town was extended again with the building of new houses and factories to accommodate the expanding population.

Tourists began to arrive in the 1930s and the first hotel on the Algarve coast opened in Praia da Rocha. An old mansion was transformed into a luxury holiday residence. It is still there today, with the same name, the Boutique Hotel Bela Vista. Today tourism is the main economy for the region, and Portimão is a busy mix of hotels and accommodation, beaches, water sports, and shopping. The area also has an active marina, and you can even go kitesurfing and paragliding, or do a parachute jump from a nearby airfield.

The main church for the town is the Igreja Matriz de Portimão, which was built in the 15th century. Partially destroyed in the 1755 earthquake, it was renovated in the 18th and 19th centuries. Its construction was based upon the then famous Batalha Monastery, which was the most important Portuguese monument of its time. The church is flamboyantly Gothic and Manueline in appearance. You certainly can't miss it. Inside, the altar is an impressive riot of gold paint and statues jostling for attention.

The Igreja Colégio dos Jesuítas (the church college of Jesuits), is located around the corner from the main church, in the Alameda da Praça da República. The church was built at the end of the 17th century under the orders of Diogo Gonçalves. He was caught up in a storm at sea and found refuge in Portimão's harbour. His way of saying thank you to God for saving his life was to build a church. I hope he liked the finished design as it became his final resting place too, as he was buried in the chancel. Work began on its construction in 1660, and Gonçalves died in 1664, before the church was completed. This is an impressive and large building, painted white with yellow trim on the outside, but is quite austere inside.

He also gave his name to the Museu Diogo Gonçalves (the museum of fine arts), which displays the artwork of almost two hundred Portuguese painters. It is home to the Centro de Apoio de Idosos home for the elderly. It's not a bad place for an artist to retire to; I shall have to keep the details stored away for the future.

One of the most interesting places to visit is Portimão Museum. Its location is a former sardine canning factory, and it includes an exhibition of how the factory used to operate. It is a beautiful building which has been sympathetically restored and uses modern technology to provide an informative museum experience. The canning factory section has life-size models to show how people used to work in there. The museum's position, right beside the waterfront, seems to bring it all to life more easily. A quick tip; they have free entry to the public on Sundays.

Carrying on with the historical theme, in the nearby parish of Mexilhoeira Grande, you can visit the Megalithic Monuments of Alcalar. This is a group of burial tombs dating from the Copper Age (2000-1600 B.C.), which have been classified as a National Monument in Portugal. It is hard to imagine that a community settled there four thousand years ago. They erected trenches and walls and developed a complex society, and their prehistoric tombs have survived to this day. The tombs reveal the different roles the individuals who once lived in Alcalar played; from specific graves for the chiefs of the tribe, to special tombs marked to honour the loved ones of a family. Some of the original pieces excavated from the site are displayed in the Museum of Portimão.

You are spoilt for choice when it comes to restaurants and food in Portimão, and it is probably most famous for its sardines. It hosts a large and popular sardine festival each summer. For the real deal, you should head to the restaurant Dona Barca on the waterfront. They have been open since 1980 and they employ old fishermen to tend the grills and cook the fish. Everything is freshly caught and prepared; it's not fancy, but the food is superb. It has a simple setting, with paper tablecloths and a relaxed atmosphere. It is almost impossible to walk past there without wanting to grab a table, with the delicious smell of the barbecue and grilled fish. It gets remarkably busy in the summer.

During the Portimão Sardine Festival, as well as the food, there is also live music every night, featuring big names in the local Portuguese music scene. This is a pleasant way to spend an evening, scoffing some tasty food, wandering along the waterfront enjoying the atmosphere, and browsing the many craft stalls and handmade goods that are for sale.

One of our favourite restaurants in Portimão is tucked away in a side street behind the post office. Head for the waterfront, turn left at the post office, and then wander around six or seven identical streets, muttering, it's round here somewhere, have they moved it? I'm sure it was just round this corner! Eventually you will find it. The Casa da Tocha restaurant is an unassuming little place from the outside, but inside is a quaint and welcoming eatery that serves fantastic Portuguese cuisine.

According to their marketing, the old building was originally a small church. Women, before they got pregnant, would visit this church, and ask for God's blessing and light a candle. In the mid-1950s it became a grocery store, where wine was sold in bulk. I'm not sure if the two things are connected. Today they have a small but excellent menu and have a fine array of wines on display and for sale. Their banoffee pie is the best I have ever tasted. The owner, Paulo, worked for many years at the Penina hotel and golf resort, and is an accomplished chef. The easiest thing to do is ask him what he would recommend, and you won't be disappointed.

❂ඛ❂ख❂

One thing you will never persuade me to experience is a trip to the local aerodrome where you can make a parachute jump. It is a lovely sight from a distance, watching the plane ascend and seeing all the little blobs falling to the ground with their colourful parachutes spinning in the breeze. But you will never catch me doing that, I'll leave it to others much dafter and braver than me.

Apparently, they jump out of the airplane at 4,300 meters altitude and 'enjoy the sensation of free fall for almost a minute'. In the tandem-jump mode, they attach you to a certified instructor who sorts out the parachute bit for you, 'leaving you free to enjoy this unforgettable experience'. Well, it doesn't matter how they market it, that is never going to encourage me to jump.

Praia da Rocha is one of the busiest towns and beaches in the Algarve, receiving thousands of visitors every year. This is a densely populated place with a host of hotels, restaurants, shops, and bars. Sadly, most of the shops seem to sell the same items. The beach is beautiful though, and enormous, so there is space for everyone. The boardwalk that runs along the length of the sand makes this a good beach for accessibility. There are several good, but expensive, restaurants here.

I admit this is just too touristy for me, although you can sometimes find us walking along the beach on a fine winter's day, when the holidaymakers have disappeared, and all is peaceful and quiet. The shops, selling their tourist tat, remain the same all year round.

Sadly, the old town of Portimão suffered with the opening of the new Aqua shopping centre on the edge of a town. The old shops that lined the streets for the most part closed, and the area took on an almost ghostly quality. Five years later, the area is being brought back to life, with small artisan suppliers, boutique shops and small delicatessens starting up. It is once again a pleasant place to wander around and explore.

If you make it to this side of town, check out the little café called A Casa da Isabel. It is like an old-fashioned tea-room from the 1930s, and their cakes are divine. It has been featured on national television —their cakes are that good!

If you want to walk off some calories from the cakes you have just eaten (you can't possibly tell me you only ate one cake at Isabel's?) then head for Praia do Vau. This is between Praia da Rocha and Alvor, and it is a great beach for strolling along, due to its easy access and sheltered location. The surrounding cliffs provide shade during the hottest hours of the day, and the beach is well organised and safe.

If you want to expend a little more energy and have a thrill, then you need to visit the Autódromo Internacional do Algarve, which is located twenty minutes from Portimão. It was opened in 2010, and is a magnet for people that like to race fast cars around a track. It has the prestige of being one of the largest kart tracks in Europe. It is known as the Algarve International Circuit, or locally referred to as the Portimão racetrack, and it has now reached the dizzy heights of being the host for Formula One racing too. It also hosts the MotoGP race championships each year. Its capacity is an impressive 100,000 spectators. As the total population of the Algarve is less than 500,000, it will be interesting to see how busy and noisy it gets when the Formula One teams arrive. I am not sure I would choose to buy a house too close to the venue, that's for sure.

✿๛✿౧✿

Alvor is a small and picturesque village about six kilometres from Portimão. Alvor's name probably comes from its old Moorish name: Al-Bûr, and this region was controlled by the Moors for several centuries. Alvor would only be conquered by the Portuguese in 1189, when the armies of Sancho I, king of Portugal, were finally able to reclaim the castle of Alvor.

The castle was built on top of an old set of ruins that predates even Roman occupation. The Moors created such an impressive structure that the castle withstood the 1755 earthquake that destroyed almost the entire village. It is still there today.

Like Ferragudo, Alvor is still a working fishing village, with the Odiáxere river forming a natural marina. The front is full of colourful boats that bob in the water and clank in the breeze. The well situated and extensive wooden boardwalk leads from the marina right round to the beautiful, long, sandy beach this area is famous for. The beach stretches for three-and-a-half kilometres from Praia de Alvor at one end of the estuary, to Praia dos Três Irmãos at the far eastern end of the beach.

The sand is soft and sweeping and perfect for families and for walking along. The area is surrounded by sand dunes and the beach is wide, flat, and unspoilt. The elevated boardwalk also takes you through the Ria de Alvor Nature Reserve, which is a peaceful place to enjoy the local wildlife, especially the estuary birds.

Alvor itself is a mix of traditional Algarvian houses, narrow streets and alleyways, with a busy selection of bars, cafés, and restaurants. You can choose from the touristy and more expensive waterfront establishments, to smaller and cheaper backstreet cafés where the locals eat.

It is a popular place for families and tourists in the summer, and there are plenty of expats, retirees, golfers, and winter holidaymakers that descend outside of the peak season. There is also a large campervan and caravan park near the marina that gets very busy in the winter.

The Igreja Matriz de Alvor is the main church in Alvor, known for its Manueline architectural details. Guidebooks will tell you it was built in the 16th century, and that its main attraction is its entrance door. The door is decorated with scenes of war, religious symbols, and motifs alluding to the region's fishing heritage. No need to go inside then with this church, you've already seen the best of it if you stand outside.

The Church of Misericórdia de Alvor is one church that is worth stepping inside, if only to see their famous stained-glass window. It depicts the 'miracle of the transformation of bread into roses' by Queen Santa Isabel, who is unsurprisingly the patron saint of the church. Of course, I wanted to know more about her, as it seems odd for a member of the Portuguese royal family to be famous for changing bread into roses.

Born in 1271, Queen Isabel was married to King Dinis. He was alleged to have been unfaithful to her and also banned her from feeding the less fortunate of the town. She was determined to help them and had filled her apron with bread to distribute to the poor. I don't know why she didn't use a basket, but there you go. One shouldn't question the story of a legend too deeply.

The king found out and asked her where she was going and what she had in her lap, and the queen replied,

"They are roses, my Lord!"

She opened her apron to show him, and the bread had been transformed into roses. Apparently, this happened in January, so King Dinis obviously didn't stop to think where she might have found a load of roses in the middle of winter. It just goes to show what a legend can do. Queen Isabel went on to dedicate her life to the poor and established orphanages and a convent in Coimbra.

I shall henceforth look more closely at the old farmer's wives who walk around the village wearing an apron that has something tucked up inside it. Obviously, it is not just the week's shopping or a pile of fresh eggs they are hiding.

---

1. Algarve Tips (s.d.). Website article *History of Portimão: a summary*. Accessed 26th August 2020 through https://www.algarvetips.com/cities/portimao/history-of-portimao/

28

Lagos and West

Lagos is a town in the western Algarve, and it is the last large urbanisation before you hit the west coast. Lacóbriga, the original name of the city, which translates as lakes, has been inhabited since 2000 BC. It was colonised by the Romans, taken over by the Moors in the 8th century, and conquered by the Christians in the 13th century. Due to its location, Lagos was fundamental to the success of the Portuguese Discoveries in the 15th and 16th centuries, and in 1577, it was made the capital of the Algarve region by King D. Sebastião.

Henry the Navigator's expeditions were organised from here, and it was from Lagos harbour that Vasco da Gama set sail for what was to be his discovery of Brazil.

This is a town with a rich history, with an old castle and fort, lots of churches, and the remains of the first slave market in Europe. Dona Ana beach, which for many is considered the best beach in the Algarve, is nearby, while further along the coast are the stunning Ponta da Piedade cliffs.

The ancient city walls are well preserved despite the devastation caused by the 1755 earthquake which destroyed much of the town.

Because of the resulting damage, Lagos lost its status as the capital of the Algarve in favour of the less affected Faro.

Today this town is famous for its stunning beaches with rock formations and rugged cliffs. It is a major tourist area, full of cafés, restaurants, shops, and entertainment. It gets very busy in the summer months and stays reasonably lively in the winter.

This is a place where people live and work as well as being a bustling holiday destination. It has a good infrastructure with a large health centre, a state secondary school, several primary and independent schools, and a hospital. It also has plenty of large supermarkets and shops on the edge of the city.

You can wander through the streets of this town enjoying its history at almost every turn. You cannot miss the Castelo de Lagos, which is also known as the Castelo de Governadores or the Governors' Castle. This is an impressive structure that would have ensured Lagos was a well-fortified city in the past.

The Forte Ponta da Bandeira was also intended to safeguard the port of Lagos and the eastern part of the old city. It is surrounded by a moat and a drawbridge, and inside today you can find an enchanting small chapel decorated with tiles.

Lagos has several impressive churches scattered around. The Igreja Paroquial de Santa Maria de Lagos is located in the Plaza Infante Dom Henrique, which is right in the centre of the town. The church dates back to 1498 and it still holds services today.

The Igreja de Santo António de Lagos is easy to miss but is worth a visit. Apart from the ceiling, the interior is lined entirely with gold. There are even intricate and ornate carvings made of Brazilian gold. This is no shy or retiring number; the decoration hits you the minute you walk through the door. It is impressive how much gold you can get inside one church. It is also believed to be the birthplace of Saint Anthony of Lisbon.

The Igreja de São Sebastião is even older than the parochial church. Built in 1325, it was renovated in the 17th and 18th centuries. This church also has a small Chapel of Bones.

For a less bling-worthy experience, the Igreja Matriz de Santa Maria (Saint Mary's Church) has been a place of worship since 1498 and has a calm and austere interior. The original building had a hospital attached to the side.

The history of the area is all around you, and no more so than in the Discoveries Wax Museum, which tells the story of the time of the Portuguese Discoveries through sixteen different scenes. The museum uses modern technology to good effect and also documents other landmarks in history, including the Treaty of Windsor.

King Richard II of England and King John I of Portugal signed the oldest alliance in the world on the 9th May 1386. The Treaty of Windsor is significant because it cemented and strengthened ties between the two countries, a bond that is unbroken almost 650 years later. What is fascinating is that the terms of this alliance are as relevant today, perhaps even more so with the looming spectre of Brexit on the horizon.

"The terms of the treaty included provisions for guaranteeing the mutual security of both nations and strengthening of commercial ties such as the right of both countries to trade on the terms enjoyed by the subjects of that country. There were even clauses encouraging freedom of movement and settlement between the two countries, as subjects of either country had the right to dwell in the domains of the other."[1]

I wonder if I will be able to quote the Treaty of Windsor at passport control in the future?

Lagos also holds the unfortunate record of being the location of the first slave market in Europe. From Lagos, the African slaves were sent to the rest of Europe, and Prince Henry the Navigator, the famous instigator of many of the Portuguese maritime conquests, received a fifth of the sale price for each of the slaves. The O Mercado de Escravos (the Slave Market) recounts this sad time in history, when from 1444, the first two hundred captured black slaves from West Africa arrived here.

During the ensuing ten years, an estimated eight hundred slaves came to Lagos. The Slave Market Museum is not an easy place to visit, recalling this tragic period in history. I think it is better to have created the museum though and attempted to record this, than to have ignored its location entirely. Surely, we can only learn from history and our mistakes if we are fully aware of them and their consequences?

૦ ౠ ૦ ૦ ૦ ૦

The historic buildings of Lagos contrast sharply with the bright and modern marina, which was opened in 1994. This is a lovely area of the town to walk around, with its stunning views, luxury boats moored up, and a profusion of cafés, bars, and restaurants. On Sunday afternoons you can listen to live music, often modern jazz, from the artists performing outside one of the many eateries.

The marina proudly displays its blue flag status and the Yacht Harbour Association's Level 5 Gold Anchor Standard. I have no idea what that means, apart from knowing that Level 5 is the highest grade possible, but it sounds impressive. The marina hosts a range of events through the year, including special sailings of the traditional 15th-century Portuguese caravel-style boat, famous for its lightness and manoeuvrability during the time of the Portuguese Discoveries. There are lots of boat-trips that set sail from the marina, luckily in more modern and technologically advanced boats than the caravel.

Duck down through the back of the marina and you will reach the sad sight of the old Lagos railway station. It was built in 1922, but has been derelict for many years. You can still wander around and imagine what it would have looked like in its heyday. Many plans have been drawn up over the years, and a British couple once tried to buy it to turn it into an art gallery and café, but it remains abandoned.

The beaches around Lagos are some of the most popular on the Algarve. Meia Praia oddly translates as 'half beach' when in fact it is an extremely long stretch of wide sand. This is an exceptionally clean beach with soft sand, ideal for families, with gentle waves in the summer and clear water. Meia Praia is a popular area for water sports including windsurfing, kite surfing, and jet skiing.

Praia Dona Ana is a beautiful beach with impressive rock formations and shimmering water. There are caves to explore, and a restaurant overlooks the beach. The only way up or down is via a series of steps.

Porto de Mós Beach has steep cliffs and fine sand with free parking and two restaurants facing the sea. This beach is slightly further away from the town and is usually less busy. You can often find surfers here as there is more of a sea breeze than at the other Lagos beaches. The headland separates this beach from the quieter Praia do Canavial round the corner.

The most impressive landmark here must be the Ponta da Piedade, which seems to gain more recognition and awards every year. There is a lighthouse, but it is the view that entices people to visit this location. The rock formations along this dramatic limestone coastline, and the view over the entire bay of Lagos stretching almost to Portimão, are worth viewing.

One experience you must decide for yourself whether to visit is Lagos Zoo. I know there are lots of people vehemently against any form of zoo experience, but Dave and I decided to visit to see it for ourselves. This is a small zoo, which is well maintained and prides itself on its conservation record and desire to educate and inform. They market the zoo as a place for all the family, and the animals seem generally well cared for. Areas for many animals, like the penguins, seem spacious, and there is a farm area where the goats, pigs, donkeys, and sheep seem most content.

I was, however, saddened to see a ridiculously small enclosure housing a large number of meerkats that didn't seem at all happy with their surroundings. It is difficult to decide whether the conservation element outweighs the disturbance to the natural habitat that most creatures would undoubtedly prefer.

○೫○೮○

Heading further west along the coast, you reach Praia da Luz, which is a welcoming and pretty town, with an excellent beachfront. Luz wraps itself around a picturesque sandy bay and was originally a small fishing village.

The name Praia da Luz (Beach of Light) was introduced

because of the fishermen's lights in the bay at night. The use of the name was first recorded in 1928, and the phrase stuck. More recently Luz has gained town status and should officially be known as Vila da Luz.

The Parish of Luz was formally constituted in 1673, however, dating back as far as the 13th century, Luz was connected with the sardine fishing industry. In the 19th century, the canning industry also became an important part of the village and surrounding areas. Three factories conserved fish in olive oil, preceding the eventual salting of sardines in the same fashion. These factories supported one hundred workers, with the majority (sixty) of them being women. Luz was also a major producer of figs, which were exported to the fine sweets industry; while wheat and barley were cultivated in many of the surrounding areas.[2]

Today, tourism has replaced fishing and figs, but fortunately this transformation has not lessened the charm of Luz. Its major wow factor is the large sandy beach with its calm sea. Although—be warned—that water may look inviting, but it will probably be shockingly cold. The main beach sits comfortably between the towering Rocha Negra headland on the east and the rocky coastline close to the Fortaleza da Luz.

The Rocha Negra, as the name suggests, is a magnificent section of black rock. Allegedly created 150 million years ago and formed by hot volcanic lava cascading over and through the sandstone cliffs; this is an impressive visual piece of geography. Suddenly all those lessons at school where the teacher tried valiantly to get me interested in rock formations and geology begin to make sense as you stand and look at this spectacle. Now I know what a basalt seam looks like.

You can also hike along the top of these cliffs and enjoy the magnificent views. The route is described as a 'challenging hiking trail' so perhaps wear something suitable on your feet.

A short walk beside the palm tree-lined promenade, which you could easily do in flip-flops, will take you to Prainha da Luz beach next to the fort. This is a small beach surrounded by rocks, favoured by people looking for some peace and quiet. The promenade walk itself is lovely, with patterns swirling in the design of the *calçadas* or pavement stones.

Look out for the ruins of some Roman baths dating from the 3rd to 5th century behind the wall that runs alongside the promenade. There is a small sign and a door in the wall which is easy to miss as you walk along. They are open to the public every day.

There are lots of restaurants, cafés, and shops situated along here. In the summer artists sometimes display their work for sale along the pavements, and there is a relaxed atmosphere to this town.

The promenade also leads to the impressive Fortaleza da Luz or Castelo da Senhora da Luz. The fortress or castle dates back to around 1640. This was another fort created to defend the region against pirates and invasions. I think the 16th and 17th centuries must have been a traumatic time. The fort originally had walls that were five metres tall, so they must have been expecting trouble. Today it is a far more genteel place, with a restaurant and bar, and live music on Sunday afternoons. Our friends are members of a local jazz band that performs there, and it is lovely to walk past and hear their music wafting out from inside the gardens.

Almost opposite the fort is the medieval Church of Nossa Senhora da Luz (Our Lady of Light). It was built around 1521, although it does seem to be rather unlucky. It was, predictably, damaged in the 1755 earthquake and restored in 1874. The work was funded by local contributions. It was then battered again by ferocious storms in 1941, and an earthquake in 1969, requiring it to be renovated again.

Praia da Luz is unfortunately probably best known for being the location of one of the largest media-reported missing child cases in recent memory. In 2007, three-year-old Madeleine McCann went missing from her holiday apartment. The case was covered globally, with a media frenzy never before witnessed by this small tourist town. The church became one of the main focal points for reporting, after her distraught parents were seen visiting the church in the days after the event occurred.

There are two excellent golf courses close to Luz. Boavista is an 18-hole championship course and the Golf Santo Antonio is another

18-hole course set within the Parque da Floresta. As you have probably guessed by now, I am not a golfer, but I am reliably informed that both these courses are worth visiting with your set of clubs in hand.

Travelling on further west are several smaller villages and lots of less-touristy beaches. Burgau is an unspoilt traditional fishing village, full of cobbled streets and pretty fishermen's cottages. As you walk down to the front, you can see tantalising glimpses of the sea at the end of each of the rows of houses. The slipway and tiny harbour are usually full of fishing boats pulled up from the tide, and you can watch fishermen mending their nets and chatting together.

Look out for the evil eye which is painted on many of the boats. This is part of an ancient legend which believes that a malevolent glare is strong enough to bring about an actual disaster. Many cultures believe that receiving the evil eye will cause injury, harm, pain, or misfortune. The idea is that by painting the eye on an object as a talisman, it will reflect the gaze back upon those wishing harm upon others.

This is a friendly village, mostly unspoilt by modern tourism, with a couple of good restaurants and cafés to choose from. In the winter it is much quieter and is a satisfying place to wander round and explore. It was known as a smugglers' hideaway in the past. As you stand in the village, you can visualise the unlit boats being drawn up onto the slipway at night, and the mysterious occupants disappearing swiftly into the maze of tiny streets behind.

The beach is surprisingly large with soft, golden sand and dramatic cliffs at either end. You need to check your tide tables before you plan a trip, as the beach all but disappears at high tide.

Towards Sagres there are several smaller beaches that are all different, despite their proximity to each other. Praia da Almádena is mostly shingle and pebbles, but the access is difficult, as you have an arduous climb down to the sand. There is a stunning old fort on the cliffs nearby, that is neither well sign-posted nor well-visited but is worth the detour. Sadly, it is often a spot for wild campers, who leave their rubbish and detritus behind them.

Salema is a small fishing village with a big wide beach. The sand is surrounded by red sandstone and yellow limestone cliffs. The ancient limestone rocks draw fossil hunters from around the world, and in 2001 dinosaur footprints were discovered in the crumbling cliff face. They are easy to spot if you head to the western end of the beach and look near to the steps that lead back up to the village.

The winding streets are a delight with the traditionally painted white fishermen's cottages. The doors and windows are all edged in the beautiful iconic Algarve-blue paint, making this a great place to take photographs.

Praia de Vale Figueira is another gem hidden away in the west. You have to park up and walk to reach this beach, which has a profusion of pebbles amongst its soft sand. The location is popular with both surfers and nudists. Although not both at the same time. I don't think I have ever seen a nude surfer. Although there is a first time for everything, I guess.

Praia do Zavial is one of my favourite beaches in the area. The high cliffs protect the beach, and the Outeiros river trickles down to the sea across the sand. In the winter, the river tends to be more vociferous, and can be a challenge to cross, although it is worth wading through to reach the soft sand on the other side. This is a lovely beach to walk along, although you need to watch out for the nudists again. I am always astounded at their tenacity to sit there in the middle of winter with everything dangling out for all to see. I would much rather view the ruins of the old Battery and Forte de Santo Ignácio do Zavial high on the cliffs, than look at some wrinkly old person's anatomy. It seems to be mostly old men I see sunbathing nude, or maybe I am just unlucky like that. So if you can avoid the less impressive anatomical sights, the western section of the Algarve is a wonderful place to explore.

---

1. Gov.UK (09.05.2016). Website article by Ben Trowbridge *History's Unparalleled Alliance: the Anglo-Portuguese Treaty of Windsor, 9th May 1386*. Accessed 1st September 2020 through https://history.blog.gov.uk/2016/05/09/historys-unparalleled-alliance-the-anglo-portuguese-treaty-of-windsor-9th-may-1386/
2. Praia da Luz (s.d.). Website article *History*. Accessed 2nd September 2020 through http://www.algarveluzbay.com/luz/history/

29

West Coast Beaches

The beaches of the Algarve win so many awards, and it is easy to see why. Although the southern Algarve region has many fantastic beaches, it is the wilder west coast that has captured our hearts. It is almost like a cross between the west of Ireland and the north Cornish coast. Dramatic cliffs, crashing Atlantic waves, pounding surf and a surprise hidden amongst almost every turn of the coastline, means the west coast reigns supreme. The Costa Vicentina is the longest stretch of protected Portuguese coastline in the entire country and has many treasures to discover, some well promoted, others more remote and secret.

We begin our beach tour just above the most south-westerly point by travelling through the small town of Vila do Bispo off the N125. Go past the petrol station and travel along the road through the town. At the T-junction after the café, look out for the brown tourist sign for *praias* and follow the narrow coastal route out of town. After a few miles you will come to a split in the road; left will take you down to Castelejo beach, and right goes to Cordoama beach. Both are fantastic.

Praia do Castelejo

This is a beautiful stretch of almost white sand, which contrasts with the smooth round black rocks you find scattered on the beach and its fabulous backdrop of rugged dark cliffs. The precipices are made of black schist metamorphic rock, and the patterns and slices of thin slabs of slate running through it are stunning.

You will need to check the tide tables before visiting Castelejo. It is the perfect beach to visit at low tide, but at high tide almost all the beach is covered. At low tide you can walk round to Cordoama enjoying the rock pools along the way. Castelejo beach has good parking and easy access, and a lifeguard in the summer. There is a restaurant beside the car park above the beach; the apt, if simply named, Restaurante O Castelejo. They serve a great fish lunch, with a basic but satisfying Portuguese menu. It's the perfect place to huddle inside on a cold winter's afternoon with a coffee and a slice of cake. They do shut early though, especially in the winter months.

This a good destination for surfing and a great beach for sunsets. It faces almost due west, so if you find a lone photographer at sunset, crouched over his tripod, getting his feet wet amongst the rocks at low tide, say hello to Dave for me.

Perched on the cliffs above Castelejo is a *miradouro* or viewpoint. These are always worth locating; they have the best vantage points to experience the spectacular views across the wild Atlantic coast. Follow the brown tourist sign, park up and enjoy the view. Just mind you don't go too close to the edge; often there is only a small low wooden barrier between you and a very large drop into the ocean. It's a great spot to watch the sunset too.

Praia da Cordoama

Cordoama is another fabulous soft sandy beach that joins Castelejo in the south. The border between these two beaches forms a series of rock formations. It includes one unique rock (or a set of scattered small rocks joined together depending on which way you look at it) that is known as Pedra da Laje. It is a favoured spot for sea anglers.

Cordoama has a bijou café restaurant, the Bar da Praia. I must be honest and say that it is nothing special, it's ok if you only want a quick coffee. Every time we have been there, I always feel like apologising to the waiter for bothering him with my order. The staff and food at Castelejo luckily make up for what Cordoama lacks in the culinary and customer service departments.

It is a shame as this is a fantastic beach, more than one kilometre in length, with plenty of space for everyone. It is a favourite for local surfers, and great for dog-walking in the winter.

Cordoama is also a famous spot for paragliding. Many of the cliffs above the beach here are over one hundred metres in height. We have been fortunate enough on several occasions to catch sight of a paraglider taking off from the cliffs right above us and sailing overhead. For me, it would be the equivalent of sitting in a tiny deck chair with a small electric fan strapped to my back. Not for the faint-hearted—and certainly not for me.

At the southern edge of the beach, look up and you will see the highest point on the Algarve coast. The Torre de Aspa was a lookout tower, situated at an altitude of one hundred and fifty-six metres. Today the tower is in ruins, but a Geodesic Landmark covers the spot. The cliffs here are prone to landslides and loose rocks that can tumble down onto the beach, so take care and keep a safe distance from the cliffs. Never sit under them.

Dave can testify to this one. He was busy with his camera on Marinha beach when a sheer slice of rock collapsed onto the sand, about one hundred metres in front of him. He said it was like watching a hot knife slice through a piece of icing on a wedding cake. The section slid down in one piece, crashing to the sand below, and scattering rocks everywhere. I have always teased him that he saunters so slowly along the beach when he is photographing, and he is always late home. On this occasion, I was just glad he wasn't further ahead. The consequences of that don't bear thinking about. Whenever we see someone sitting under the cliffs, we go over and say something politely to them. I am often astounded at the response we receive, with people blatantly ignoring the warning signs attached to the cliff face above them.

Praia da Barriga

This beach is situated north of Cordoama. This is a more hidden and isolated location, and it is often deserted, mainly because of the rough track road you have to drive along to reach the beach. It is worth the effort, and once you have climbed down the steps onto the soft sand, you can enjoy some stunning scenery. The rock formations and black rocks form a magnificent backdrop to a pretty beach. There are no facilities here though, so pack a picnic.

Prainha

This is a wide flat beach, which is extremely popular with surfers. It leads onto Praia do Amado with the busy Algarve International Surf School straddling the two beaches. This is not the quietest place in the summer; it is best visited in the winter months if you like peaceful surroundings and space to walk.

The beach is surrounded by magnificent cliffs and the colour of the rocks is striking, with deep reds and glints of gold.

Praia do Amado

Leading on from Prainha, Amado beach is a lovely long stretch of sand, famous for its surfing conditions. They host international surf competitions here, and the waves in the winter are not for the fainthearted or the beginner surfer. The beach faces west-northwest and has wonderful large open skies. Perfect for sunsets, too.

The cliffs above the beach are ideal for hiking, and there are several signposted walking trails to follow. Look out for Pedra do Cavaleiro (Knight's Rock) which stands tall and proud above the waves. You can walk from Amado beach all the way to Bordeira and enjoy the spectacular views along the way.

Praia da Bordeira

A wooden boardwalk and lots of steps will lead you down to Bordeira beach. This is one of the longest beaches in the whole of the Algarve, stretching to almost three kilometres. It has a river running down to the sea and there is a surf school and a beach bar. There are wonderful sand dunes at the back of the beach to explore, and behind them is a forest of ancient pine trees. You feel that you are miles from civilisation when you sit enjoying the space and freedom here.

There is also a viewpoint along the walking trail to the left of the beach with stupendous views over the coast. Look out for the fishermen perched precariously on the edge of the cliffs, busy catching their supper. I have held my breath so many times watching them at work, seemingly unperturbed by the crashing waves around them and the sheer drop to the sea below them.

CNN ranked Bordeira 31st in their Top Fifty Surf Spots in the World in 2013 and it is easy to see why.[1] This is an unspoilt beach, despite its popularity, and there is plenty of room for surfers, sunbathers and walkers. The Atlantic waves can be powerful here, so take care if you want to go for a swim. Although I think you would have to be daft to bathe here, the water is usually very, very cold!

If you hunt around, you can even see the ruins of a fort here, built in the 17th century to protect the beach and surrounding area from attackers.

Arrifana

Praia da Arrifana is one of Dave's favourite beaches. This is a long narrow beach, stretching for more than half a kilometre. It is in a small bay surrounded by impressive black cliffs and picture-perfect little white houses. On the right side of the shore there is a small fishing port. This is a great place to watch the sunset. The approach is via a steep and winding single-lane road. Only local vehicles are allowed to travel down the road to the beach, so you will need to park at the top and walk down. Just remember you have to climb back up to the car at the end of the day.

On the left side of the coast (when you are looking out to sea), there is a big tall rock standing proud in the water. The rock is called Pedra da Agulha (Needle Rock) and has become a famous landmark of the area.

Arrifana is one of many Blue Flag beaches along the Algarve, which means the beach complies with recognised environmental and quality standards. There are restaurants and toilets in the area and a café at the bottom near the beach. In the summer, there are lifeguards in attendance.

Our favourite restaurant, O Paulo's, where we had our special New Year's Eve meal, is above Arrifana beach.

Praia de Monte Clérigo

This is our nearest beach and one we love to walk along, especially in the winter. Kat adores the rock pools to the left of the shore, and at low tide this is a wonderful area to explore. The rocks here are spectacular, with a combination of towering cliffs at each end of the beach and sand dunes. At high tide it can be fun trying to skip or wade through the shallow river that cuts the beach in half. The water can sometimes reach as far as the main road in the winter. The backdrop of the village with its tiny houses tumbling down to the beach makes this a perfect place to bring a camera. Sadly, the rocks are prone to crumbling and there are several houses that look like they are in danger of disappearing soon.

Monte Clérigo is a relatively large beach, which stretches for about five hundred metres. The walk along the edge of the soft golden sand can be a gentle stroll one day, and a bracing battle against the elements the next. The current and tides show little mercy here, and we have often watched surfers battling against the waves as they head out to sea.

The coast is punctuated by ancient rock formations, ending at the appropriately named Ponta da Atalaia, or Lookout Point. There are a couple of cafés, a restaurant, toilets, and lifeguards in the summer. There is also excellent access onto the beach from the main car park.

Praia da Amoreira

Amoreira is a big wide stretch of sand backed by large sand dunes, high cliffs, and granite rocks. According to local legend, the black rock formation on the northern side of the beach is a giant lying down. The smaller rock on the left side is the head of the giant (complete with an impressive pointed nose) and the enormous cliff to the right is the giant's belly. Once seen, you cannot unsee it.

When the tide is low, a shallow lagoon appears which is lovely to paddle in, or for children to play safely in. There is also a surf school here.

At the southern end of Praia da Amoreira you reach the mouth of the Aljezur River as it reaches the sea. The river runs for almost ten kilometres from Aljezur until it finally arrives at Amoreira. Above the beach is a restaurant with a great menu and a stupendous view over the cliffs and out to sea. The perfect place for a late-afternoon coffee as you watch the sunset in the winter months. And then it is oh so tempting to stay on for dinner too. Well, once they have brought you the menu, it would be rude to refuse.

Praia de Vale dos Homens

This beach is often deserted because of its remote location. However, this is the ideal location for nature lovers who seek peace and solitude. At low tide, the shore is littered with natural rock pools, full of small sea creatures. This is a beautiful beach to walk along.

The downside to this? There are two hundred and eighty steps to climb down to reach the beach. Which is bad enough until you remember there are the same number of steps to climb back up to the car park at the end of your stay. Ask Dave, he has counted each one as he trekked back up carrying his camera equipment on numerous occasions.

Odeceixe

Praia de Odeceixe is a beautiful beach with a unique horseshoe shape. It is surrounded by the Ribeira de Seixe river. It is backed by steep cliffs. On the west side of the beach is a big rock that looks like the fin of a shark. This beach is popular amongst both surfers and families due to the impressive waves and safe lagoon. In 2012, this beach was chosen as one of the seven wonders of Portugal in the category of cliff beaches and it is easy to see why.[2]

The river is what makes Praia de Odeceixe so beautiful. On one side of the beach you have the ocean and on the other side the river. The river Seixe separates the Algarve from the Alentejo, so if you take a dip in both the sea and the river you will have swum in both regions in one session.

Be aware that the area around the southern cliffs, which is accessible during lower tides, is a stretch of sand designated for nudists. There is a good selection of cafés and restaurants on the cliff top overlooking the beach, and the tiny village of Odeceixe nearby is also worth a trip too.

Praia da Amália

This beach requires a trek across streams, sandy paths, and bamboo clearings before you reach the cliff edge and the steps down to the sand. Once there, you will most likely have the entire place to yourself, and you can explore a marvellous natural phenomenon right on the beach. Amália is famous for its waterfall, which in the winter has a magnificent display of tumbling water that cascades down the cliffs.

Praia do Carvalhal

Carvalhal has soft sand, wide open spaces, and splendid views. There are wooden walkways that lead to the beach, lots of parking, and a few restaurants. The high cliffs at either side protect the shore from the elements and the wind, making this a lovely place to settle down and read a book or have a snooze. It is also known for being a great spot for competitive fishing too and often hosts competitions.

Zambujeira do Mar

Famous for its annual music festival, this is a hippie laid-back hangout of a village and beach. For four days in August, thousands of young people descend on the village to enjoy live music and bands. For the rest of the year, the village sleeps quietly, bothered only by surfers and beach-lovers who revel in the stunning beaches in the area. You can rent a body board or take surfing lessons here, and in the evening enjoy a sumptuous meal of freshly caught and grilled fish in one of the local establishments.

At the northern end of the beach, overlooking the sea, is the little chapel of Nossa Senhora do Mar. Below this, the beach divides into two sections with a rocky outcrop in the middle. At the far end the rocks are known as the Palheirão.

We were walking along the area in front of the chapel one Sunday afternoon, enjoying the sunshine, when we noticed an incident happening down on the beach. Suddenly a huge Sea King helicopter flew overhead, and we watched as they lowered a rescue team onto the rocks. It was eerie to stand there, alongside so many other people who had gathered beside the cliff wall in front of the church and all the way down to the beach. The helicopter remained balanced in the air, hovering above the rocks, as they winched up first one stretcher, then a second. They quickly spun around and then landed on the nearby cliffs to a waiting ambulance.

Locals told us that a woman had got into difficulty in the sea. A man went in after her to help her but was also battered against the rocks. Local surfers tried to save them both, and then the emergency services were called. Initially, it seemed as if the rescue had been successful, so I was really saddened to read later that the woman and the man, who were both British, had died.

It is a sobering reminder that the sea can appear calm and welcoming, but hidden rip tides and submerged rocks can be lethal. It was awful to think we had watched the rescue attempt, in good faith, along with many others. Inwardly I felt relieved when we saw they had landed safely for the waiting ambulance to rush them away, and I was upset when we heard the tragic news later that evening.

Vila Nova de Milfontes

This is as far north as we are going to travel for this beach guide; however, I couldn't resist including this picturesque and upcoming town with its amazing beaches. This is predominantly a Portuguese resort, with many Lisbonites travelling down here for a weekend break. It gets busy in the summer, but there are plenty of restaurants and hotels to cater for everyone. There are also several remarkably diverse but equally wonderful beaches to explore and enjoy.

The town itself is charming, full of cobbled streets, and views across the Mira river. It is on the Rota Vicentina hiking trail, on the suitably named Fisherman's Route. This is a superb stretch of coastline with spectacular views.

You are spoilt for choice with beaches in this location, here are some of the best:

Praia da Franquia

This is the main beach of Vila Nova de Milfontes and extends along the Mira River, from the lifeboat station to the lighthouse headland. Franquia is a sheltered space, perfect for families and sunbathing, although it gets busy in the summer months. You can hire stand up paddleboards or kayaks and enjoy exploring the river.

Praia do Farol

This is located at the mouth of the river Mira estuary. This is another protected calm sandy beach with rock pools at low tide full of sea life.

Praia do Carreiro das Fazendas

A much wilder and less protected beach. It is surrounded by sand dunes and is a great place to enjoy nature and the fierce Atlantic waves.

Praia das Furnas

This is the beach you can see from Vila Nova de Milfontes, on the opposite side of the Mira River. Furnas is divided into two distinct areas, the first section overlooks the estuary and is similar to Praia da Franquia. The second half faces the Atlantic Ocean and is a much larger and more rugged expanse of sand. You can reach Furnas beach via the little ferry that departs from the mooring below the castle. You can also walk or drive to the beach via the N393 road bridge, then follow the gravel track along the estuary.

Praia do Patacho

A small beach that is famous for one thing. It has a rusting old shipwreck grounded on the rocks, which can be seen at low tide. If you are in the area, it is worth a detour.

Praia de Almograve

This is only fourteen kilometres from Vila Nova de Milfontes and is considered to be one of the finest beaches in Portugal. A fitting beach to end with. This is a vast expanse of soft golden sand, split into two distinct areas. The north end of the beach has gentle sand dunes in the background with rock pools, whereas the southern end has dramatic black shale rocks and cliffs. This beach showcases the full force of the Atlantic Ocean and is great for surfing and bodyboarding.

Almograve town has a good selection of restaurants and is popular with both local people and the Portuguese on holiday.

Explore the southern end of town to see the pretty traditional fishing harbour, called the Porto das Lapas das Pombas.

So there you are. A total of twenty-one beaches, along the western Algarve and Alentejo coast, and all within an easy driving distance of our new home. Is it any wonder we love living here so much?

---

1. CNN Travel (01.07.2013). Website article by Jade Bremner *World's 50 best surf spots: No 31 Carrapateira / Bordeira.* Accessed 25th July 2020 through https://edition.cnn.com/travel/article/50-surf-spots/index.html
2. Wikipédia (s.d.). Website article *Sete Maravilhas de Portugal.* Accessed 25th July 2020 through https://pt.wikipedia.org/wiki/Sete_Maravilhas_de_Portugal

Living the Dream - in the Algarve, Portugal

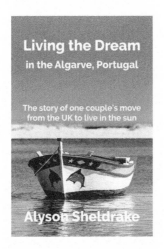

Could you leave everything behind and start a new life in the sun? Have you ever been on holiday abroad and wondered what it would be like to live there?

Alyson and Dave Sheldrake did. They fell in love with a little fishing village in the Algarve, Portugal, and were determined to realise their dream of living abroad. They bought a house there, ended their jobs, packed up everything they owned and moved to the Algarve to start a new life.

Follow them as they battle with Portuguese bureaucracy, set up their own businesses, adopt a rescue dog and learn to adapt to a slower pace of life. Laugh with them as Alyson propositions a builder, they try to master the Portuguese language, and successfully navigate the 'expat' world.

Part guidebook, mostly memoir; this is a refreshingly honest and often hilarious account of life abroad.

Available to purchase now in eBook, Paperback and Large Print Book on Amazon Worldwide.

A New Life in the Algarve, Portugal

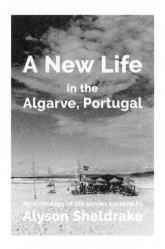

What makes a person decide to move abroad to start a new life? And why do so many people choose the Algarve in Portugal as their dream destination?

In this compilation of life stories, you can read about a whole range of different people who have made the Algarve their home.

Read about the families that moved to live in the Algarve in the early 1970s, before tourism was even an idea.

Find out more about the people who packed up everything they owned to follow their dreams of a new life in the sun.

Funny moments, heartfelt journeys, and real-life modern adventures are all covered in this new and fascinating anthology.

Read their stories - and be inspired.

Includes a foreword written by the British Ambassador to Portugal.

Available to purchase now on Amazon worldwide.

For more information visit:
www.alysonsheldrake.com/books

Further Reading

If you are interested in finding out more about moving to live in Portugal, I can recommend the following sites:

The British Embassy in Portugal website
www.gov.uk/world/portugal
And the Embassy's Facebook Page: Brits in Portugal
www.facebook.com/BritsInPortugal

Also on Facebook – there is a particularly good and supportive group called British Expats in Portugal. The group has an excellent Files Section with information covering a wide range of 'need to know' hints, tips, and guides for anyone considering a move to Portugal.
www.facebook.com/groups/265570920476558

For Americans considering a move to Portugal I can recommend the Facebook group Americans and FriendsPT. They have a similar range of files covering everything specific to the American visa scheme and related information.
www.facebook.com/groups/americansandfriendsPT

If you are not on Facebook, then check out the Expats Portugal Community Forum. They have an active membership with lots of questions and answers about all things Portugal. www.expatsportugal.com/community/

Dave Sheldrake Photography. He has a selection of high-quality images of Portugal, and especially his favourite beaches, for you to enjoy. You can view them on his website: www.davesheldrake.photography/portugal/

If this book has whetted your appetite and you are considering buying in the Algarve, then the article *Where to Buy a Property in the Algarve* on our Algarve Blog will be a good starting point for you: www.algarveblog.net/2015/06/10/where-to-buy-a-property-in-the-algarve/

Live and Invest Overseas have a wealth of information and advice for people looking to live or invest abroad. They have in-depth guides, a vast network of correspondents, and free reports and newsletters. They also host regular conferences across the world, including in the Algarve, for which I am their designated 'western Algarve expert'. You can find out more on their website: www.liveandinvestoverseas.com

Contacts and Links

My artist and author website:
www.alysonsheldrake.com

Email:
author@alysonsheldrake.com

Our Algarve Blog is full of information, photographs, stories, and guides.
Algarve Blog website:
www.algarveblog.net

Algarve Blog on Facebook:
www.facebook.com/AlgarveBlog

Dave's photography website:
www.davesheldrake.photography

Acknowledgements

My special thanks go to those friends who contributed to this book, in particular, Dave D and Merja, Yayeri and Kyle, and Gerty and Raymond. Thank you for your honesty and willingness to share your thoughts and views with me. Thank you to everyone for supporting me and indulging my crazy ideas.

To the beta readers that helped to shape this book, namely Susan Spector, Sue Raymond, Jude Mossad, Lisa Rose Wright, and Susan Jackson – thank you. To Val Poore, Beth Haslam, and Julie Haigh, who went above and beyond the call of beta reading, my sincere and heartfelt thanks.

Thank you to the wonderful members of the Facebook Group We Love Memoirs. This really is the best bunch of friendly authors and memoir readers. I have made new friends and read so many wonderful books through this group.

My special thanks must also go to Victoria Twead, of Ant Press publishing company, for her support, advice, and encouragement. You have made the journey to being an author far less daunting.

To Nicole, April, Caroline, Susan, Holly, Sharon, Kay, and Victoria – my wonderful friends and fellow members of our Zoom Memoir Writing Accountability Group. Thank you all for your support and for cheering me on. Knowing we are meeting each afternoon is such a positive thing. Here's to the day every single one of us has at least one book with their name on the cover.

✧⁍✧⁌✧

As always, thank you to Dave, my long-suffering, supportive and hilarious husband. I love you.

To everyone that has a dream, my advice is simple. Go for it. You will only regret the things you did not do, not the times you scaled the heights and dared to imagine. May you have dreams that are as big as the sky.

Free Photo Book

To view a series of free photographs which accompany this book, please visit my website:
    www.alysonsheldrake.com/books/

Keeping in Touch

If you would like to be notified when I publish my next book, please contact me via email and I will add you to my mailing list.

author@alysonsheldrake.com

I also write a monthly newsletter with Dave, which is full of art, photographs, book reviews, and articles about the Algarve. You can sign up to this free via the link here:

www.alysonsheldrake.com/news/

About the Author

Alyson Sheldrake was born in Birmingham in 1968. She has an honours degree in sport and has a PGCE (Secondary) qualification in physical education, English, and drama. She has always loved art and painting, although she found little time for such pleasures, working full-time after graduation. She joined the Devon and Cornwall Police in 1992 and served for thirteen years, before leaving and working her way up the education ladder, rapidly reaching the dizzy heights of Director of Education for the Church of England in Devon in 2008.

Managing over 130 schools in the Devon area was a challenging and demanding role, however after three years her husband Dave retired from the Police, and their long-held dream of living in the sun became a reality.

Alyson handed in her notice, and with her dusty easel and set of acrylic paints packed and ready to move, they started their new adventure living in the beautiful Algarve in Portugal in 2011.

Alyson is the author of the award-winning and popular Algarve Blog, and has also been a keynote speaker for several years at the annual Live and Invest in Portugal international conference. She is also a feature writer for the Tomorrow Magazine in the Algarve.

She is an accomplished and sought-after artist working alongside her husband Dave, a professional photographer. Being able to bring their much-loved hobbies and creative interests to life has been a wonderful bonus to their life in the Algarve. She is also delighted to be able to add the title 'author' to her CV, with the publication of her first book, *Living the Dream – in the Algarve, Portugal*, in April 2020. When she is not painting or writing, she can be found walking Kat the dog along the river in Aljezur.

Your Review

I do hope you have enjoyed reading this book. If you have a moment, I would love it if you could leave a review online, even if it is just a star rating. I read and learn something from every review that is posted, and I do a happy little dance for every lovely comment that is shared.

Thank you.

Made in United States
Orlando, FL
16 April 2022